Something was grabbing the edge of the mirror, as if from the inside of the glass, as if the glass surface were an open window and something or somebody were just climbing through it.

Don Juan and I fought desperately; the loud thrashing continued unremittingly like an enormous fish in our bare hands. A strange shape was actually trying to climb up through it . . .

I vacillated a second and the mirror flew out of my hands.

"Grab it! Grab it!" Don Juan yelled . . .

"A VISION OF THE SORCERER'S WORLD THAT IS FULL OF MIND-SPINNING IMPLICATIONS IN THE CASTANEDA TRADITION."

—*United Press International*

"HIS STORIES OF INITIATION INTO THE WORLD OF MAGIC AND SORCERY . . . CAN BE BOTH MOCKING AND TERRIFYING. . . . *THE FIRE FROM WITHIN* WILL FASCINATE YOU."

—*The Nashville Tennessean*

"ONE CAN'T EXAGGERATE THE SIGNIFICANCE OF WHAT CASTANEDA HAS DONE."

—*The New York Times*

Books by Carlos Castaneda

The Eagle's Gift
The Fire from Within
Journey to Ixtlan
The Second Ring of Power
Tales of Power

Published by POCKET BOOKS

CARLOS CASTANEDA

THE FIRE FROM WITHIN

PUBLISHED BY POCKET BOOKS NEW YORK

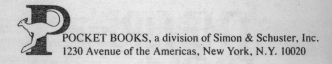

POCKET BOOKS, a division of Simon & Schuster, Inc.
1230 Avenue of the Americas, New York, N.Y. 10020

Copyright © 1984 by Carlos Castaneda
Cover artwork copyright © 1985 Robert Giusti

Published by arrangement with Simon & Schuster, Inc.
Library of Congress Catalog Card Number: 84-3896

ISBN: 0-671-54214-1

First Pocket Books printing September, 1985

10 9 8 7 6 5 4 3 2 1

POCKET and colophon are registered trademarks
of Simon & Schuster, Inc.

Printed in the U.S.A.

I WANT TO EXPRESS MY ADMIRATION AND GRAT-
ITUDE TO A MASTERFUL TEACHER, H.Y.L., FOR
HELPING ME RESTORE MY ENERGY, AND FOR
TEACHING ME AN ALTERNATE WAY TO PLENI-
TUDE AND WELL-BEING.

Contents

Foreword

I have written extensive descriptive accounts of my apprentice relationship with a Mexican Indian sorcerer, don Juan Matus. Due to the foreignness of the concepts and practices don Juan wanted me to understand and internalize, I have had no other choice but to render his teachings in the form of a narrative, a narrative of what happened, as it happened.

The organization of don Juan's instruction was predicated on the idea that man has two types of awareness. He labeled them the right side and the left side. He described the first as the state of normal awareness necessary for everyday life. The second, he said, was the mysterious side of man, the state of awareness needed to function as sorcerer and seer. Don Juan divided his instruction, accordingly, into teachings for the right side and teachings for the left side.

He conducted his teachings for the right side when I was in my state of normal awareness, and I have described those teachings in all my accounts. In my state of normal awareness don Juan told me that he was a sorcerer. He even introduced me to another sorcerer, don Genaro Flores, and because of the nature of our association, I logically concluded that they had taken me as their apprentice.

That apprenticeship ended with an incomprehensible act that both don Juan and don Genaro led me to perform. They made me jump from the top of a flat mountain into an abyss.

I have described in one of my accounts what took place on that mountaintop. The last drama of don Juan's teachings for the right side was played there by don Juan himself; don Genaro; two apprentices, Pablito and Nestor; and me. Pablito, Nestor, and I jumped from that mountaintop into an abyss.

For years afterward I thought that just my total trust in don Juan and don Genaro had been sufficient to obliterate all my rational fears on facing actual annihilation. I know now that it wasn't so; I know that the secret was in don Juan's teachings for the left side, and that it took tremendous discipline and perseverance for don Juan, don Genaro, and their companions to conduct those teachings.

It has taken me nearly ten years to recollect what exactly took place in his teachings for the left side that led me to be so willing to perform such an incomprehensible act: jumping into an abyss.

It was in his teachings for the left side that don Juan let on what he, don Genaro, and their companions were really doing to me, and who they were. They were not teaching me sorcery, but how to master three aspects of an ancient knowledge they possessed: awareness, *stalking,* and *intent.* And they were not sorcerers; they were seers. And don Juan was not only a seer, but also a nagual.

Don Juan had already explained to me, in his teachings for the right side, a great deal about the nagual and about *seeing.* I had understood *seeing* to be the capacity of human beings to enlarge their perceptual field until they are capable of assessing not only the outer appearances but the essence of everything. He had also explained that seers *see* man as a field of energy, which looks like a luminous egg. The majority of people, he said, have their fields of energy divided into two parts. A few men and women have four or sometimes three parts. Because these people are more resilient than the average man, they can become naguals after learning to *see*.

In his teachings for the left side, don Juan explained to me the intricacies of *seeing* and of being a nagual. To be a nagual, he said, is something more complex and far-reaching than being merely a more resilient man who has learned to *see*. To be a nagual entails being a leader, being a teacher and a guide.

As a nagual, don Juan was the leader of a group of seers known as the nagual's party, which was composed of eight female seers, Cecilia, Delia, Hermelinda, Carmela, Nelida, Florinda, Zuleica, and Zoila; three male seers, Vicente, Silvio Manuel, and Genaro; and four couriers or messengers, Emilito, John Tuma, Marta, and Teresa.

In addition to leading the nagual's party, don Juan also taught and guided a group of apprentice seers known as the new nagual's party. It consisted of four young men, Pablito, Nestor, Eligio, and Benigno, along with five women, Soledad, la Gorda, Lidia, Josefina, and Rosa. I was the nominal leader of the new nagual's party together with the nagual woman Carol.

In order for don Juan to impart to me his teachings for the left side it was necessary for me to enter into a unique state of perceptual clarity known as heightened awareness. Throughout the years of my association with him, he had me repeatedly shift into such a state by means of a blow that he delivered with the palm of his hand on my upper back.

Don Juan explained that in a state of heightened awareness apprentices can behave almost as naturally as in everyday life, but can bring their minds to focus on anything with uncommon force and clarity. Yet, an inherent quality of heightened awareness is that it is not susceptible to normal recall. What transpires in such a state becomes part of the apprentice's everyday awareness only through a staggering effort of recovery.

My interaction with the nagual's party was an example of this difficulty of recall. With the exception of don Genaro, I had contact with them only when I was in a state of heightened awareness; hence in my normal everyday life I could not remember them, not even as vague characters in dreams. The manner in which I met with them every time was almost a ritual. I would drive to don Genaro's house in a small town in the southern part of Mexico. Don Juan would join us immediately and the three of us would then get busy with don Juan's teachings for the right side. After that, don Juan would make me change levels of awareness and then we would drive to a larger, nearby town where he and the other fifteen seers were living.

Every time I entered into heightened awareness I could not cease marveling at the difference between my two sides. I always felt as if a veil had been lifted from my eyes, as if I had been partially blind before and now I could see. The freedom, the sheer joy that used to possess me on those occasions cannot be compared with anything else I have ever experienced. Yet at the same time, there was a frightening feeling of sadness and longing that went hand in hand with that freedom and joy. Don Juan had told me that there is no completeness without sadness and longing, for without them there is no sobriety, no kindness. Wisdom without kindness, he said, and knowledge without sobriety are useless.

The organization of his teachings for the left side also required that don Juan, together with some of his fellow seers, explain to me the three facets of their knowledge: the mastery of awareness, the mastery of *stalking,* and the mastery of *intent.*

This work deals with the mastery of awareness, which is part of his total set of teachings for the left side; the set he used in order to prepare me for performing the astonishing act of jumping into an abyss.

Due to the fact that the experiences I narrate here took place in heightened awareness, they cannot have the texture of daily life. They are lacking in worldly context, although I have tried my best to supply it without fictionalizing it. In heightened awareness one is minimally conscious of the surroundings, because one's total concentration is taken by the details of the action at hand.

In this case the action at hand was, naturally, the elucidation of the mastery of awareness. Don Juan understood the mastery of awareness as being the modern-day version of an extremely old tradition, which he called the tradition of the ancient Toltec seers.

Although he felt that he was inextricably linked to that old tradition, he considered himself to be one of the seers of a new cycle. When I asked him once what was the essential character of the seers of the new cycle, he said that they are the warriors of total freedom, that they are such masters of awareness, *stalking*, and *intent* that they are not caught by death, like the rest of mortal men, but choose the moment and the way of their departure from this world. At that moment they are consumed by a fire from within and vanish from the face of the earth, free, as if they had never existed.

THE FIRE
FROM
WITHIN

1
The New Seers

I had arrived in the city of Oaxaca in southern Mexico on my way to the mountains to look for don Juan. On my way out of town in the early morning, I had the good sense to drive by the main square, and there I found him sitting on his favorite bench, as if waiting for me to go by.

I joined him. He told me that he was in the city on business, that he was staying at a local boardinghouse, and that I was welcome to stay with him because he had to remain in town for two more days. We talked for a while about my activities and problems in the academic world.

As was customary with him, he suddenly hit me on my back when I least expected it, and the blow shifted me into a state of heightened awareness.

We sat in silence for a very long time. I anxiously waited for him to begin talking, yet when he did, he caught me by surprise.

"Ages before the Spaniards came to Mexico," he said, "there were extraordinary Toltec seers, men capable of inconceivable deeds. They were the last link in a chain of knowledge that extended over thousands of years.

"The Toltec seers were extraordinary men—powerful sorcerers, somber, driven men who unraveled mysteries and possessed secret knowledge that they used to influence and victimize people by fixating the awareness of their victims on whatever they chose."

He stopped talking and looked at me intently. I felt that he was waiting for me to ask a question, but I did not know what to ask.

"I have to emphasize an important fact," he continued, "the fact that those sorcerers knew how to fixate the awareness of their victims. You didn't pick up on that. When I mentioned it, it didn't mean anything to you. That's not surprising. One of the hardest things to acknowledge is that awareness can be manipulated."

I felt confused. I knew that he was leading me toward something. I felt a familiar apprehension—the same feeling I had whenever he began a new round of his teachings.

I told him how I felt. He smiled vaguely. Usually when he smiled he exuded happiness; this time he was definitely preoccupied. He seemed to consider for a moment whether or not to go on talking. He stared at me intently again, slowly moving his gaze over the entire length of my body. Then, apparently satisfied, he nodded and said that I was ready for my final exercise, something that all warriors go through before considering themselves fit to be on their own. I was more mystified than ever.

"We are going to be talking about awareness," he continued. "The Toltec seers knew the art of handling awareness. As a matter of fact, they were the supreme masters of that art. When I say that they knew how to fixate the awareness of their victims, I mean that their secret knowledge and secret practices allowed them to pry open the mystery of being aware. Enough of their practices have survived to this day, but fortunately in a modified form. I say fortunately because

2

those activities, as I will explain, did not lead the ancient Toltec seers to freedom, but to their doom."

"Do you know those practices yourself?" I asked.

"Why, certainly," he replied. "There is no way for us not to know those techniques, but that doesn't mean that we practice them ourselves. We have other views. We belong to a new cycle."

"But you don't consider yourself a sorcerer, don Juan, do you?" I asked.

"No, I don't," he said. "I am a warrior who *sees*. In fact, all of us are *los nuevos videntes*—the new seers. The old seers were the sorcerers.

"For the average man," he continued, "sorcery is a negative business, but it is fascinating all the same. That's why I encouraged you, in your normal awareness, to think of us as sorcerers. It's advisable to do so. It serves to attract interest. But for us to be sorcerers would be like entering a dead-end street."

I wanted to know what he meant by that, but he refused to talk about it. He said that he would elaborate on the subject as he proceeded with his explanation of awareness.

I asked him then about the origin of the Toltecs' knowledge.

"The way the Toltecs first started on the path of knowledge was by eating power plants," he replied. "Whether prompted by curiosity, or hunger, or error, they ate them. Once the power plants had produced their effects on them, it was only a matter of time before some of them began to analyze their experiences. In my opinion, the first men on the path of knowledge were very daring, but very mistaken."

"Isn't all this a conjecture on your part, don Juan?"

"No, this is no conjecture of mine. I am a seer, and when I focus my *seeing* on that time I know everything that took place."

"Can you *see* the details of things of the past?" I asked.

"*Seeing* is a peculiar feeling of knowing," he replied, "of knowing something without a shadow of doubt. In this case, I know what those men did, not only because of my *seeing,* but because we are so closely bound together."

Don Juan explained then that his use of the term "Toltec" did not correspond to what I understood it to mean. To me it meant a culture, the Toltec Empire. To him, the term "Toltec" meant "man of knowledge."

He said that in the time he was referring to, centuries or perhaps even millennia before the Spanish Conquest, all such men of knowledge lived within a vast geographical area, north and south of the valley of Mexico, and were employed in specific lines of work: curing, bewitching, storytelling, dancing, being an oracle, preparing food and drink. Those lines of work fostered specific wisdom, wisdom that distinguished them from average men. These Toltecs, moreover, were also people who fitted into the structure of everyday life, very much as doctors, artists, teachers, priests, and merchants in our own time do. They practiced their professions under the strict control of organized brotherhoods and became proficient and influential, to such an extent that they even dominated groups of people who lived outside the Toltecs' geographical regions.

Don Juan said that after some of these men had finally learned to *see*—after centuries of dealing with power plants—the most enterprising of them then began to teach other men of knowledge how to *see*. And that was the beginning of their end. As time passed, the number of seers increased, but their obsession with what they *saw,* which filled them with reverence and fear, became so intense that they ceased to be men of knowledge. They became extraordinarily proficient in *seeing* and could exert great control over the strange worlds they were witnessing. But

4

it was to no avail. *Seeing* had undermined their strength and forced them to be obsessed with what they *saw*.

"There were seers, however, who escaped that fate," don Juan continued, "great men who, in spite of their *seeing*, never ceased to be men of knowledge. Some of them endeavored to use *seeing* positively and to teach it to their fellow men. I'm convinced that under their direction, the populations of entire cities went into other worlds and never came back.

"But the seers who could only *see* were fiascos, and when the land where they lived was invaded by a conquering people they were as defenseless as everyone else.

"Those conquerors," he went on, "took over the Toltec world—they appropriated everything—but they never learned to *see*."

"Why do you think they never learned to *see*?" I asked.

"Because they copied the procedures of the Toltec seers without having the Toltecs' inner knowledge. To this day there are scores of sorcerers all over Mexico, descendants of those conquerors, who follow the Toltec ways but don't know what they're doing, or what they're talking about, because they're not seers."

"Who were those conquerors, don Juan?"

"Other Indians," he said. "When the Spaniards came, the old seers had been gone for centuries, but there was a new breed of seers who were starting to secure their place in a new cycle."

"What do you mean, a new breed of seers?"

"After the world of the first Toltecs was destroyed, the surviving seers retreated and began a serious examination of their practices. The first thing they did was to establish *stalking, dreaming,* and *intent* as the key procedures and to deemphasize the use of power plants; perhaps that gives us a hint as to what really happened to them with power plants.

5

"The new cycle was just beginning to take hold when the Spanish conquerors swept the land. Fortunately, by that time the new seers were thoroughly prepared to face that danger. They were already consummate practitioners of the art of *stalking*."

Don Juan said that the subsequent centuries of subjugation provided for these new seers the ideal circumstances in which to perfect their skills. Oddly enough, it was the extreme rigor and coercion of that period that gave them the impetus to refine their new principles. And, owing to the fact that they never divulged their activities, they were left alone to map their findings.

"Were there a great many new seers during the Conquest?" I asked.

"At the beginning there were. Near the end there were only a handful. The rest had been exterminated."

"What about in our day, don Juan?" I asked.

"There are a few. They are scattered all over, you understand."

"Do you know them?" I asked.

"Such a simple question is the hardest one to answer," he replied. "There are some we know very well. But they are not exactly like us because they have concentrated on other specific aspects of knowledge, such as dancing, curing, bewitching, talking, instead of what the new seers recommend, *stalking, dreaming,* and *intent*. Those who are exactly like us would not cross our path. The seers who lived during the Conquest set it up that way so as to avoid being exterminated in the confrontation with the Spaniards. Each of those seers founded a lineage. And not all of them had descendants, so the lines are few."

"Do you know any who are exactly like us?" I asked.

"A few," he replied laconically.

I asked him then to give me all the information he

could, for I was vitally interested in the topic; to me it was of crucial importance to know names and addresses for purposes of validation and corroboration.

Don Juan did not seem inclined to oblige me. "The new seers went through that bit of corroboration," he said. "Half of them left their bones in the corroborating room. So now they are solitary birds. Let's leave it that way. All we can talk about is our line. About that, you and I can say as much as we please."

He explained that all the lines of seers were started at the same time and in the same fashion. Around the end of the sixteenth century every nagual deliberately isolated himself and his group of seers from any overt contact with other seers. The consequence of that drastic segregation, he said, was the formation of the individual lineages. Our lineage consisted of fourteen naguals and one hundred and twenty-six seers, he said. Some of those fourteen naguals had as few as seven seers with them, others had eleven, and some up to fifteen.

He told me that his teacher—or his benefactor, as he called him—was the nagual Julian, and the one who came before Julian was the nagual Elias. I asked him if he knew the names of all fourteen naguals. He named and enumerated them for me, so I could learn who they were. He also said that he had personally known the fifteen seers who formed his benefactor's group and that he had also known his benefactor's teacher, the nagual Elias, and the eleven seers of his party.

Don Juan assured me that our line was quite exceptional, because it underwent a drastic change in the year 1723 as a result of an outside influence that came to bear on us and inexorably altered our course. He did not want to discuss the event itself at the moment, but he said that a new beginning is counted from that time; and that the eight naguals who have ruled the

7

line since then are considered intrinsically different from the six who preceded them.

Don Juan must have had business to take care of the next day, for I did not see him until around noon. In the meantime, three of his apprentices had come to town, Pablito, Nestor, and la Gorda. They were shopping for tools and materials for Pablito's carpentry business. I accompanied them and helped them to complete all their errands. Then all of us went back to the boardinghouse.

All four of us were sitting around talking when don Juan came into my room. He announced that we were leaving after lunch, but that before we went to eat he still had something to discuss with me, in private. He wanted the two of us to take a stroll around the main square and then all of us would meet at a restaurant.

Pablito and Nestor stood up and said that they had some errands to run before meeting us. La Gorda seemed very displeased.

"What are you going to talk about?" she blurted out, but quickly realized her mistake and giggled.

Don Juan gave her a strange look but did not say anything.

Encouraged by his silence, la Gorda proposed that we take her along. She assured us that she would not bother us in the least.

"I'm sure you won't bother us," don Juan said to her, "but I really don't want you to hear anything of what I have to say to him."

La Gorda's anger was very obvious. She blushed and, as don Juan and I walked out of the room, her entire face clouded with anxiety and tension, becoming instantly distorted. Her mouth was open and her lips were dry.

La Gorda's mood made me very apprehensive. I felt an actual discomfort. I didn't say anything, but don Juan seemed to notice my feelings.

8

"You should thank la Gorda day and night," he said all of a sudden. "She's helping you destroy your self-importance. She's the petty tyrant in your life, but you still haven't caught on to that."

We strolled around the plaza until all my nervousness had vanished. Then we sat down on his favorite bench again.

"The ancient seers were very fortunate indeed," don Juan began, "because they had plenty of time to learn marvelous things. Let me tell you, they knew wonders that we can't even imagine today."

"Who taught them all that?" I asked.

"They learned everything by themselves through *seeing*," he replied. "Most of the things we know in our lineage were figured out by them. The new seers corrected the mistakes of the old seers, but the basis of what we know and do is lost in Toltec time."

He explained. One of the simplest and yet most important findings, from the point of view of instruction, he said, is the knowledge that man has two types of awareness. The old seers called them the right and the left side of man.

"The old seers figured out," he went on, "that the best way to teach their knowledge was to make their apprentices shift to their left side, to a state of heightened awareness. Real learning takes place there.

"Very young children were given to the old seers as apprentices," don Juan continued, "so that they wouldn't know any other way of life. Those children, in turn, when they came of age took other children as apprentices. Imagine the things they must have uncovered in their shifts to the left and to the right, after centuries of that kind of concentration."

I remarked how disconcerting those shifts were to me. He said that my experience was similar to his own. His benefactor, the nagual Julian, had created a profound schism in him, by making him shift back and forth from one type of awareness to the other. He said that the clarity and freedom he experienced in heightened awareness were in total contrast to the rationalizations, the defenses, the anger, and the fear of his normal state of awareness.

The old seers used to create this polarity to suit their own particular purposes; with it, they forced their apprentices to achieve the concentration needed to learn sorcery techniques. But the new seers, he said, use it to lead their apprentices to the conviction that there are unrealized possibilities in man.

"The best effort of the new seers," don Juan continued, "is their explanation of the mystery of awareness. They condensed it all into some concepts and actions which are taught while the apprentices are in heightened awareness."

He said that the value of the new seers' method of teaching is that it takes advantage of the fact that no one can remember anything that happens while being in a state of heightened awareness. This inability to remember sets up an almost insurmountable barrier for warriors, who have to recollect all the instruction given to them if they are to go on. Only after years of struggle and discipline can warriors recollect their instruction. By then the concepts and the procedures that were taught to them have been internalized and have thus acquired the force the new seers meant them to have.

2
Petty Tyrants

Don Juan did not discuss the mastery of awareness with me until months later. We were at that time in the house where the nagual's party lived.

"Let's go for a walk," don Juan said to me, placing his hand on my shoulder. "Or better yet, let's go to the town's square, where there are a lot of people, and sit down and talk."

I was surprised when he spoke to me, as I had been in the house for a couple of days then and he had not said so much as hello.

As don Juan and I were leaving the house, la Gorda intercepted us and demanded that we take her along. She seemed determined not to take no for an answer. Don Juan in a very stern voice told her that he had to discuss something in private with me.

"You're going to talk about me," la Gorda said, her tone and gestures betraying both suspicion and annoyance.

"You're right," don Juan replied dryly. He moved past her without turning to look at her.

I followed him, and we walked in silence to the town's square. When we sat down I asked him what on earth we would find to discuss about la Gorda. I was still smarting from her look of menace when we left the house.

"We have nothing to discuss about la Gorda or anybody else," he said. "I told her that just to provoke her enormous self-importance. And it worked. She is furious with us. If I know her, by now she will have talked to herself long enough to have built up her confidence and her righteous indignation at having been refused and made to look like a fool. I wouldn't be surprised if she barges in on us here, at the park bench."

"If we're not going to talk about la Gorda, what are we going to discuss?" I asked.

"We're going to continue the discussion we started in Oaxaca," he replied. "To understand the explanation of awareness will require your utmost effort and your willingness to shift back and forth between levels of awareness. While we are involved in our discussion I will demand your total concentration and patience."

Half-complaining, I told him that he had made me feel very uncomfortable by refusing to talk to me for the past two days. He looked at me and arched his brows. A smile played on his lips and vanished. I realized that he was letting me know I was no better than la Gorda.

"I was provoking your self-importance," he said with a frown. "Self-importance is our greatest enemy. Think about it—what weakens us is feeling offended by the deeds and misdeeds of our fellow men. Our self-importance requires that we spend most of our lives offended by someone.

"The new seers recommended that every effort should be made to eradicate self-importance from the lives of warriors. I have followed that recommendation, and much of my endeavors with you has been geared to show you that without self-importance we are invulnerable."

As I listened his eyes suddenly became very shiny.

I was thinking to myself that he seemed to be on the verge of laughter and there was no reason for it when I was startled by an abrupt, painful slap on the right side of my face.

I jumped up from the bench. La Gorda was standing behind me, her hand still raised. Her face was flushed with anger.

"Now you can say what you like about me and with more justification," she shouted. "If you have anything to say, however, say it to my face!"

Her outburst appeared to have exhausted her, because she sat down on the cement and began to weep. Don Juan was transfixed with inexpressible glee. I was frozen with sheer fury. La Gorda glared at me and then turned to don Juan and meekly told him that we had no right to criticize her.

Don Juan laughed so hard he doubled over almost to the ground. He couldn't even speak. He tried two or three times to say something to me, then finally got up and walked away, his body still shaking with spasms of laughter.

I was about to run after him, still glowering at la Gorda—at that moment I found her despicable—when something extraordinary happened to me. I realized what don Juan had found so hilarious. La Gorda and I were horrendously alike. Our self-importance was monumental. My surprise and fury at being slapped were just like la Gorda's feelings of anger and suspicion. Don Juan was right. The burden of self-importance is a terrible encumbrance.

I ran after him then, elated, the tears flowing down my cheeks. I caught up with him and told him what I had realized. His eyes were shining with mischievousness and delight.

"What should I do about la Gorda?" I asked.

"Nothing," he replied. "Realizations are always personal."

He changed the subject and said that the omens

were telling us to continue our discussion back at his house, either in a large room with comfortable chairs or in the back patio, which had a roofed corridor around it. He said that whenever he conducted his explanation inside the house those two areas would be off limits to everyone else.

We went back to the house. Don Juan told everyone what la Gorda had done. The delight all the seers showed in taunting her made la Gorda's position extremely uncomfortable.

"Self-importance can't be fought with niceties," don Juan commented when I expressed my concern about la Gorda.

He then asked everyone to leave the room. We sat down and don Juan began his explanations.

He said that seers, old and new, are divided into two categories. The first one is made up of those who are willing to exercise self-restraint and can channel their activities toward pragmatic goals, which would benefit other seers and man in general. The other category consists of those who don't care about self-restraint or about any pragmatic goals. It is the consensus among seers that the latter have failed to resolve the problem of self-importance.

"Self-importance is not something simple and naive," he explained. "On the one hand, it is the core of everything that is good in us, and on the other hand, the core of everything that is rotten. To get rid of the self-importance that is rotten requires a masterpiece of strategy. Seers, through the ages, have given the highest praise to those who have accomplished it."

I complained that the idea of eradicating self-importance, although very appealing to me at times, was really incomprehensible; I told him that I found his directives for getting rid of it so vague I could not follow them.

"I've said to you many times," he said, "that in order to follow the path of knowledge one has to be

14

very imaginative. You see, in the path of knowledge nothing is as clear as we'd like it to be."

My discomfort made me argue that his admonitions about self-importance reminded me of Catholic dictums. After a lifetime of being told about the evils of sin, I had become callous.

"Warriors fight self-importance as a matter of strategy, not principle," he replied. "Your mistake is to understand what I say in terms of morality."

"I see you as a highly moral man, don Juan," I insisted.

"You've noticed my impeccability, that's all," he said.

"Impeccability, as well as getting rid of self-importance, is too vague a concept to be of any value to me," I remarked.

Don Juan choked with laughter, and I challenged him to explain impeccability.

"Impeccability is nothing else but the proper use of energy," he said. "My statements have no inkling of morality. I've saved energy and that makes me impeccable. To understand this, you have to save enough energy yourself."

We were quiet for a long time. I wanted to think about what he had said. Suddenly, he started talking again.

"Warriors take strategic inventories," he said. "They list everything they do. Then they decide which of those things can be changed in order to allow themselves a respite, in terms of expending their energy."

I argued that their list would have to include everything under the sun. He patiently answered that the strategic inventory he was talking about covered only behavioral patterns that were not essential to our survival and well-being.

I jumped at the opportunity to point out that survival and well-being were categories that could be interpreted in endless ways, hence, there was no way of agreeing what was or was not essential to survival and well-being.

As I kept on talking I began to lose momentum. Finally, I stopped because I realized the futility of my arguments.

Don Juan said then that in the strategic inventories of warriors, self-importance figures as the activity that consumes the greatest amount of energy, hence, their effort to eradicate it.

"One of the first concerns of warriors is to free that energy in order to face the unknown with it," don Juan went on. "The action of rechanneling that energy is impeccability."

He said that the most effective strategy was worked out by the seers of the Conquest, the unquestionable masters of *stalking*. It consists of six elements that interplay with one another. Five of them are called the attributes of warriorship: control, discipline, forbearance, timing, and *will*. They pertain to the world of the warrior who is fighting to lose self-importance. The sixth element, which is perhaps the most important of all, pertains to the outside world and is called the petty tyrant.

He looked at me as if silently asking me whether or not I had understood.

"I'm really mystified," I said. "You keep on saying that la Gorda is the petty tyrant of my life. Just what is a petty tyrant?"

"A petty tyrant is a tormentor," he replied. "Someone who either holds the power of life and death over warriors or simply annoys them to distraction."

Don Juan had a beaming smile as he spoke to me. He said that the new seers developed their own classification of petty tyrants; although the concept is one of their most serious and important findings, the new seers had a sense of humor about it. He assured me that there was a tinge of malicious humor in every one of their classifications, because humor was the only means of counteracting the compulsion of human awareness to take inventories and to make cumbersome classifications.

The new seers, in accordance with their practice, saw fit to head their classification with the primal source of energy, the one and only ruler in the universe, and they called it simply the tyrant. The rest of the despots and authoritarians were found to be, naturally, infinitely below the category of tyrant. Compared to the source of everything, the most fearsome, tyrannical men are buffoons; consequently, they were classified as petty tyrants, *pinches tiranos*.

He said that there were two subclasses of minor petty tyrants. The first subclass consisted of the petty tyrants who persecute and inflict misery but without actually causing anybody's death. They were called little petty tyrants, *pinches tiranitos*. The second consisted of the petty tyrants who are only exasperating and bothersome to no end. They were called small-fry petty tyrants, *repinches tiranitos,* or teensy-weensy petty tyrants, *pinches tiranitos chiquititos*.

I thought his classifications were ludicrous. I was sure that he was improvising the Spanish terms. I asked him if that was so.

"Not at all," he replied with an amused expression. "The new seers were great ones for classifications. Genaro is doubtless one of the greatest; if you'd observe him carefully, you'd realize exactly how the new seers feel about their classifications."

He laughed uproariously at my confusion when I asked him if he was pulling my leg.

"I wouldn't dream of doing that," he said, smiling. "Genaro may do that, but not I, especially when I know how you feel about classifications. It's just that the new seers were terribly irreverent."

He added that the little petty tyrants are further divided into four categories. One that torments with brutality and violence. Another that does it by creating unbearable apprehension through deviousness. Another which oppresses with sadness. And the last, which torments by making warriors rage.

"La Gorda is in a class of her own," he added. "She is an acting, small-fry petty tyrant. She annoys you to pieces and makes you rage. She even slaps you. With all that she is teaching you detachment."

"That's not possible!" I protested.

"You haven't yet put together all the ingredients of the new seers' strategy," he said. "Once you do that, you'll know how efficient and clever is the device of using a petty tyrant. I would certainly say that the strategy not only gets rid of self-importance; it also prepares warriors for the final realization that impeccability is the only thing that counts in the path of knowledge."

He said that what the new seers had in mind was a deadly manuever in which the petty tyrant is like a mountain peak and the attributes of warriorship are like climbers who meet at the summit.

"Usually, only four attributes are played," he went on. "The fifth, *will*, is always saved for an ultimate confrontation, when warriors are facing the firing squad, so to speak."

"Why is it done that way?"

"Because *will* belongs to another sphere, the unknown. The other four belong to the known, exactly where the petty tyrants are lodged. In fact, what turns human beings into petty tyrants is precisely the obsessive manipulation of the known."

Don Juan explained that the interplay of all the five attributes of warriorship is done only by seers who are also impeccable warriors and have mastery over *will*. Such an interplay is a supreme maneuver that cannot be performed on the daily human stage.

"Four attributes are all that is needed to deal with the worst of petty tyrants," he continued. "Provided, of course, that a petty tyrant has been found. As I said, the petty tyrant is the outside element, the one we cannot control and the element that is perhaps the most important of them all. My benefactor used to say that the warrior who stumbles on a petty tyrant is a lucky one. He meant that you're fortunate if you come upon one in your path, because if you don't, you have to go out and look for one."

He explained that one of the greatest accomplishments of the seers of the Conquest was a construct he called the three-phase progression. By understanding the nature of man, they were able to reach the incontestable conclusion that if seers can hold their own in facing petty tyrants, they can certainly face the unknown with impunity, and then they can even stand the presence of the unknowable.

"The average man's reaction is to think that the order of that statement should be reversed," he went on. "A seer who can hold his own in the face of the unknown can certainly face petty tyrants. But that's not so. What destroyed the superb seers of ancient times was that assumption. We know better now. We know that nothing can temper the spirit of a warrior as much as the challenge of dealing with impossible people in positions of power. Only under those conditions can warriors acquire the sobriety and serenity to stand the pressure of the unknowable."

I vociferously disagreed with him. I told him that in my opinion tyrants can only render their victims helpless or make them as brutal as they themselves are. I pointed out that countless studies had been done on the effects of physical and psychological torture on such victims.

"The difference is in something you just said," he retorted. "They are victims, not warriors. Once I felt just as you do. I'll tell you what made me change, but first let's go back again to what I said about the Conquest. The seers of that time couldn't have found a better ground. The Spaniards were the petty tyrants who tested the seers' skills to the limit; after dealing with the conquerors, the seers were capable of facing anything. They were the lucky ones. At that time there were petty tyrants everywhere.

"After all those marvelous years of abundance things changed a great deal. Petty tyrants never again had that scope; it was only during those times that their authority was unlimited. The perfect ingredient for the making of a superb seer is a petty tyrant with unlimited prerogatives.

"In our times, unfortunately, seers have to go to extremes to find a worthy one. Most of the time they have to be satisfied with very small fry."

"Did you find a petty tyrant yourself, don Juan?"

"I was lucky. A king-size one found me. At the time, though, I felt like you; I couldn't consider myself fortunate."

Don Juan said that his ordeal began a few weeks before he met his benefactor. He was barely twenty years old at the time. He had gotten a job at a sugar mill working as a laborer. He had always been very strong, so it was easy for him to get jobs that required muscle. One day when he was moving some heavy sacks of sugar a woman came by. She was very well dressed and seemed to be a woman of means. She was perhaps in her fifties, don Juan said, and very domineering. She looked at don Juan and then spoke to the foreman and left. Don Juan was then approached by the foreman, who told him that for a fee he would recommend him for a job in the boss's house. Don Juan told the man that he had no money. The foreman smiled and said not to worry because he would have plenty on payday. He patted don Juan's back and assured him it was a great honor to work for the boss.

Don Juan said that being a lowly ignorant Indian living hand-to-mouth, not only did he believe every word, he thought a good fairy had touched him. He promised to pay the foreman anything he wished. The foreman named a large sum, which had to be paid in installments.

Immediately thereafter the foreman himself took don Juan to the house, which was quite a distance from the town, and left him there with another foreman, a huge, somber, ugly man who asked a lot of questions. He wanted to know about don Juan's family. Don Juan answered that he didn't have any. The man was so pleased that he even smiled through his rotten teeth.

He promised don Juan that they would pay him plenty, and that he would even be in a position to save money, because he didn't have to spend any, for he was going to live and eat in the house.

The way the man laughed was terrifying. Don Juan knew that he had to escape immediately. He ran for the gate, but the man cut in front of him with a revolver in his hand. He cocked it and rammed it into don Juan's stomach. "You're here to work yourself to the bone," he said. "And don't you forget it." He shoved don Juan around with a billy club. Then he took him to the side of the house and, after observing that he worked his men every day from sunrise to sunset without a break, he put don Juan to work digging out two enormous tree stumps. He also told don Juan that if he ever tried to escape or went to the authorities he would shoot him dead—and that if don Juan should ever get away, he would swear in court that don Juan had tried to murder the boss. "You'll work here until you die," he said. "Another Indian will get your job then, just as you're taking a dead Indian's place."

Don Juan said that the house looked like a fortress, with armed men with machetes everywhere. So he got busy working and tried not to think about his predicament. At the end of the day, the man came back and kicked him all the way to the kitchen, because he did not like the defiant look in don Juan's eyes. He threatened to cut the tendons of don Juan's arms if he didn't obey him.

In the kitchen an old woman brought food, but don Juan was so upset and afraid that he couldn't eat. The old woman advised him to eat as much as he could. He had to be strong, she said, because his work would never end. She warned him that the man who had held his job had died just a day earlier. He was too weak to work and had fallen from a second-story window.

Don Juan said that he worked at the boss's place for three weeks and that the man bullied him every moment of every day. He made him work under the most dangerous conditions, doing the heaviest work imaginable, under the constant threat of his knife, gun, or billy club. He sent him daily to the stables to clean the stalls while the nervous stallions were in them. At the beginning of every day don Juan thought it would be his last one on earth. And surviving meant only that he had to go through the same hell again the next day.

What precipitated the end was don Juan's request to have some time off. The pretext was that he needed to go to town to pay the foreman of the sugar mill the money that he owed him. The other foreman retorted that don Juan could not stop working, not even for a minute, because he was in debt up to his ears just for the privilege of working there.

Don Juan knew that he was done for. He understood the man's maneuvers. Both he and the other foreman were in cahoots to get lowly Indians from the mill, work them to death, and divide their salaries. That realization angered him so intensely that he ran through the kitchen screaming and got inside the main house. The foreman and the other workers were caught totally by surprise. He ran out the front door and almost got away, but the foreman caught up with him on the road and shot him in the chest. He left him for dead.

Don Juan said that it was not his destiny to die; his benefactor found him there and tended him until he got well.

"When I told my benefactor the whole story," don Juan said, "he could hardly contain his excitement. 'That foreman is really a prize,' my benefactor said. 'He is too good to be wasted. Someday you must go back to that house.'

"He raved about my luck in finding a one-in-a-million petty tyrant with almost unlimited power. I thought the old man was nuts. It was years before I fully understood what he was talking about."

"That is one of the most horrible stories I have ever heard," I said. "Did you really go back to that house?"

"I certainly did, three years later. My benefactor was right. A petty tyrant like that one was one in a million and couldn't be wasted."

"How did you manage to go back?"

"My benefactor developed a strategy using the four attributes of warriorship: control, discipline, forbearance, and timing."

Don Juan said that his benefactor, in explaining to him what he had to do to profit from facing that ogre of a man, also told him what the new seers considered to be the four steps on the path of knowledge. The first step is the decision to become apprentices. After the apprentices change their views about themselves and the world they take the second step and become warriors, which is to say, beings capable of the utmost discipline and control over themselves. The third step, after acquiring forbearance and timing, is to become men of knowledge. When men of knowledge learn to *see* they have taken the fourth step and have become seers.

His benefactor stressed the fact that don Juan had been on the path of knowledge long enough to have acquired a minimum of the first two attributes: control

23

and discipline. Don Juan emphasized that both of these attributes refer to an inner state. A warrior is self-oriented, not in a selfish way, but in the sense of a total and continuous examination of the self.

"At that time, I was barred from the other two attributes," don Juan went on. "Forbearance and timing are not quite an inner state. They are in the domain of the man of knowledge. My benefactor showed them to me through his strategy."

"Does this mean that you couldn't have faced the petty tyrant by yourself?" I asked.

"I'm sure that I could have done it myself, although I have always doubted that I would have carried it off with flair and joyfulness. My benefactor was simply enjoying the encounter by directing it. The idea of using a petty tyrant is not only for perfecting the warrior's spirit, but also for enjoyment and happiness."

"How could anyone enjoy the monster you described?"

"He was nothing in comparison to the real monsters that the new seers faced during the Conquest. By all indications those seers enjoyed themselves blue dealing with them. They proved that even the worst tyrants can bring delight, provided, of course, that one is a warrior."

Don Juan explained that the mistake average men make in confronting petty tyrants is not to have a strategy to fall back on; the fatal flaw is that average men take themselves too seriously; their actions and feelings, as well as those of the petty tyrants, are all-important. Warriors, on the other hand, not only have a well-thought-out strategy, but are free from self-importance. What restrains their self-importance is that they have understood that reality is an interpretation we make. That knowledge was the definitive advantage that the new seers had over the simple-minded Spaniards.

He said that he became convinced he could defeat

the foreman using only the single realization that petty tyrants take themselves with deadly seriousness while warriors do not.

Following his benefactor's strategic plan, therefore, don Juan got a job in the same sugar mill as before. Nobody remembered that he had worked there in the past; peons came to that sugar mill and left it without leaving a trace.

His benefactor's strategy specified that don Juan had to be solicitous of whoever came to look for another victim. As it happened, the same woman came and spotted him, as she had done years ago. This time he was physically even stronger than before.

The same routine took place. The strategy, however, called for refusing payment to the foreman from the outset. The man had never been turned down and was taken aback. He threatened to fire don Juan from the job. Don Juan threatened him back, saying that he would go directly to the lady's house and see her. Don Juan knew that the woman, who was the wife of the owner of the mill, did not know what the two foremen were up to. He told the foreman that he knew where she lived, because he had worked in the surrounding fields cutting sugar cane. The man began to haggle, and don Juan demanded money from him before he would accept going to the lady's house. The foreman gave in and handed him a few bills. Don Juan was perfectly aware that the foreman's acquiescence was just a ruse to get him to go to the house.

"He himself once again took me to the house," don Juan said. "It was an old hacienda owned by the people of the sugar mill—rich men who either knew what was going on and didn't care, or were too indifferent even to notice.

"As soon as we got there, I ran into the house to look for the lady. I found her and dropped to my knees and kissed her hand to thank her. The two foremen were livid.

"The foreman at the house followed the same pattern as before. But I had the proper equipment to deal with him; I had control, discipline, forbearance, and timing. It turned out as my benefactor had planned it. My control made me fulfill the man's most asinine demands. What usually exhausts us in a situation like that is the wear and tear on our self-importance. Any man who has an iota of pride is ripped apart by being made to feel worthless.

"I gladly did everything he asked of me. I was joyful and strong. And I didn't give a fig about my pride or my fear. I was there as an impeccable warrior. To tune the spirit when someone is trampling on you is called control."

Don Juan explained that his benefactor's strategy required that instead of feeling sorry for himself as he had done before, he immediately go to work mapping the man's strong points, his weaknesses, his quirks of behavior.

He found that the foreman's strongest points were his violent nature and his daring. He had shot don Juan in broad daylight and in sight of scores of onlookers. His great weakness was that he liked his job and did not want to endanger it. Under no circumstances could he attempt to kill don Juan inside the compound in the daytime. His other weakness was that he was a family man. He had a wife and children who lived in a shack near the house.

"To gather all this information while they are beating you up is called discipline," don Juan said. "The man was a regular fiend. He had no saving grace. According to the new seers, a perfect petty tyrant has no redeeming feature."

Don Juan said that the other two attributes of warriorship, forbearance and timing, which he did not yet have, had been automatically included in his benefactor's strategy. Forbearance is to wait patiently—no

26

rush, no anxiety—a simple, joyful holding back of what is due.

"I groveled daily," don Juan continued, "sometimes crying under the man's whip. And yet I was happy. My benefactor's strategy was what made me go from day to day without hating the man's guts. I was a warrior. I knew that I was waiting and I knew what I was waiting for. Right there is the great joy of warriorship."

He added that his benefactor's strategy called for a systematic harassment of the man by taking cover with a higher order, just as the seers of the new cycle had done during the Conquest by shielding themselves with the Catholic church. A lowly priest was sometimes more powerful than a nobleman.

Don Juan's shield was the lady who got him the job. He kneeled in front of her and called her a saint every time he saw her. He begged her to give him the medallion of her patron saint so he could pray to him for her health and well-being.

"She gave me one," don Juan went on, "and that rattled the foreman to pieces. And when I got the servants to pray at night he nearly had a heart attack. I think he decided then to kill me. He couldn't afford to let me go on.

"As a countermeasure I organized a rosary among all the servants of the house. The lady thought I had the makings of a most pious man.

"I didn't sleep soundly after that, nor did I sleep in my bed. I climbed to the roof every night. From there I saw the man twice looking for me in the middle of the night with murder in his eyes.

"Daily he shoved me into the stallions' stalls hoping that I would be crushed to death, but I had a plank of heavy boards that I braced against one of the corners and protected myself behind it. The man never knew because he was nauseated by the horses—another of

27

his weaknesses, the deadliest of all, as things turned out."

Don Juan said that timing is the quality that governs the release of all that is held back. Control, discipline, and forbearance are like a dam behind which everything is pooled. Timing is the gate in the dam.

The man knew only violence, with which he terrorized. If his violence was neutralized he was rendered nearly helpless. Don Juan knew that the man would not dare to kill him in view of the house, so one day, in the presence of the other workers but in sight of his lady as well, don Juan insulted the man. He called him a coward, who was mortally afraid of the boss's wife.

His benefactor's strategy had called for being on the alert for a moment like that and using it to turn the tables on the petty tyrant. Unexpected things always happen that way. The lowest of the slaves suddenly makes fun of the tyrant, taunts him, makes him feel ridiculous in front of significant witnesses, and then rushes away without giving the tyrant time to retaliate.

"A moment later, the man went crazy with rage, but I was already solicitously kneeling in front of the lady," he continued.

Don Juan said that when the lady went inside the house, the man and his friends called him to the back, allegedly to do some work. The man was very pale, white with anger. From the sound of his voice don Juan knew what the man was really planning to do. Don Juan pretended to acquiesce, but instead of heading for the back, he ran for the stables. He trusted that the horses would make such a racket the owners would come out to see what was wrong. He knew that the man would not dare shoot him. That would have been too noisy and the man's fear of endangering his job was too overpowering. Don Juan also knew that the man would not go where the horses were—that is, unless he had been pushed beyond his endurance.

"I jumped inside the stall of the wildest stallion,"

don Juan said, "and the petty tyrant, blinded by rage, took out his knife and jumped in after me. I went instantly behind my planks. The horse kicked him once and it was all over.

"I had spent six months in that house and in that period of time I had exercised the four attributes of warriorship. Thanks to them, I had succeeded. Not once had I felt sorry for myself or wept in impotence. I had been joyful and serene. My control and discipline were as keen as they'd ever been, and I had had a firsthand view of what forbearance and timing did for impeccable warriors. And I had not once wished the man to die.

"My benefactor explained something very interesting. Forbearance means holding back with the spirit something that the warrior knows is rightfully due. It doesn't mean that a warrior goes around plotting to do anybody mischief, or planning to settle past scores. Forbearance is something independent. As long as the warrior has control, discipline, and timing, forbearance assures giving whatever is due to whoever deserves it."

"Do petty tyrants sometimes win, and destroy the warrior facing them?" I asked.

"Of course. There was a time when warriors died like flies at the beginning of the Conquest. Their ranks were decimated. The petty tyrants could put anyone to death, simply acting on a whim. Under that kind of pressure seers reached sublime states."

Don Juan said that that was the time when the surviving seers had to exert themselves to the limit to find new ways.

"The new seers used petty tyrants," don Juan said, staring at me fixedly, "not only to get rid of their self-importance, but to accomplish the very sophisticated maneuver of moving themselves out of this world. You'll understand that maneuver as we keep on discussing the mastery of awareness."

I explained to don Juan that what I had wanted to know was whether, in the present, in our times, the petty tyrants he had called small fry could ever defeat a warrior.

"All the time," he replied. "The consequences aren't as dire as those in the remote past. Today it goes without saying that warriors always have a chance to recuperate or to retrieve and come back later. But there is another side to this problem. To be defeated by a small-fry petty tyrant is not deadly, but devastating. The degree of mortality, in a figurative sense, is almost as high. By that I mean that warriors who succumb to a small-fry petty tyrant are obliterated by their own sense of failure and unworthiness. That spells high mortality to me."

"How do you measure defeat?"

"Anyone who joins the petty tyrant is defeated. To act in anger, without control and discipline, to have no forbearance, is to be defeated."

"What happens after warriors are defeated?"

"They either regroup themselves or they abandon the quest for knowledge and join the ranks of the petty tyrants for life."

3

The Eagle's Emanations

The next day, don Juan and I went for a walk along the road to the city of Oaxaca. The road was deserted at that hour. It was 2:00 P.M.

As we strolled leisurely, don Juan suddenly began to talk. He said that our discussion about the petty tyrants had been merely an introduction to the topic of awareness. I remarked that it had opened a new view for me. He asked me to explain what I meant.

I told him that it had to do with an argument we had had some years before about the Yaqui Indians. In the course of his teachings for the right side, he had tried to tell me about the advantages that the Yaquis could find in being oppressed. I had passionately argued that there were no possible advantages in the wretched conditions in which they lived. And I had told him that I could not understand how, being a Yaqui himself, he did not react against such a flagrant injustice.

He had listened attentively. Then, when I was sure he was going to defend his point, he agreed that the conditions of the Yaqui Indians were indeed wretched. But he pointed out that it was useless to single out the Yaquis when life conditions of man in general were horrendous.

"Don't just feel sorry for the poor Yaqui Indians," he had said. "Feel sorry for mankind. In the case of the Yaqui Indians, I can even say they're the lucky ones. They are oppressed, and because of that, some of them may come out triumphant in the end. But the oppressors, the petty tyrants that tread upon them, they don't have a chance in hell."

I had immediately answered him with a barrage of political slogans. I had not understood his point at all. He again tried to explain to me the concept of petty tyrants, but the whole idea bypassed me. It was only now that everything fit into place.

"Nothing has fit into place yet," he said, laughing at what I had told him. "Tomorrow, when you are in your normal state of awareness, you won't even remember what you've realized now."

I felt utterly depressed, for I knew he was right.

"What's going to happen to you is what happened to me," he continued. "My benefactor, the nagual Julian, made me realize in heightened awareness what you have realized yourself about petty tyrants. And I ended up, in my daily life, changing my opinions without knowing why.

"I had always been oppressed, so I had real venom toward my oppressors. Imagine my surprise when I found myself seeking the company of petty tyrants. I thought I had lost my mind."

We came to a place, on the side of the road, where some large boulders were half buried by an old landslide; don Juan headed for them and sat down on a flat rock. He signaled me to sit down, facing him. And then without further preliminaries, he started his explanation of the mastery of awareness.

He said that there were a series of truths that seers, old and new, had discovered about awareness, and that such truths had been arranged in a specific sequence for purposes of comprehension.

He explained that the mastery of awareness consisted in internalizing the total sequence of such truths. The first truth, he said, was that our familiarity with the world we perceive compels us to believe that we are surrounded by objects, existing by themselves and as themselves, just as we perceive them, whereas, in fact, there is no world of objects, but a universe of the Eagle's emanations.

He told me then that before he could explain the Eagle's emanations, he had to talk about the known, the unknown, and the unknowable. Most of the truths about awareness were discovered by the old seers, he said. But the order in which they were arranged had been worked out by the new seers. And without that order those truths were nearly incomprehensible.

He said that not to seek order was one of the great mistakes that the ancient seers made. A deadly consequence of that mistake was their assumption that the unknown and the unknowable are the same thing. It was up to the new seers to correct that error. They set up boundaries and defined the unknown as something that is veiled from man, shrouded perhaps by a terrifying context, but which, nonetheless, is within man's reach. The unknown becomes the known at a given time. The unknowable, on the other hand, is the indescribable, the unthinkable, the unrealizable. It is something that will never be known to us, and yet it is there, dazzling and at the same time horrifying in its vastness.

"How can seers make the distinction between the two?" I asked.

"There is a simple rule of thumb," he said. "In the face of the unknown, man is adventurous. It is a quality of the unknown to give us a sense of hope and happiness. Man feels robust, exhilarated. Even the apprehension that it arouses is very fulfilling. The new seers *saw* that man is at his best in the face of the unknown."

He said that whenever what is taken to be the un-

33

known turns out to be the unknowable the results are disastrous. Seers feel drained, confused. A terrible oppression takes possession of them. Their bodies lose tone, their reasoning and sobriety wander away aimlessly, for the unknowable has no energizing effects whatsoever. It is not within human reach; therefore, it should not be intruded upon foolishly or even prudently. The new seers realized that they had to be prepared to pay exorbitant prices for the faintest contact with it.

Don Juan explained that the new seers had had formidable barriers of tradition to overcome. At the time when the new cycle began, none of them knew for certain which procedures of their immense tradition were the right ones and which were not. Obviously, something had gone wrong with the ancient seers, but the new seers did not know what. They began by assuming that everything their predecessors had done was erroneous. Those ancient seers had been the masters of conjecture. They had, for one thing, assumed that their proficiency in *seeing* was a safeguard. They thought that they were untouchable—that is, until the invaders smashed them, and put most of them to horrendous deaths. The ancient seers had no protection whatsoever, despite their total certainty that they were invulnerable.

The new seers did not waste their time in speculations about what went wrong. Instead, they began to map the unknown in order to separate it from the unknowable.

"How did they map the unknown, don Juan?" I asked.

"Through the controlled use of *seeing*," he replied.

I said that what I had meant to ask was, what was entailed in mapping the unknown?

He answered that mapping the unknown means making it available to our perception. By steadily practicing *seeing*, the new seers found that the unknown and the known are really on the same footing, because both are within the reach of human perception. Seers, in fact, can leave the known at a given moment and enter into the unknown.

Whatever is beyond our capacity to perceive is the unknowable. And the distinction between it and the knowable is crucial. Confusing the two would put seers in a most precarious position whenever they are confronted with the unknowable.

"When this happened to the ancient seers," don Juan went on, "they thought their procedures had gone haywire. It never occurred to them that most of what's out there is beyond our comprehension. It was a terrifying error of judgment on their part, for which they paid dearly."

"What happened after the distinction between the unknown and the unknowable was realized?" I asked.

"The new cycle began," he replied. "That distinction is the frontier between the old and the new. Everything that the new seers have done stems from understanding that distinction."

Don Juan said that *seeing* was the crucial element in both the destruction of the ancient seers' world and in the reconstruction of the new view. It was through *seeing* that the new seers discovered certain undeniable facts, which they used to arrive at certain conclusions, revolutionary to them, about the nature of man and the world. These conclusions, which made the new cycle possible, were the truths about awareness he was explaining to me.

Don Juan asked me to accompany him to the center of town for a stroll around the square. On our way, we began to talk about machines and delicate instruments. He said that instruments are extensions of our senses, and I maintained that there are instruments that are not in that category, because they perform

35

functions that we are not physiologically capable of performing.

"Our senses are capable of everything," he asserted.

"I can tell you offhand that there are instruments that can detect radio waves that come from outer space," I said. "Our senses cannot detect radio waves."

"I have a different idea," he said. "I think our senses can detect everything we are surrounded by."

"What about the case of ultrasonic sounds?" I insisted. "We don't have the organic equipment to hear them."

"It is the seers' conviction that we've tapped a very small portion of ourselves," he replied.

He immersed himself in thought for a while as if he were trying to decide what to say next. Then he smiled.

"The first truth about awareness, as I have already told you," he began, "is that the world out there is not really as we think it is. We think it is a world of objects and it's not."

He paused as if to measure the effect of his words. I told him that I agreed with his premise, because everything could be reduced to being a field of energy. He said that I was merely intuiting a truth, and that to reason it out was not to verify it. He was not interested in my agreement or disagreement, he said, but in my attempt to comprehend what was involved in that truth.

"You cannot witness fields of energy," he went on. "Not as an average man, that is. Now, if you were able to *see* them, you would be a seer, in which case you would be explaining the truths about awareness. Do you understand what I mean?"

He went on to say that conclusions arrived at through reasoning had very little or no influence in altering the course of our lives. Hence, the countless examples of people who have the clearest convictions and yet act diametrically against them time and time again; and have as the only explanation for their behavior the idea that to err is human.

"The first truth is that the world is as it looks and yet it isn't," he went on. "It's not as solid and real as our perception has been led to believe, but it isn't a mirage either. The world is not an illusion, as it has been said to be; it's real on the one hand, and unreal on the other. Pay close attention to this, for it must be understood, not just accepted. We perceive. This is a hard fact. But what we perceive is not a fact of the same kind, because we learn what to perceive.

"Something out there is affecting our senses. This is the part that is real. The unreal part is what our senses tell us is there. Take a mountain, for instance. Our senses tell us that it is an object. It has size, color, form. We even have categories of mountains, and they are downright accurate. Nothing wrong with that; the flaw is simply that it has never occurred to us that our senses play only a superficial role. Our senses perceive the way they do because a specific feature of our awareness forces them to do so."

I began to agree with him again, but not because I wanted to, for I had not quite understood his point. Rather, I was reacting to a threatening situation. He made me stop.

"I've used the term 'the world,' " don Juan went on, "to mean everything that surrounds us. I have a better term, of course, but it would be quite incomprehensible to you. Seers say that we think there is a world of objects out there only because of our awareness. But what's really out there are the Eagle's emanations, fluid, forever in motion, and yet unchanged, eternal."

He stopped me with a gesture of his hand just as I was about to ask him what the Eagle's emanations were. He explained that one of the most dramatic legacies the old seers had left us was their discovery that the reason for the existence of all sentient beings is to enhance awareness. Don Juan called it a colossal discovery.

In a half-serious tone he asked me if I knew of a better answer to the question that has always haunted man: the reason for our existence. I immediately took a defensive position and began to argue about the meaninglessness of the question because it cannot be logically answered. I told him that in order to discuss that subject we would have to talk about religious beliefs and turn it all into a matter of faith.

"The old seers were not just talking about faith," he said. "They were not as practical as the new seers, but they were practical enough to know what they were *seeing*. What I was trying to point out to you with that question, which has rattled you so badly, is that our rationality alone cannot come up with an answer about the reason for our existence. Every time it tries, the answer turns into a matter of beliefs. The old seers took another road, and they did find an answer which doesn't involve faith alone."

He said that the old seers, risking untold dangers, actually *saw* the indescribable force which is the source of all sentient beings. They called it the Eagle, because in the few glimpses that they could sustain, they *saw* it as something that resembled a black-and-white eagle of infinite size.

They *saw* that it is the Eagle who bestows awareness. The Eagle creates sentient beings so that they will live and enrich the awareness it gives them with life. They also *saw* that it is the Eagle who devours that same enriched awareness after making sentient beings relinquish it at the moment of death.

"For the old seers," don Juan went on, "to say that the reason for existence is to enhance awareness is not a matter of faith or deduction. They *saw* it.

"They *saw* that the awareness of sentient beings

flies away at the moment of death and floats like a luminous cotton puff right into the Eagle's beak to be consumed. For the old seers that was the evidence that sentient beings live only to enrich the awareness that is the Eagle's food.''

Don Juan's elucidation was interrupted because he had to leave on a short business trip. Nestor drove him to Oaxaca. As I saw them off, I remembered that at the beginning of my association with don Juan, every time he mentioned a business trip I thought he was employing a euphemism for something else. I eventually realized that he meant what he said. Whenever such a trip was about to take place, he would put on one of his many immaculately tailored three-piece suits and would look like anything but the old Indian I knew. I had commented to him about the sophistication of his metamorphosis.

"A nagual is someone flexible enough to be anything," he had said. "To be a nagual, among other things, means to have no points to defend. Remember this—we'll come back to it over and over."

We had come back to it over and over, in every possible way; he did indeed seem to have no points to defend, but during his absence in Oaxaca I was given to just a shadow of doubt. Suddenly I realized that a nagual did have one point to defend—the description of the Eagle and what it does required, in my opinion, a passionate defense.

I tried to pose that question to some of don Juan's companions, but they eluded my probings. They told me that I was in quarantine from that kind of discussion until don Juan had finished his explanation.

The moment he returned, we sat down to talk and I asked him about it.

"Those truths are not something to defend passionately," he replied. "If you think that I'm trying to defend them, you are mistaken. Those truths were put

39

together for the delight and enlightenment of warriors, not to engage any proprietary sentiments. When I told you that a nagual has no points to defend, I meant, among other things, that a nagual has no obsessions."

I told him that I was not following his teachings, for I had become obsessed with his description of the Eagle and what it does. I remarked over and over about the awesomeness of such an idea.

"It is not just an idea," he said. "It is a fact. And a damn scary one if you ask me. The new seers were not simply playing with ideas."

"But what kind of a force would the Eagle be?"

"I wouldn't know how to answer that. The Eagle is as real for the seers as gravity and time are for you, and just as abstract and incomprehensible."

"Wait a minute, don Juan. Those are abstract concepts, but they do refer to real phenomena that can be corroborated. There are whole disciplines dedicated to that."

"The Eagle and its emanations are equally corroboratable," don Juan retorted. "And the discipline of the new seers is dedicated to doing just that."

I asked him to explain what the Eagle's emanations are.

He said that the Eagle's emanations are an immutable thing-in-itself, which engulfs everything that exists, the knowable and the unknowable.

"There is no way to describe in words what the Eagle's emanations really are," don Juan continued. "A seer must witness them."

"Have you witnessed them yourself, don Juan?"

"Of course I have, and yet I can't tell you what they are. They are a presence, almost a mass of sorts, a pressure that creates a dazzling sensation. One can catch only a glimpse of them, as one can catch only a glimpse of the Eagle itself."

"Would you say, don Juan, that the Eagle is the source of the emanations?"

"It goes without saying that the Eagle is the source of its emanations."

"I meant to ask if that is so visually."

"There is nothing visual about the Eagle. The entire body of a seer senses the Eagle. There is something in all of us that can make us witness with our entire body. Seers explain the act of *seeing* the Eagle in very simple terms: because man is composed of the Eagle's emanations, man need only revert back to his components. The problem arises with man's awareness; it is his awareness that becomes entangled and confused. At the crucial moment when it should be a simple case of the emanations acknowledging themselves, man's awareness is compelled to interpret. The result is a vision of the Eagle and the Eagle's emanations. But there is no Eagle and no Eagle's emanations. What is out there is something that no living creature can grasp."

I asked him if the source of the emanations was called the Eagle because eagles in general have important attributes.

"This is simply the case of something unknowable vaguely resembling something known," he replied. "On account of that, there have certainly been attempts to imbue eagles with attributes they don't have. But that always happens when impressionable people learn to perform acts that require great sobriety. Seers come in all sizes and shapes."

"Do you mean to say that there are different kinds of seers?"

"No. I mean that there are scores of imbeciles who become seers. Seers arc human beings full of foibles, or rather, human beings full of foibles are capable of becoming seers. Just as in the case of miserable people who become superb scientists.

"The characteristic of miserable seers is that they are willing to forget the wonder of the world. They become overwhelmed by the fact that they *see* and

41

believe that it's their genius that counts. A seer must be a paragon in order to override the nearly invincible laxness of our human condition. More important than *seeing* itself is what seers do with what they *see*."

"What do you mean by that, don Juan?"

"Look at what some seers have done to us. We are stuck with their vision of an Eagle that rules us and devours us at the moment of our death."

He said that there is a definite laxness in that version, and that personally he did not appreciate the idea of something devouring us. For him, it would be more accurate to say that there is a force that attracts our consciousness, much as a magnet attracts iron shavings. At the moment of dying, all of our being disintegrates under the attraction of that immense force.

That such an event was interpreted as the Eagle devouring us he found grotesque, because it turns an indescribable act into something as mundane as eating.

"I'm a very average man," I said. "The description of an Eagle that devours us had a great impact on me."

"The real impact can't be measured until the moment when you *see* it yourself," he said. "But you must bear in mind that our flaws remain with us even after we become seers. So when you *see* that force, you may very well agree with the lax seers who called it the Eagle, as I did myself. On the other hand, you may not. You may resist the temptation to ascribe human attributes to what is incomprehensible, and actually improvise a new name for it, a more accurate one."

"Seers who *see* the Eagle's emanations often call them commands," don Juan said. "I wouldn't mind calling them commands myself if I hadn't got used to calling them emanations. It was a reaction to my benefactor's preference; for him they were commands. I thought that term was more in keeping with his forceful personality than with mine. I wanted something impersonal. 'Commands' sounds too human to me, but that's what they really are, commands.''

Don Juan said that to *see* the Eagle's emanations is to court disaster. The new seers soon discovered the tremendous difficulties involved, and only after great tribulations in trying to map the unknown and separate it from the unknowable did they realize that everything is made out of the Eagle's emanations. Only a small portion of those emanations is within reach of human awareness, and that small portion is still further reduced, to a minute fraction, by the constraints of our daily lives. That minute fraction of the Eagle's emanations is the known; the small portion within possible reach of human awareness is the unknown, and the incalculable rest is the unknowable.

He went on to say that the new seers, being pragmatically oriented, became immediately cognizant of the compelling power of the emanations. They realized that all living creatures are forced to employ the Eagle's emanations without ever knowing what they are. They also realized that organisms are constructed to grasp a certain range of those emanations and that every species has a definite range. The emanations exert great pressure on organisms, and through that pressure organisms construct their perceivable world.

"In our case, as human beings," don Juan said, "we employ those emanations and interpret them as reality. But what man senses is such a small portion of the Eagle's emanations that it's ridiculous to put much stock in our perceptions, and yet it isn't possible for us to disregard our perceptions. The new seers found this out the hard way—after courting tremendous dangers.''

Don Juan was sitting where he usually sat in the large room. Ordinarily there was no furniture in that room—people sat on mats on the floor—but Carol, the nagual woman, had managed to furnish it with very comfortable armchairs for the sessions when she and I took turns reading to him from the works of Spanish-speaking poets.

"I want you to be very aware of what we are doing," he said as soon as I sat down. "We are discussing the mastery of awareness. The truths we're discussing are the principles of that mastery."

He added that in his teachings for the right side he had demonstrated those principles to my normal awareness with the help of one of his seer companions, Genaro, and that Genaro had played around with my awareness with all the humor and irreverence for which the new seers were known.

"Genaro is the one who should be here telling you about the Eagle," he said, "except that his versions are too irreverent. He thinks that the seers who called that force the Eagle were either very stupid or were making a grand joke, because eagles not only lay eggs, they also lay turds."

Don Juan laughed and said that he found Genaro's comments so appropriate that he couldn't resist laughter. He added that if the new seers had been the ones to describe the Eagle the description would certainly have been made half in fun.

I told don Juan that on one level I took the Eagle as a poetic image, and as such it delighted me, but on another level I took it literally, and that terrified me.

"One of the greatest forces in the lives of warriors is fear," he said. "It spurs them to learn."

He reminded me that the description of the Eagle came from the ancient seers. The new seers were through with description, comparison, and conjecture of any sort. They wanted to get directly to the source of things and consequently risked unlimited danger to get to it. They did *see* the Eagle's emanations. But they never tampered with the description of the Eagle.

They felt that it took too much energy to *see* the Eagle, and that the ancient seers had already paid heavily for their scant glimpse of the unknowable.

"How did the old seers come around to describing the Eagle?" I asked.

"They needed a minimal set of guidelines about the unknowable for purposes of instruction," he replied. "They resolved it with a sketchy description of the force that rules all there is, but not of its emanations, because the emanations cannot be rendered at all in a language of comparisons. Individual seers may feel the urge to make comments about certain emanations, but that will remain personal. In other words, there is no pat version of the emanations, as there is of the Eagle."

"The new seers seem to have been very abstract," I commented. "They sound like modern-day philosophers."

"No. The new seers were terribly practical men," he replied. "They weren't involved in concocting rational theories."

He said that the ancient seers were the ones who were the abstract thinkers. They built monumental edifices of abstractions proper to them and their time. And just like the modern-day philosophers, they were not at all in control of their concatenations. The new seers, on the other hand, imbued with practicality, were able to *see* a flux of emanations and to *see* how man and other living beings utilize them to construct their perceivable world.

"How are those emanations utilized by man, don Juan?"

"It's so simple it sounds idiotic. For a seer, men are luminous beings. Our luminosity is made up of that portion of the Eagle's emanations which is encased in our egglike cocoon. That particular portion, that handful of emanations that is encased, is what makes us

45

men. To perceive is to match the emanations contained inside our cocoon with those that are outside.

"Seers can *see*, for instance, the emanations inside any living creature and can tell which of the outside emanations would match them."

"Are the emanations like beams of light?" I asked.

"No. Not at all. That would be too simple. They are something indescribable. And yet, my personal comment would be to say that they are like filaments of light. What's incomprehensible to normal awareness is that the filaments are aware. I can't tell you what that means, because I don't know what I am saying. All I can tell you with my personal comments is that the filaments are aware of themselves, alive and vibrating, that there are so many of them that numbers have no meaning and that each of them is an eternity in itself."

4
The Glow of Awareness

Don Juan, don Genaro, and I had just returned from gathering plants in the surrounding mountains. We were at don Genaro's house, sitting around the table, when don Juan made me change levels of awareness. Don Genaro had been staring at me and began to chuckle. He remarked how odd he thought it was that I had two completely different standards for dealing with the two sides of awareness. My relation with him was the most obvious example. On my right side, he was the respected and feared sorcerer don Genaro, a man whose incomprehensible acts delighted me and at the same time filled me with mortal terror. On my left side, he was plain Genaro, or Genarito, with no don attached to his name, a charming and kind seer whose acts were thoroughly comprehensible and coherent with what I myself did or tried to do.

I agreed with him and added that on my left side, the man whose mere presence made me shake like a leaf was Silvio Manuel, the most mysterious of don Juan's companions. I also said that don Juan, being a true nagual, transcended arbitrary standards and was respected and admired by me in both states.

"But is he feared?" Genaro asked in a quivering voice.

"Very feared," don Juan interjected in a falsetto voice.

We all laughed, but don Juan and Genaro laughed with such abandon that I immediately suspected they knew something they were holding back.

Don Juan was reading me like a book. He explained that in the intermediate stage, before one enters fully into the left-side awareness, one is capable of tremendous concentration, but one is also susceptible to every conceivable influence. I was being influenced by suspicion.

"La Gorda is always at this stage," he said. "She learns beautifully, but she's a royal pain in the neck. She can't help being driven by anything that comes her way, including, of course, very good things, like keen concentration."

Don Juan explained that the new seers discovered that the transition period is the time when the deepest learning takes place, and that it is also the time when warriors must be supervised and explanations must be given to them so they can evaluate them properly. If no explanations are given to them before they enter into the left side, they will be great sorcerers but poor seers, as the ancient Toltecs were.

Female warriors in particular fall prey to the lure of the left side, he said. They are so nimble that they can go into the left side with no effort, often too soon for their own good.

After a long silence, Genaro fell asleep. Don Juan began to speak. He said that the new seers had had to invent a number of terms in order to explain the second truth about awareness. His benefactor had changed some of those terms to suit himself, and he himself had done the same, guided by the seers' belief that it does not make any difference what terms are used as long as the truths have been verified by *seeing*.

I was curious to know what terms he had changed, but I didn't know quite how to word my question. He took it that I was doubting his right or his ability to change them and explained that if the terms we propose originate in our reason they can only communicate the mundane agreement of everyday life. When seers propose a term, on the other hand, it is never a figure of speech because it stems from *seeing* and embraces everything that seers can attain.

I asked him why he had changed the terms.

"It's a nagual's duty always to look for better ways to explain," he replied. "Time changes everything, and every new nagual has to incorporate new words, new ideas, to describe his *seeing*."

"Do you mean that a nagual takes ideas from the world of everyday life?" I asked.

"No. I mean that a nagual talks about *seeing* in ever new ways," he said. "For instance, as the new nagual, you'd have to say that awareness gives rise to perception. You'd be saying the same thing my benefactor said, but in a different way."

"What do the new seers say perception is, don Juan?"

"They say that perception is a condition of alignment; the emanations inside the cocoon become aligned with those outside that fit them. Alignment is what allows awareness to be cultivated by every living creature. Seers make these statements because they *see* living creatures as they really are: luminous beings that look like bubbles of whitish light."

I asked him how the emanations inside the cocoon fit those outside so as to accomplish perception.

"The emanations inside and the emanations outside," he said, "are the same filaments of light. Sentient beings are minute bubbles made out of those filaments, microscopic points of light, attached to the infinite emanations."

He went on to explain that the luminosity of living

49

beings is made by the particular portion of the Eagle's emanations they happen to have inside their luminous cocoons. When seers *see* perception, they witness that the luminosity of the Eagle's emanations outside those creatures' cocoons brightens the luminosity of the emanations inside their cocoons. The outside luminosity attracts the inside one; it traps it, so to speak, and fixes it. That fixation is the awareness of every specific being.

Seers can also *see* how the emanations outside the cocoon exert a particular pressure on the portion of emanations inside. This pressure determines the degree of awareness that every living being has.

I asked him to clarify how the Eagle's emanations outside the cocoon exert pressure on those inside.

"The Eagle's emanations are more than filaments of light," he replied. "Each one of them is a source of boundless energy. Think of it this way: since some of the emanations outside the cocoon are the same as the emanations inside, their energies are like a continuous pressure. But the cocoon isolates the emanations that are inside its web and thereby directs the pressure.

"I've mentioned to you that the old seers were masters of the art of handling awareness," he went on. "What I can add now is that they were the masters of that art because they learned to manipulate the structure of man's cocoon. I've said to you that they unraveled the mystery of being aware. By that I meant that they *saw* and realized that awareness is a glow in the cocoon of living beings. They rightly called it the glow of awareness."

He explained that the old seers *saw* that man's awareness is a glow of amber luminosity more intense than the rest of the cocoon. That glow is on a narrow, vertical band on the extreme right side of the cocoon, running along its entire length. The mastery of the old seers was to move that glow, to make it spread from its original setting on the surface of the cocoon inward across its width.

He stopped talking and looked at Genaro, who was still sound asleep.

"Genaro doesn't give a fig about explanations," he said. "He's a doer. My benefactor pushed him constantly to face insoluble problems. So he entered into the left side proper and never had a chance to ponder and wonder."

"Is it better to be that way, don Juan?"

"It depends. For him, it's perfect. For you and for me, it wouldn't be satisfactory, because in one way or another we are called upon to explain. Genaro or my benefactor are more like the old than the new seers: they can control and do what they want with the glow of awareness."

He stood up from the mat where we were sitting and stretched his arms and legs. I pressed him to continue talking. He smiled and said that I needed to rest, that my concentration was waning.

There was a knock at the door. I woke up. It was dark. For a moment I could not remember where I was. There was something in me that was far away, as if part of me were still asleep, yet I was fully awake. Enough moonlight came through the open window so that I could see.

I saw don Genaro get up and go to the door. I realized then that I was at his house. Don Juan was sound asleep on a mat on the floor. I had the distinct impression that the three of us had fallen asleep after returning dead tired from a trip to the mountains.

Don Genaro lit his kerosene lantern. I followed him into the kitchen. Someone had brought him a pot of hot stew and a stack of tortillas.

"Who brought you food?" I asked him. "Do you have a woman around here that cooks for you?"

Don Juan had come into the kitchen. Both of them

looked at me, smiling. For some reason their smiles were terrifying to me. I was about to scream in terror, in fact, when don Juan hit me on the back and made me shift into a state of heightened awareness. I realized then that perhaps during my sleep, or as I woke up, I had drifted back to everyday awareness.

The sensation I experienced then, once I was back in heightened awareness, was a mixture of relief and anger and the most acute sadness. I was relieved that I was myself again, for I had come to regard those incomprehensible states as being my true self. There was one simple reason for that—in those states I felt complete; nothing was missing from me. The anger and the sadness were a reaction to impotence. I was more aware than ever of the limitations of my being.

I asked don Juan to explain to me how it was possible for me to do what I was doing. In states of heightened awareness I could look back and remember everything about myself; I could give an account of everything I had done in either state; I could even remember my incapacity to recollect. But once I had returned to my normal, everyday level of awareness I could not recall anything I had done in heightened awareness, even if my life depended on it.

"Hold it, hold it there," he said. "You haven't remembered anything yet. Heightened awareness is only an intermediate state. There is infinitely more beyond that, and you have been there many, many times. Right now you can't remember, even if your life depends on it."

He was right. I had no idea what he was talking about. I pleaded for an explanation.

"The explanation is coming," he said. "It's a slow process, but we'll get to it. It is slow because I am just like you: I like to understand. I am the opposite of my benefactor, who was not given to explaining. For him there was only action. He used to put us squarely against incomprehensible problems and let us resolve them for ourselves. Some of us never did resolve anything, and we ended up very much in the same boat with the old seers: all action and no real knowledge."

"Are those memories trapped in my mind?" I asked.

"No. That would make it too simple," he replied. "The actions of seers are more complex than dividing a man into mind and body. You have forgotten what you've done, or what you've witnessed, because when you were performing what you've forgotten you were *seeing*."

I asked don Juan to reinterpret what he had just said.

Patiently, he explained that everything I had forgotten had taken place in states in which my everyday awareness had been enhanced, intensified, a condition that meant that other areas of my total being were used.

"Whatever you've forgotten is trapped in those areas of your total being," he said. "To be using those other areas is to *see*."

"I'm more confused than ever, don Juan," I said.

"I don't blame you," he said. "*Seeing* is to lay bare the core of everything, to witness the unknown and to glimpse into the unknowable. As such, it doesn't bring one solace. Seers ordinarily go to pieces on finding out that existence is incomprehensibly complex and that our normal awareness maligns it with its limitations."

He reiterated that my concentration had to be total, that to understand was of crucial importance, that the new seers placed the highest value on deep, unemotional realizations.

"For instance, the other day," he went on, "when you understood about la Gorda's and your self-importance, you didn't understand anything really. You had an emotional outburst, that was all. I say this because the next day you were back on your high horse of self-importance as if you never had realized anything.

"The same thing happened to the old seers. They were given to emotional reactions. But when the time came for them to understand what they had *seen,* they couldn't do it. To understand one needs sobriety, not emotionality. Beware of those who weep with realization, for they have realized nothing.

"There are untold dangers in the path of knowledge for those without sober understanding," he continued. "I am outlining the order in which the new seers arranged the truths about awareness, so it will serve you as a map, a map that you have to corroborate with your *seeing,* but not with your eyes."

There was a long pause. He stared at me. He was definitely waiting for me to ask him a question.

"Everybody falls prey to the mistake that *seeing* is done with the eyes," he continued. "But don't be surprised that after so many years you haven't realized yet that *seeing* is not a matter of the eyes. It's quite normal to make that mistake."

"What is *seeing,* then?" I asked.

He replied that *seeing* is alignment. And I reminded him that he had said that perception is alignment. He explained then that the alignment of emanations used routinely is the perception of the day-to-day world, but the alignment of emanations that are never used ordinarily is *seeing.* When such an alignment occurs one *sees. Seeing,* therefore, being produced by alignment out of the ordinary, cannot be something one could merely look at. He said that in spite of the fact that I had *seen* countless times, it had not occurred to me to disregard my eyes. I had succumbed to the way *seeing* is labeled and described.

"When seers *see,* something explains everything as the new alignment takes place," he continued. "It's a voice that tells them in their ear what's what. If that voice is not present, what the seer is engaged in isn't *seeing.*"

After a moment's pause, he continued explaining

the voice of *seeing*. He said that it was equally falla-
cious to say that *seeing* was hearing, because it was
infinitely more than that, but that seers had opted for
using sound as a gauge of a new alignment.

He called the voice of *seeing* a most mysterious
inexplicable thing. "My personal conclusion is that
the voice of *seeing* belongs only to man," he said. "It
may happen because talking is something that no one
else besides man does. The old seers believed it was
the voice of an overpowering entity intimately related
to mankind, a protector of man. The new seers found
out that that entity, which they called the mold of
man, doesn't have a voice. The voice of *seeing* for the
new seers is something quite incomprehensible; they
say it's the glow of awareness playing on the Eagle's
emanations as a harpist plays on a harp."

He refused to explain it any further, arguing that
later on, as he proceeded with his explanation, everything would become clear to me.

My concentration had been so total while don Juan
spoke that I actually did not remember sitting down at
the table to eat. When don Juan stopped talking, I
noticed that his plate of stew was nearly finished.

Genaro was staring at me with a beaming smile. My
plate was in front of me on the table, and it too was
empty. There was only a tiny residue of stew left in it,
as if I had just finished eating. I did not remember
eating it at all, but neither did I remember walking to
the table or sitting down.

"Did you like the stew?" Genaro asked me and
looked away.

I said I did, because I did not want to admit that I
was having problems recollecting.

"It had too much chile for my taste," Genaro said.
"You never eat hot food yourself, so I'm sort of worried about what it will do to you. You shouldn't have

eaten two servings. I suppose you're a little more pig-
gish when you're in heightened awareness, eh?''

I admitted that he was probably right. He handed
me a large pitcher of water to quench my thirst and
soothe my throat. When I eagerly drank all of it, both
of them broke into howling laughter.

Suddenly, I realized what was going on. My realization was physical. It was a flash of yellowish light
that hit me as if a match had been struck right between
my eyes. I knew then that Genaro was joking. I had
not eaten. I had been so absorbed in don Juan's explanation that I had forgotten about everything else. The
plate in front of me was Genaro's.

After dinner don Juan went on with his explanation
about the glow of awareness. Genaro sat by me, listening as if he had never heard the explanation before.

Don Juan said that the pressure that the emanations
outside the cocoon, which are called emanations at
large, exert on the emanations inside the cocoon is the
same in all sentient beings. Yet the results of that pressure are vastly different among them, because their
cocoons react to that pressure in every conceivable
way. There are, however, degrees of uniformity
within certain boundaries.

"Now," he went on, "when seers *see* that the pressure of the emanations at large bears down on the
emanations inside, which are always in motion, and
makes them stop moving, they know that the luminous
being at that moment is fixated by awareness.

"To say that the emanations at large bear down on
those inside the cocoon and make them stop moving
means that seers *see* something indescribable, the
meaning of which they know without a shadow of
doubt. It means that the voice of *seeing* has told them
that the emanations inside the cocoon are completely
at rest and match some of those which are outside."

He said that seers maintain, naturally, that awareness always comes from outside ourselves, that the

real mystery is not inside us. Since by nature the emanations at large are made to fixate what is inside the cocoon, the trick of awareness is to let the fixating emanations merge with what is inside us. Seers believe that if we let that happen we become what we really are—fluid, forever in motion, eternal.

There was a long pause. Don Juan's eyes had an intense shine. They seemed to be looking at me from a great depth. I had the feeling that each of his eyes was an independent point of brilliance. For an instant he appeared to be struggling against an invisible force, a fire from within that intended to consume him. It passed and he went on talking.

"The degree of awareness of every individual sentient being," he continued, "depends on the degree to which it is capable of letting the pressure of the emanations at large carry it."

After a long interruption, don Juan continued explaining. He said that seers *saw* that from the moment of conception awareness is enhanced, enriched, by the process of being alive. He said that seers *saw*, for instance, that the awareness of an individual insect or that of an individual man grows from the moment of conception in astoundingly different ways, but with equal consistency.

"Is it from the moment of conception or from the moment of birth that awareness develops?" I asked.

"Awareness develops from the moment of conception," he replied. "I have always told you that sexual energy is something of ultimate importance and that it has to be controlled and used with great care. But you have always resented what I said, because you thought I was speaking of control in terms of morality; I always meant it in terms of saving and rechanneling energy."

Don Juan looked at Genaro. Genaro nodded his head in approval.

"Genaro is going to tell you what our benefactor, the nagual Julian, used to say about saving and re-channeling sexual energy," don Juan said to me.

"The nagual Julian used to say that to have sex is a matter of energy," Genaro began. "For instance, he never had any problems having sex, because he had bushels of energy. But he took one look at me and prescribed right away that my peter was just for peeing. He told me that I didn't have enough energy to have sex. He said that my parents were too bored and too tired when they made me; he said that I was the result of very boring sex, *cojida aburrida*. I was born like that, bored and tired. The nagual Julian recommended that people like me should never have sex; this way we can store the little energy we have.

"He said the same thing to Silvio Manuel and to Emilito. He *saw* that the others had enough energy. They were not the result of bored sex. He told them that they could do anything they wanted with their sexual energy, but he recommended that they control themselves and understand the Eagle's command that sex is for bestowing the glow of awareness. We all said we had understood.

"One day, without any warning at all, he opened the curtain of the other world with the help of his own benefactor, the nagual Elias, and pushed all of us inside, with no hesitation whatsoever. All of us, except Silvio Manuel, nearly died in there. We had no energy to withstand the impact of the other world. None of us, except Silvio Manuel, had followed the nagual's recommendation."

"What is the curtain of the other world?" I asked don Juan.

"What Genaro said—it is a curtain," don Juan replied. "But you're getting off the subject. You always do. We're talking about the Eagle's command about sex. It is the Eagle's command that sexual energy be used for creating life. Through sexual energy, the eagle bestows awareness. So when sentient beings are engaged in sexual intercourse, the emanations inside their cocoons do their best to bestow awareness to the new sentient being they are creating."

He said that during the sexual act, the emanations encased inside the cocoon of both partners undergo a profound agitation, the culminating point of which is a merging, a fusing of two pieces of the glow of awareness, one from each partner, that separate from their cocoons.

"Sexual intercourse is always a bestowal of awareness even though the bestowal may not be consolidated," he went on. "The emanations inside the cocoon of human beings don't know of intercourse for fun."

Genaro leaned over toward me from his chair across the table and talked to me in a low voice, shaking his head for emphasis.

"The nagual is telling you the truth," he said and winked at me. "Those emanations really don't know."

Don Juan fought not to laugh and added that the fallacy of man is to act with total disregard for the mystery of existence and to believe that such a sublime act of bestowing life and awareness is merely a physical drive that one can twist at will.

Genaro made obscene sexual gestures, twisting his pelvis around, on and on. Don Juan nodded and said that that was exactly what he meant. Genaro thanked him for acknowledging his one and only contribution to the explanation of awareness.

Both of them laughed like idiots, saying that if I had known how serious their benefactor was about the explanation of awareness, I would be laughing with them.

I earnestly asked don Juan what all this meant for an average man in the day-to-day world.

"You mean what Genaro is doing?" he asked me in mock seriousness.

Their glee was always contagious. It took a long time for them to calm down. Their level of energy was so high that next to them, I seemed old and decrepit.

"I really don't know," don Juan finally answered me. "All I know is what it means to warriors. They know that the only real energy we possess is a life-bestowing sexual energy. This knowledge makes them permanently conscious of their responsibility.

"If warriors want to have enough energy to *see*, they must become misers with their sexual energy. That was the lesson the nagual Julian gave us. He pushed us into the unknown, and we all nearly died. Since everyone of us wanted to *see*, we, of course, abstained from wasting our glow of awareness."

I had heard him voice that belief before. Every time he did, we got into an argument. I always felt compelled to protest and raise objections to what I thought was a puritanical attitude toward sex.

I again raised my objections. Both of them laughed to tears.

"What can be done with man's natural sensuality?" I asked don Juan.

"Nothing," he replied. "There is nothing wrong with man's sensuality. It's man's ignorance of and disregard for his magical nature that is wrong. It's a mistake to waste recklessly the life-bestowing force of sex and not have children, but it's also a mistake not to know that in having children one taxes the glow of awareness."

"How do seers know that having children taxes the glow of awareness?" I asked.

"They *see* that on having a child, the parents' glow of awareness diminishes and the child's increases. In some supersensitive, frail parents, the glow of awareness almost disappears. As children enhance their awareness, a big dark spot develops in the luminous

60

cocoon of the parents, on the very place from which the glow was taken away. It is usually on the midsection of the cocoon. Sometimes those spots can even be *seen* superimposed on the body itself."

I asked him if there was anything that could be done to give people a more balanced understanding of the glow of awareness.

"Nothing," he said. "At least, there is nothing that seers can do. Seers aim to be free, to be unbiased witnesses incapable of passing judgment; otherwise they would have to assume the responsibility for bringing about a more adjusted cycle. No one can do that. The new cycle, if it is to come, must come of itself."

5

The First Attention

The following day we ate breakfast at dawn, then don Juan made me shift levels of awareness.

"Today, let's go to an original setting," don Juan said to Genaro.

"By all means," Genaro said gravely. He glanced at me and then added in a low voice, as if not wanting me to overhear him, "Does he have to . . . perhaps it's too much . . ."

In a matter of seconds my fear and suspicion escalated to unbearable heights. I was sweating and panting. Don Juan came to my side and, with an expression of almost uncontrollable amusement, assured me that Genaro was just entertaining himself at my expense, and that we were going to a place where the original seers had lived thousands of years ago.

As don Juan was speaking to me, I happened to glance at Genaro. He slowly shook his head from side to side. It was an almost imperceptible gesture, as if he were letting me know that don Juan was not telling the truth. I went into a state of nervous frenzy, near hysteria—and stopped only when Genaro burst into laughter.

I marveled how easily my emotional states could

escalate to nearly unmanageable heights or drop to nothing.

Don Juan, Genaro, and I left Genaro's house in the early morning and traveled a short distance into the surrounding eroded hills. Presently we stopped and sat down on top of an enormous flat rock, on a gradual slope, in a corn field that seemed to have been recently harvested.

"This is the original setting," don Juan said to me. "We'll come back here a couple more times, during the course of my explanation."

"Very weird things happen here at night," Genaro said. "The nagual Julian actually caught an ally here. Or rather, the ally . . ."

Don Juan made a noticeable gesture with his eyebrows and Genaro stopped in midsentence. He smiled at me.

"It's too early in the day for scary stories," Genaro said. "Let's wait until dark."

He stood up and began creeping all around the rock, tiptoeing with his spine arched backward.

"What was he saying about your benefactor's catching an ally here?" I asked don Juan.

He did not answer right away. He was ecstatic, watching Genaro's antics.

"He was referring to some sophisticated use of awareness," he finally replied, still staring at Genaro.

Genaro completed a circle around the rock and came back and sat down by me. He was panting heavily, almost wheezing, out of breath.

Don Juan seemed fascinated by what Genaro had done. Again I had the feeling that they were amusing themselves at my expense, that both of them were up to something I knew nothing about.

Suddenly, don Juan began his explanation. His voice soothed me. He said that after much toiling, seers arrived at the conclusion that the consciousness

63

of adult human beings, matured by the process of growth, can no longer be called awareness, because it has been modified into something more intense and complex, which seers call attention.

"How do seers know that man's awareness is being cultivated and that it grows?" I asked.

He said that at a given time in the growth of human beings a band of the emanations inside their cocoons becomes very bright; as human beings accumulate experience, it begins to glow. In some instances, the glow of this band of emanations increases so dramatically that it fuses with the emanations from the outside. Seers, witnessing an enhancement of this kind, had to surmise that awareness is the raw material and attention the end product of maturation.

"How do seers describe attention?" I asked.

"They say that attention is the harnessing and enhancing of awareness through the process of being alive," he replied.

He said that the danger of definitions is that they simplify matters to make them understandable; in this case, in defining attention, one runs the risk of transforming a magical, miraculous accomplishment into something commonplace. Attention is man's greatest single accomplishment. It develops from raw animal awareness until it covers the entire gamut of human alternatives. Seers perfect it even further until it covers the whole scope of human possibilities.

I wanted to know if there was a special significance to alternatives and possibilities in the seers' view.

Don Juan replied that human alternatives are everything we are capable of choosing as persons. They have to do with the level of our day-to-day range, the known; and owing to that fact, they are quite limited in number and scope. Human possibilities belong to the unknown. They are not what we are capable of choosing but what we are capable of attaining. He said that an example of human alternatives is our choice to believe that the human body is an object among objects. An example of human possibilities is the seers' achievement in viewing man as an egglike luminous being. With the body as an object one tackles the known, with the body as a luminous egg one tackles the unknown; human possibilities have, therefore, nearly an inexhaustible scope.

"Seers say that there are three types of attention," don Juan went on. "When they say that, they mean it just for human beings, not for all the sentient beings in existence. But the three are not just types of attention, they are rather three levels of attainment. They are the first, second, and third attention, each of them an independent domain, complete in itself."

He explained that the first attention in man is animal awareness, which has been developed, through the process of experience, into a complex, intricate, and extremely fragile faculty that takes care of the day-to-day world in all its innumerable aspects. In other words, everything that one can think about is part of the first attention.

"The first attention is everything we are as average men," he continued. "By virtue of such an absolute rule over our lives, the first attention is the most valuable asset that the average man has. Perhaps it is even our only asset.

"Taking into account its true value, the new seers started a rigorous examination of the first attention through *seeing*. Their findings molded their total outlook and the outlook of all their descendants, even though most of them do not understand what those seers really *saw*."

He emphatically warned me that the conclusions of the new seers' rigorous examination had very little to do with reason or rationality, because in order to examine and explain the first attention, one must *see* it.

Only seers can do that. But to examine what seers *see* in the first attention is essential. It allows the first attention the only opportunity it will ever have to realize its own workings.

"In terms of what seers *see*, the first attention is the glow of awareness developed to an ultra shine," he continued. "But it is a glow fixed on the surface of the cocoon, so to speak. It is a glow that covers the known.

"The second attention, on the other hand, is a more complex and specialized state of the glow of awareness. It has to do with the unknown. It comes about when unused emanations inside man's cocoon are utilized.

"The reason I called the second attention specialized is that in order to utilize those unused emanations, one needs uncommon, elaborate tactics that require supreme discipline and concentration."

He said that he had told me before, when he was teaching me the art of *dreaming*, that the concentration needed to be aware that one is having a dream is the forerunner of the second attention. That concentration is a form of consciousness that is not in the same category as the consciousness needed to deal with the daily world.

He said that the second attention is also called the left-side awareness; and it is the vastest field that one can imagine, so vast in fact that it seems limitless.

"I wouldn't stray into it for anything in this world," he went on. "It is a quagmire so complex and bizarre that sober seers go into it only under the strictest conditions.

"The great difficulty is that the entrance into the second attention is utterly easy and its lure nearly irresistible."

He said that the old seers, being the masters of awareness, applied their expertise to their own glows of awareness and made them expand to inconceivable limits. They actually aimed at lighting up all the emanations inside their cocoons, one band at a time. They succeeded, but oddly enough the accomplishment of lighting up one band at a time was instrumental in their becoming imprisoned in the quagmire of the second attention.

"The new seers corrected that error," he continued, "and let the mastery of awareness develop to its natural end, which is to extend the glow of awareness beyond the bounds of the luminous cocoon in one single stroke.

"The third attention is attained when the glow of awareness turns into the fire from within: a glow that kindles not one band at a time but all the Eagle's emanations inside man's cocoon."

Don Juan expressed his awe for the new seers' deliberate effort to attain the third attention while they are alive and conscious of their individuality.

He did not consider it worthwhile to discuss the random cases of men and other sentient beings who enter into the unknown and the unknowable without being aware of it; he referred to this as the Eagle's gift. He asserted that for the new seers to enter into the third attention is also a gift, but has a different meaning. It is more like a reward for an attainment.

He added that at the moment of dying all human beings enter into the unknowable and some of them do attain the third attention, but altogether too briefly and only to purify the food for the Eagle.

"The supreme accomplishment of human beings," he said, "is to attain that level of attention while retaining the life-force, without becoming a disembodied awareness moving like a flicker of light up to the Eagle's beak to be devoured."

* * *

While listening to don Juan's explanation I had again completely lost sight of everything that surrounded me. Genaro apparently had gotten up and left us, and was nowhere in sight. Strangely, I found myself crouching on the rock, with don Juan squatting by me holding me down by gently pushing on my shoulders. I reclined on the rock and closed my eyes. There was a soft breeze blowing from the west.

"Don't fall asleep," don Juan said. "Not for any reason should you fall asleep on this rock."

I sat up. Don Juan was staring at me.

"Just relax," he went on. "Let the internal dialogue die out."

All my concentration was involved in following what he was saying when I got a jolt of fright. I did not know what it was at first; I thought I was going through another attack of distrust. But then it struck me, like a bolt, that it was very late in the afternoon. What I had thought was an hour's conversation had consumed an entire day.

I jumped up, fully aware of the incongruity, although I could not conceive what had happened to me. I felt a strange sensation that made my body want to run. Don Juan jumped me, restraining me forcefully. We fell to the soft ground, and he held me there with an iron grip. I had had no idea that don Juan was so strong.

My body shook violently. My arms flew every which way as they shook. I was having something like a seizure. Yet some part of me was detached to the point of becoming fascinated with watching my body vibrate, twist, and shake.

The spasms finally died out and don Juan let go of me. He was panting with the exertion. He recommended that we climb back up on the rock and sit there until I was all right.

I could not help pressing him with my usual question: What had happened to me? He answered that as he talked to me I had pushed beyond a certain limit and had entered very deeply into the left side. He and Genaro had followed me in there. And then I had rushed out in the same fashion I had rushed in.

"I caught you right on time," he said. "Otherwise you would have gone straight out to your normal self."

I was totally confused. He explained that the three of us had been playing with awareness. I must have gotten scared and run out on them.

"Genaro is the master of awareness," don Juan went on. "Silvio Manuel is the master of *will*. The two of them were mercilessly pushed into the unknown. My benefactor did to them what his benefactor did to him. Genaro and Silvio Manuel are very much like the old seers in some respects. They know what they can do, but they don't care to know how they do it. Today, Genaro seized the opportunity to push your glow of awareness and we all ended up in the weird confines of the unknown."

I begged him to tell me what had happened in the unknown.

"You'll have to remember that yourself," a voice said just by my ear.

I was so convinced that it was the voice of *seeing* that it did not frighten me at all. I did not even obey the impulse to turn around.

"I am the voice of *seeing* and I tell you that you are a peckerhead," the voice said again and chuckled.

I turned around. Genaro was sitting behind me. I was so surprised that I laughed perhaps a bit more hysterically than they did.

"It's getting dark now," Genaro said to me. "As I promised you earlier today, we are going to have a ball here."

Don Juan intervened and said that we should stop

for the day, because I was the kind of nincompoop who could die of fright.

"Nah, he's all right," Genaro said, patting me on the shoulder.

"You'd better ask him," don Juan said to Genaro. "He himself will tell you that he's that kind of nincompoop."

"Are you really that kind of nincompoop?" Genaro asked me with a frown.

I didn't answer him. And that made them roll around laughing. Genaro rolled all the way to the ground.

"He's caught," Genaro said to don Juan, referring to me, after don Juan had swiftly jumped down and helped him to stand up. "He'll never say he's a nincompoop. He's too self-important for that, but he's shivering in his pants with fear of what might happen because he didn't confess he's a nincompoop."

Watching them laugh, I was convinced that only Indians could laugh with such joyfulness. But I also became convinced that there was a mile-wide streak of maliciousness in them. They were poking fun at a non-Indian.

Don Juan immediately caught my feelings.

"Don't let your self-importance run rampant," he said. "You're not special by any standards. None of us are, Indians and non-Indians. The nagual Julian and his benefactor added years of enjoyment to their lives laughing at us."

Genaro nimbly climbed back onto the rock and came to my side.

"If I were you, I'd feel so frigging embarrassed I'd cry," he said to me. "Cry, cry. Have a good cry and you'll feel better."

To my utter amazement I began to weep softly. Then I got so angry that I roared with fury. Only then I felt better.

Don Juan patted my back gently. He said that usually anger is very sobering, or sometimes fear is, or humor. My violent nature made me respond only to anger.

He added that a sudden shift in the glow of awareness makes us weak. They had been trying to reinforce me, to bolster me. Apparently, Genaro had succeeded by making me rage.

It was twilight by then. Suddenly Genaro pointed to a flicker in midair at eye level. In the twilight it appeared to be a large moth flying around the place where we sat.

"Be very gentle with your exaggerated nature," don Juan said to me. "Don't be eager. Just let Genaro guide you. Don't take your eyes from that spot."

The flickering point was definitely a moth. I could clearly distinguish all its features. I followed its convoluted, tired flight, until I could *see* every speck of dust on its wings.

Something got me out of my total absorption. I sensed a flurry of soundless noise, if that could be possible, just behind me. I turned around and caught sight of an entire row of people on the other edge of the rock, an edge that was a bit higher than the one on which we were sitting. I supposed that the people who lived nearby must have gotten suspicious of us hanging around all day and had climbed onto the rock intending to harm us. I knew about their intentions instantly.

Don Juan and Genaro slid down from the rock and told me to hurry down. We left immediately without turning back to see if the men were following us. Don Juan and Genaro refused to talk while we walked back to Genaro's house. Don Juan even made me hush with a fierce grunt, putting his finger to his lips. Genaro did not come into the house, but kept on walking as don Juan dragged me inside.

"Who were those people, don Juan?" I asked him,

when the two of us were safely inside the house and he had lit the lantern.

"They were not people," he replied.

"Come on, don Juan, don't mystify me," I said. "They were men; I saw them with my own eyes."

"Of course, you saw them with your own eyes," he retorted, "but that doesn't say anything. Your eyes misled you. Those were not people and they were following you. Genaro had to draw them away from you."

"What were they, then, if not people?"

"Oh, there is the mystery," he said. "It's a mystery of awareness and it can't be solved rationally by talking about it. The mystery can only be witnessed."

"Let me witness it then," I said.

"But you already have, twice in one day," he said. "You don't remember now. You will, however, when you rekindle the emanations that were glowing when you witnessed the mystery of awareness I'm referring to. In the meantime, let's go back to our explanation of awareness."

He reiterated that awareness begins with the permanent pressure that the emanations at large exert on the ones trapped inside the cocoon. This pressure produces the first act of consciousness; it stops the motion of the trapped emanations, which are fighting to break the cocoon, fighting to die.

"For a seer, the truth is that all living beings are struggling to die," he went on. "What stops death is awareness."

Don Juan said that the new seers were profoundly disturbed by the fact that awareness forestalls death and at the same time induces it by being food for the Eagle. Since they could not explain it, for there is no rational way to understand existence, seers realized that their knowledge is composed of contradictory propositions.

72

"Why did they develop a system of contradictions?" I asked.

"They didn't develop anything," he said. "They found unquestionable truths by means of their *seeing*. Those truths are arranged in terms of supposedly blatant contradictions, that's all.

"For example, seers have to be methodical, rational beings, paragons of sobriety, and at the same time they must shy away from all of those qualities in order to be completely free and open to the wonders and mysteries of existence."

His example left me baffled, but not to the extreme. I understood what he meant. He himself had sponsored my rationality only to crush it and demand a total absence of it. I told him how I understood his point.

"Only a feeling of supreme sobriety can bridge the contradictions," he said.

"Could you say, don Juan, that art is that bridge?"

"You may call the bridge between contradictions anything you want—art, affection, sobriety, love, or even kindness."

Don Juan continued his explanation and said that in examining the first attention, the new seers realized that all organic beings, except man, quiet down their agitated trapped emanations so that those emanations can align themselves with their matching ones outside. Human beings do not do that; instead, their first attention takes an inventory of the Eagle's emanations inside their cocoons.

"What is an inventory, don Juan?" I asked.

"Human beings take notice of the emanations they have inside their cocoons," he replied. "No other creatures do that. The moment the pressure from the emanations at large fixates the emanations inside, the first attention begins to watch itself. It notes everything about itself, or at least it tries to, in whatever aberrant ways it can. This is the process seers call taking an inventory.

"I don't mean to say that human beings choose to take an inventory, or that they can refuse to take it. To take an inventory is the Eagle's command. What is subject to volition, however, is the manner in which the command is obeyed."

He said that although he disliked calling the emanations commands, that is what they are: commands that no one can disobey. Yet the way out of obeying the commands is in obeying them.

"In the case of the inventory of the first attention," he went on, "seers take it, for they can't disobey. But once they have taken it they throw it away. The Eagle doesn't command us to worship our inventory; it commands us to take it, that's all."

"How do seers *see* that man takes an inventory?" I asked.

"The emanations inside the cocoon of man are not quieted down for purposes of matching them with those outside," he replied. "This is evident after *seeing* what other creatures do. On quieting down, some of them actually merge themselves with the emanations at large and move with them. Seers can *see*, for instance, the light of the scarabs' emanations expanding to great size.

"But human beings quiet down their emanations and then reflect on them. The emanations focus on themselves."

He said that human beings carry the command of taking an inventory to its logical extreme and disregard everything else. Once they are deeply involved in the inventory, two things may happen. They may ignore the impulses of the emanations at large, or they may use them in a very specialized way.

The end result of ignoring those impulses after taking an inventory is a unique state known as reason.

The result of using every impulse in a specialized way is known as self-absorption.

Human reason appears to a seer as an unusually homogeneous dull glow that rarely if ever responds to the constant pressure from the emanations at large—a glow that makes the egglike shell become tougher, but more brittle.

Don Juan remarked that reason in the human species should be bountiful, but that in actuality it is very rare. The majority of human beings turn to self-absorption.

He asserted that the awareness of all living beings has a degree of self-reflection in order for them to interact. But none except man's first attention has such a degree of self-absorption. Contrary to men of reason, who ignore the impulse of the emanations at large, the self-absorbed individuals use every impulse and turn them all into a force to stir the trapped emanations inside their cocoons.

Observing all this, seers arrived at a practical conclusion. They *saw* that men of reason are bound to live longer, because by disregarding the impulse of the emanations at large, they quiet down the natural agitation inside their cocoons. The self-absorbed individuals, on the other hand, by using the impulse of the emanations at large to create more agitation, shorten their lives.

"What do seers *see* when they gaze at self-absorbed human beings?" I asked.

"They *see* them as intermittent bursts of white light, followed by long pauses of dullness," he said.

Don Juan stopped talking. I had no more questions to ask, or perhaps I was too tired to ask about anything. There was a loud bang that made me jump. The front door flew open and Genaro came in, out of breath. He slumped on the mat. He was actually covered with perspiration.

"I was explaining about the first attention," don Juan said to him.

"The first attention works only with the known," Genaro said. "It isn't worth two plugged nickels with the unknown."

"That is not quite right," don Juan retorted. "The first attention works very well with the unknown. It blocks it; it denies it so fiercely that in the end, the unknown doesn't exist for the first attention.

"Taking an inventory makes us invulnerable. That is why the inventory came into existence in the first place."

"What are you talking about?" I asked don Juan.

He didn't reply. He looked at Genaro as if waiting for an answer.

"But if I open the door," Genaro said, "would the first attention be capable of dealing with what will come in?"

"Yours and mine wouldn't, but his will," don Juan said, pointing at me. "Let's try it."

"Even though he's in heightened awareness?" Genaro asked don Juan.

"That won't make any difference," don Juan answered.

Genaro got up and went to the front door and threw it open. He instantly jumped back. A gust of cold wind came in. Don Juan came to my side, and so did Genaro. Both of them looked at me in amazement.

I wanted to close the front door. The cold was making me uncomfortable. But as I moved toward the door, don Juan and Genaro jumped in front of me and shielded me.

"Do you notice anything in the room?" Genaro asked me.

"No, I don't," I said, and I really meant it.

Except for the cold wind pouring in through the open door, there was nothing to notice in there.

"Weird creatures came in when I opened the door," he said. "Don't you notice anything?"

There was something in his voice that told me he was not joking this time.

The three of us, with both of them flanking me, walked out of the house. Don Juan picked up the kerosene lantern, and Genaro locked the front door. We got inside the car, through the passenger's side. They pushed me in first. And then we drove to don Juan's house in the next town.

6

Inorganic Beings

The next day I repeatedly asked don Juan to explain
our hasty departure from Genaro's house. He refused
even to mention the incident. Genaro was no help
either. Every time I asked him he winked at me, grin-
ning like a fool.

In the afternoon, don Juan came to the back patio
of his house, where I was talking with his apprentices.
As if on cue, all the young apprentices left instantly.

Don Juan took me by the arm, and we began to walk
along the corridor. He did not say anything; for a
while we just strolled around, very much as if we were
in the public square.

Don Juan stopped walking and turned to me. He
circled me, looking over my entire body. I knew that
he was *seeing* me. I felt a strange fatigue, a laziness I
had not felt until his eyes swept over me. He began to
talk all of a sudden.

"The reason Genaro and I didn't want to focus on
what happened last night," he said, "was that you had
been very frightened during the time you were in the
unknown. Genaro pushed you, and things happened
to you in there."

"What things, don Juan?"

"Things that are still difficult if not impossible to explain to you now," he said. "You don't have enough surplus energy to enter into the unknown and make sense of it. When the new seers arranged the order of the truths about awareness, they *saw* that the first attention consumes all the glow of awareness that human beings have, and not an iota of energy is left free. That's your problem now. So, the new seers proposed that warriors, since they have to enter into the unknown, have to save their energy. But where are they going to get energy, if all of it is taken? They'll get it, the new seers say, from eradicating unnecessary habits."

He stopped talking and solicited questions. I asked him what eradicating unnecessary habits did to the glow of awareness.

He replied that it detaches awareness from self-reflection and allows it the freedom to focus on something else.

"The unknown is forever present," he continued, "but it is outside the possibility of our normal awareness. The unknown is the superfluous part of the average man. And it is superfluous because the average man doesn't have enough free energy to grasp it.

"After all the time you've spent in the warrior's path, you have enough free energy to grasp the unknown, but not enough energy to understand it or even to remember it."

He explained that at the site of the flat rock, I had entered very deeply into the unknown. But I indulged in my exaggerated nature and became terrified, which was about the worst thing anyone can do. So I had rushed out of the left side, like a bat out of hell; unfortunately, taking a legion of strange things with me.

I told don Juan that he was not getting to the point, that he should come out and tell me exactly what he meant by a legion of strange things.

He took me by the arm and continued strolling around with me.

"In explaining awareness," he said, "I am presumably fitting everything or nearly everything into place. Let's talk a little bit about the old seers. Genaro, as I've told you, is very much like them."

He led me then to the big room. We sat down there and he began his elucidation.

"The new seers were simply terrified by the knowledge that the old seers had accumulated over the years," don Juan said. "It's understandable. The new seers knew that that knowledge leads only to total destruction. Yet they were also fascinated by it—especially by the practices."

"How did the new seers know about those practices?" I asked.

"They are the legacy of the old Toltecs," he said. "The new seers learn about them as they go along. They hardly ever use them, but the practices are there as part of their knowledge."

"What kind of practices are they, don Juan?"

"They are very obscure formulas, incantations, lengthy procedures that have to do with the handling of a very mysterious force. At least it was mysterious to the ancient Toltecs, who masked it and made it more horrifying than it really is."

"What is that mysterious force?" I asked.

"It's a force that is present throughout everything there is," he said. "The old seers never attempted to unravel the mystery of the force that made them create their secret practices; they simply accepted it as something sacred. But the new seers took a close look and called it *will*, the *will* of the Eagle's emanations, or *intent*."

Don Juan went on explaining that the ancient Toltecs had divided their secret knowledge into five sets of two categories each: the earth and the dark regions, fire and water, the above and the below, the loud and the silent, the moving and the stationary. He speculated that there must have been thousands of different techniques, which became more and more intricate as time passed.

"The secret knowledge of the earth," he went on, "had to do with everything that stands on the ground. There were particular sets of movements, words, unguents, potions that were applied to people, animals, insects, trees, small plants, rocks, soil.

"These were techniques that made the old seers into horrid beings. And their secret knowledge of the earth was employed either to groom or to destroy anything that stands on the ground.

"The counterpart of the earth was what they knew as the dark regions. These practices were by far the most dangerous. They dealt with entities without organic life. Living creatures that are present on the earth and populate it together with all organic beings.

"Doubtlessly, one of the most worthwhile findings of the ancient seers, especially for them, was the discovery that organic life is not the only form of life present on this earth."

I did not quite comprehend what he had said. I waited for him to clarify his statements.

"Organic beings are not the only creatures that have life," he said and paused again as if to allow me time to think his statements over.

I countered with a long argument about the definition of life and being alive. I talked about reproduction, metabolism, and growth, the processes that distinguish live organisms from inanimate things.

"You're drawing from the organic," he said. "But that's only one instance. You shouldn't draw all you have to say from one category alone."

"But how else can it be?" I asked.

"For seers, to be alive means to be aware," he replied. "For the average man, to be aware means to be an organism. This is where seers are different. For them, to be aware means that the emanations that cause awareness are encased inside a receptacle.

"Organic living beings have a cocoon that encloses the emanations. But there are other creatures whose receptacles don't look like a cocoon to a seer. Yet they have the emanations of awareness in them and characteristics of life other than reproduction and metabolism."

"Such as what, don Juan?"

"Such as emotional dependency, sadness, joy, wrath, and so forth and so on. And I forgot the best yet, love; a kind of love man can't even conceive."

"Are you serious, don Juan?" I asked in earnest.

"Inanimately serious," he answered with a deadpan expression and then broke into laughter.

"If we take as our clue what seers *see*," he continued, "life is indeed extraordinary."

"If those beings are alive, why don't they make themselves known to man?" I asked.

"They do, all the time. And not only to seers but also to the average man. The problem is that all the energy available is consumed by the first attention. Man's inventory not only takes it all, but it also toughens the cocoon to the point of making it inflexible. Under those circumstances there is no possible interaction."

He reminded me of the countless times, in the course of my apprenticeship with him, when I had had a firsthand view of inorganic beings. I retorted that I had explained away nearly every one of those instances. I had even formulated the hypothesis that his teachings, through the use of hallucinogenic plants, were geared to force an agreement, on the part of the apprentice, about a primitive interpretation of the world. I told him that I had not formally called it primitive interpretation but in anthropological terms I had labeled it a "world view more proper to hunting and gathering societies."

Don Juan laughed until he was out of breath.

"I really don't know whether you're worse in your normal state of awareness or in a heightened one," he said. "In your normal state you're not suspicious, but boringly reasonable. I think I like you best when you are way inside the left side, in spite of the fact that you are terribly afraid of everything, as you were yesterday."

Before I had time to say anything at all, he stated that he was pitting what the old seers did against the accomplishments of the new seers, as a sort of counterpoint, with which he intended to give me a more inclusive view of the odds I was up against.

He continued then with his elucidation of the practices of the old seers. He said that another of their great findings had to do with the next category of secret knowledge: fire and water. They discovered that flames have a most peculiar quality; they can transport man bodily, just as water does.

Don Juan called it a brilliant discovery. I remarked that there are basic laws of physics that would prove that to be impossible. He asked me to wait until he had explained everything before drawing any conclusions. He remarked that I had to check my excessive rationality, because it constantly affected my states of heightened awareness. It was not a case of reacting every which way to external influences, but of succumbing to my own devices.

He went on explaining that the ancient Toltecs, although they obviously *saw,* did not understand what they *saw.* They merely used their findings without bothering to relate them to a larger picture. In the case of their category of fire and water, they divided fire into heat and flame, and water into wetness and fluidity. They correlated heat and wetness and called them lesser properties. They considered flames and fluidity to be higher, magical properties, and they used them as a means for bodily transportation to the realm of nonorganic life. Between their knowledge of that kind of life and their fire and water practices, the ancient seers became bogged down in a quagmire with no way out.

Don Juan assured me that the new seers agreed that the discovery of nonorganic living beings was indeed extraordinary, but not in the way the old seers believed it to be. To find themselves in a one-to-one relation with another kind of life gave the ancient seers a false feeling of invulnerability, which spelled their doom.

I wanted him to explain the fire and water techniques in greater detail. He said that the old seers' knowledge was as intricate as it was useless and that he was only going to outline it.

Then he summarized the practices of the above and the below. The above dealt with secret knowledge about wind, rain, sheets of lightning, clouds, thunder, daylight, and the sun. The knowledge of the below had to do with fog, water of underground springs, swamps, lightning bolts, earthquakes, the night, moonlight, and the moon.

The loud and the silent were a category of secret knowledge that had to do with the manipulation of sound and quiet. The moving and the stationary were practices concerned with mysterious aspects of motion and motionlessness.

I asked him if he could give me an example of any of the techniques he had outlined. He replied that he had already given me dozens of demonstrations over the years. I insisted that I had rationally explained away everything he had done to me.

He did not answer. He seemed to be either angry at me for asking questions or seriously involved in searching for a good example. After a while he smiled and said that he had visualized the proper example.

"The technique I have in mind has to be put in

action in the shallow depths of a stream," he said. "There is one near Genaro's house."

"What will I have to do?"

"You'll have to get a medium-size mirror."

I was surprised at his request. I remarked that the ancient Toltecs did not know about mirrors.

"They didn't," he admitted, smiling. "This is my benefactor's addition to the technique. All the ancient seers needed was a reflecting surface."

He explained that the technique consisted of submerging a shiny surface into the shallow water of a stream. The surface could be any flat object that had some capacity to reflect images.

"I want you to construct a solid frame made of sheet metal for a medium-size mirror," he said. "It has to be waterproof, so you must seal it with tar. You must make it yourself with your own hands. When you have made it, bring it over and we'll proceed."

"What's going to happen, don Juan?"

"Don't be apprehensive. You yourself have asked me to give you an example of an ancient Toltec practice. I asked the same thing of my benefactor. I think everybody asks for one at a certain moment. My benefactor said that he did the same thing himself. His benefactor, the nagual Elías, gave him an example; my benefactor in turn gave the same one to me, and now I am going to give it to you.

"At the time my benefactor gave me the example I didn't know how he did it. I know now. Someday you yourself will also know how the technique works; you will understand what's behind all this."

I thought that don Juan wanted me to go back home to Los Angeles and construct the frame for the mirror there. I commented that it would be impossible for me to remember the task if I did not remain in heightened awareness.

"There are two things out of kilter with your comment," he said. "One is that there is no way for you to remain in heightened awareness, because you won't be able to function unless I or Genaro or any of the warriors in the nagual's party nurse you every minute of the day, as I do now. The other is that Mexico is not the moon. There are hardware stores here. We can go to Oaxaca and buy anything you need."

We drove to the city the next day and I bought all the pieces for the frame. I assembled it myself in a mechanic's shop for a minimal fee. Don Juan told me to put it in the trunk of my car. He did not so much as glance at it.

We drove back to Genaro's house in the late afternoon and arrived there in the early morning. I looked for Genaro. He was not there. The house seemed deserted.

"Why does Genaro keep this house?" I asked don Juan. "He lives with you, doesn't he?"

Don Juan did not answer. He gave me a strange look and went to light the kerosene lantern. I was alone in the room in total darkness. I felt a great tiredness that I attributed to the long, tortuous drive up the mountains. I wanted to lie down. In the darkness, I could not see where Genaro had put the mats. I stumbled over a pile of them. And then I knew why Genaro kept that house; he took care of the male apprentices Pablito, Nestor, and Benigno, who lived there when they were in their state of normal awareness.

I felt exhilarated; I was no longer tired. Don Juan came in with a lantern. I told him about my realization, but he said that it did not matter, that I would not remember it for too long.

He asked me to show him the mirror. He seemed pleased and remarked about its being light yet solid. He noticed that I had used metal screws to affix an aluminum frame to a piece of sheet metal that I had used as a backing for a mirror eighteen inches long by fourteen inches wide.

"I made a wooden frame for my mirror," he said. "This looks much better than mine. My frame was too cumbersome and at the same time frail.

"Let me explain what we're going to do," he continued after he had finished examining the mirror. "Or perhaps I should say, what we're going to attempt to do. The two of us together are going to place this mirror on the surface of the stream near the house. It is wide enough and shallow enough to serve our purposes.

"The idea is to let the fluidity of the water exert pressure on us and transport us away."

Before I could make any remarks or ask any questions, he reminded me that in the past I had utilized the water of a similar stream and accomplished extraordinary feats of perception. He was referring to the aftereffects of ingesting hallucinogenic plants, which I had experienced various times while being submerged in the irrigation ditch behind his house in northern Mexico.

"Save any questions until I explain to you what the seers knew about awareness," he said. "Then you'll understand everything we're doing in a different light. But first let's go on with our procedure."

We walked to the nearby stream, and he selected a place with flat, exposed rocks. He said that there the water was shallow enough for our purposes.

"What do you expect to happen?" I asked in the midst of a gripping apprehension.

"I don't know. All I know is what we are going to attempt. We will hold the mirror very carefully, but very firmly. We will gently place it on the surface of the water and then let it submerge. We will then hold it on the bottom. I've checked it. There is enough silt there to allow us to dig our fingers underneath the mirror to hold it firmly."

He asked me to squat on a flat rock above the surface in the middle of the gentle stream and made me

87

hold the mirror with both hands, almost at the corners on one side. He squatted facing me and held the mirror the same way I did. We let the mirror sink and then we held it by plunging our arms in the water almost to our elbows.

He commanded me to empty myself of thoughts and stare at the surface of the mirror. He repeated over and over that the trick was not to think at all. I looked intently into the mirror. The gentle current mildly disarranged the reflection of don Juan's face and mine. After a few minutes of steady gazing into the mirror it seemed to me that gradually the image of his face and mine became much clearer. And the mirror grew in size until it was at least a yard square. The current seemed to have stopped, and the mirror looked as clear as if it were placed on top of the water. Even more odd was the crispness of our reflections. It was as if my face had been magnified, not in size but in focus. I could see the pores in the skin of my forehead.

Don Juan gently whispered not to stare at my eyes or his, but to let my gaze wander around without focusing on any part of our reflections.

"Gaze fixedly without staring!" he repeatedly ordered in a forceful whisper.

I did what he said without stopping to ponder about the seeming contradiction. At that moment something inside me was caught in that mirror and the contradiction actually made sense. "It is possible to gaze fixedly without staring," I thought, and the instant that thought was formulated another head appeared next to don Juan's and mine. It was on the lower side of the mirror, to my left.

My whole body trembled. Don Juan whispered to calm down and not show fear or surprise. He again commanded me to gaze without staring at the newcomer. I had to make an unimaginable effort not to gasp and release the mirror. My body was shaking from head to toe. Don Juan whispered again to get hold of myself. He nudged me repeatedly with his shoulder.

Slowly I got my fear under control. I gazed at the third head and gradually realized that it was not a human head, or an animal head either. In fact, it was not a head at all. It was a shape that had no inner mobility. As the thought occurred to me, I instantly realized that I was not thinking it myself. The realization was not a thought either. I had a moment of tremendous anxiety and then something incomprehensible became known to me. The thoughts were a voice in my ear!

"I am *seeing!*" I yelled in English, but there was no sound. "Yes, you're *seeing,*" the voice in my ear said in Spanish.

I felt that I was encased in a force greater than myself. I was not in pain or even anguished. I felt nothing. I knew beyond the shadow of a doubt, because the voice was telling me so, that I could not break the grip of that force by an act of will or strength. I knew I was dying. I lifted my eyes automatically to look at don Juan, and at the instant our eyes met the force let go of me. I was free. Don Juan was smiling at me as if he knew exactly what I had gone through.

I realized that I was standing up. Don Juan was holding the mirror edgewise to let the water drip off.

We walked back to the house in silence.

"The ancient Toltecs were simply mesmerized by their findings," don Juan said.

"I can understand why," I said.

"So can I," don Juan retorted.

The force that had enveloped me had been so powerful as to incapacitate me for speech, even for thought, for hours afterward. It had frozen me with a total lack of volition. And I had thawed out only by tiny degrees.

"Without any deliberate intervention on our part," don Juan continued, "this ancient Toltec technique has been divided into two parts for you. The first was just enough to familiarize you with what takes place. In the second, we will try to accomplish what the old seers pursued."

"What really took place out there, don Juan?" I asked.

"There are two versions. I'll give you the old seers' version first. They thought that the reflecting surface of a shiny object submerged in water enlarges the power of the water. What they used to do was gaze into bodies of water, and the reflecting surface served them as an aid to accelerate the process. They believed that our eyes are the keys to entering into the unknown; by gazing into water, they were allowing the eyes to open the way."

Don Juan said that the old seers observed that the wetness of water only dampens or soaks, but that the fluidity of water moves. It runs, they surmised, in search of other levels underneath us. They believed that water had been given to us not only for life, but also as a link, a road to the other levels below.

"Are there many levels below?" I asked.

"The ancient seers counted seven levels," he replied.

"Do you know them yourself, don Juan?"

"I am a seer of the new cycle, and consequently I have a different view," he said. "I am just showing you what the old seers did and I'm telling you what they believed."

He asserted that just because he had different views did not mean the old seers' practices were invalid; their interpretations were wrong, but their truths had practical value for them. In the instance of the water practices, they were convinced that it was humanly possible to be transported bodily by the fluidity of water anywhere between this level of ours and the other seven levels below; or to be transported in essence anywhere on this level, along the watercourse of a river in either direction. They used, accordingly, running water to be transported on this level of ours and the water of deep lakes or that of waterholes to be transported to the depths.

"What they pursued with the technique I'm showing you was twofold," he went on. "On the one hand they used the fluidity of the water to be transported to the first level below. On the other, they used it to have a face-to-face meeting with a living being from that first level. The headlike shape in the mirror was one of those creatures that came to look us over."

"So, they really exist!" I exclaimed.

"They certainly do," he retorted.

He said that ancient seers were damaged by their aberrant insistence on staying glued to their procedures, but that whatever they found was valid. They found out that the surest way to meet one of those creatures is through a body of water. The size of the body of water is not relevant; an ocean or a pond serves the same purpose. He had chosen a small stream because he hated to get wet. We could have gotten the same results in a lake or a large river.

"The other life comes to find out what's going on when human beings call," he continued. "That Toltec technique is like a knock on their door. The old seers said the shiny surface on the bottom of the water served as a bait and a window. So humans and those creatures meet at a window."

"Is that what happened to me there?" I asked.

"The old seers would've said that you were being pulled by the power of the water and the power of the first level, plus the magnetic influence of the creature at the window."

"But I heard a voice in my ear saying that I was dying," I said.

"The voice was right. You were dying, and you

would have if I hadn't been there. That is the danger of practicing the Toltecs' techniques. They are extremely effective but most of the time they are deadly."

I told him that I was ashamed to confess that I was terrified. *Seeing* that shape in the mirror and having the sensation of an enveloping force around me had proved too much for me the day before.

"I don't want to alarm you," he said, "but nothing has happened to you yet. If what happened to me is going to be the guideline of what will happen to you, you'd better prepare yourself for the shock of your life. It's better to shake in your boots now than to die of fright tomorrow."

My fear was so terrifying that I couldn't even voice the questions that came to my mind. I had a hard time swallowing. Don Juan laughed until he was coughing. His face got purple. When I got my voice back, every one of my questions prompted another attack of coughing laughter.

"You have no idea how funny this all is to me," he finally said. "I'm not laughing at you. It's just the situation. My benefactor made me go through the same motions, and looking at you I can't help seeing myself."

I told him that I felt sick to my stomach. He said that that was fine, that it was natural to be scared, and that to control fear was wrong and senseless. The ancient seers got trapped by suppressing their terror when they should have been scared out of their wits. Since they did not want to stop their pursuits or abandon their comforting constructs they controlled their fear instead.

"What else are we going to do with the mirror?" I asked.

"That mirror is going to be used for a face-to-face meeting between you and that creature you only gazed at yesterday."

"What happens in a face-to-face meeting?"

"What happens is that one form of life, the human form, meets another form of life. The old seers said that in this case, it is a creature from the first level of the fluidity of water."

He explained that the ancient seers surmised that the seven levels below ours were levels of the fluidity of water. For them a spring had untold significance, because they thought that in such a case the fluidity of water is reversed and goes from the depth to the surface. They took that to be the means whereby creatures from other levels, these other forms of life, come to our plane to peer at us, to observe us.

"In this respect those old seers were not mistaken," he went on. "They hit the nail right on the head. Entities that the new seers call allies do appear around waterholes."

"Was the creature in the mirror an ally?" I asked.

"Of course. But not one that can be utilized. The tradition of the allies, which I have acquainted you with in the past, comes directly from the ancient seers. They did wonders with allies, but nothing they did was worth anything when the real enemy came along: their fellow men."

"Since those creatures are allies, they must be very dangerous," I said.

"As dangerous as we men are, no more, no less."

"Can they kill us?"

"Not directly, but they certainly can frighten us to death. They can cross the boundaries themselves, or they can just come to the window. As you may have realized by now, the ancient Toltecs didn't stop at the window, either. They found weird ways to go beyond it."

The second stage of the technique proceeded very much as had the first except that it took perhaps twice as long for me to relax and stop my internal turmoil.

When that was done, the reflection of don Juan's face and mine became instantly clear. I gazed from his reflection to mine for perhaps an hour. I expected the ally to appear any moment, but nothing happened. My neck hurt. My back was stiff and my legs were numb. I wanted to kneel on the rock to relieve the pain in my lower back. Don Juan whispered that the moment the ally showed its shape my discomfort would vanish.

He was absolutely right. The shock of witnessing a round shape appear on the edge of the mirror dispelled every discomfort of mine.

"What do we do now?" I whispered.

"Relax and don't focus your gaze on anything, not even for an instant," he replied. "Watch everything that appears in the mirror. Gaze without staring."

I obeyed him. I glanced at everything within the frame of the mirror. There was a peculiar buzzing in my ears. Don Juan whispered that I should move my eyes in a clockwise direction if I felt that I was being enveloped by an unusual force; but under no circumstances, he stressed, should I lift my head to look at him.

After a moment I noticed that the mirror was reflecting more than the reflection of our faces and the round shape. Its surface had become dark. Spots of an intense violet light appeared. They grew large. There were also spots of jet blackness. Then it turned into something like a flat picture of a cloudy sky at night, in the moonlight. Suddenly, the whole surface came into focus, as if it were a moving picture. The new sight was a three-dimensional, breathtaking view of the depths.

I knew that it was absolutely impossible for me to fight off the tremendous attraction of that sight. It began to pull me in.

Don Juan whispered forcefully that I should roll my eyes for dear life. The movement brought immediate relief. I could again distinguish our reflections and that of the ally. Then the ally disappeared and reappeared again on the other end of the mirror.

Don Juan commanded me to grip the mirror with all my might. He warned me to be calm and not make any sudden movements.

"What's going to happen?" I whispered.

"The ally will try to come out," he replied.

As soon as he had said that I felt a powerful tug. Something jerked my arms. The tug was from underneath the mirror. It was like a suction force that created a uniform pressure all around the frame.

"Hold the mirror tightly but don't break it," don Juan ordered. "Fight the suction. Don't let the ally sink the mirror too deep."

The force pulling down on us was enormous. I felt that my fingers were going to break or be crushed against the rocks on the bottom. Don Juan and I both lost our balance at one point and had to step down from the flat rocks into the stream. The water was quite shallow, but the thrashing of the ally's force around the frame of the mirror was as frightening as if we had been in a large river. The water around our feet was being swirled around madly, but the images in the mirror were undisturbed.

"Watch out!" don Juan yelled. "Here it comes!"

The tugging changed into a thrust from underneath. Something was grabbing the edge of the mirror; not the outer edge of the frame where we were holding it, but from the inside of the glass. It was as if the glass surface were indeed an open window and something or somebody were just climbing through it.

Don Juan and I fought desperately either to push the mirror down when it was being thrust up or pull it up when it was being tugged downward. In a stooped-over position we slowly moved downstream from the original spot. The water was deeper and the bottom was covered with slippery rocks.

"Let's lift the mirror out of the water and shake him loose," don Juan said in a harsh voice.

The loud thrashing continued unremittingly. It was as if we had caught an enormous fish with our bare hands and it was swimming around wildly.

It occurred to me that the mirror was in essence a hatch. A strange shape was actually trying to climb up through it. It was leaning on the edge of the hatch with a mighty weight and was big enough to displace the reflection of don Juan's face and mine. I could not see us anymore. I could only distinguish a mass trying to push itself up.

The mirror was not resting on the bottom anymore. My fingers were not compressed against the rocks. The mirror was in mid-depth, held by the opposing forces of the ally's tugs and ours. Don Juan said he was going to extend his hands underneath the mirror and that I should very quickly grab them in order to have a better leverage to lift the mirror with our forearms. When he let go it tilted to his side. I quickly reached for his hands but there was nothing underneath. I vacillated a second too long and the mirror flew out of my hands.

"Grab it! Grab it!" don Juan yelled.

I caught the mirror just as it was going to land on the rocks. I lifted it out of the water, but not quickly enough. The water seemed to be like glue. As I pulled the mirror out, I also pulled a portion of a heavy rubbery substance that simply pulled the mirror out of my hands and back into the water.

Don Juan, displaying extraordinary nimbleness, caught the mirror and lifted it up edgewise without any difficulty.

Never in my life had I had such an attack of melancholy. It was a sadness that had no precise foundation; I associated it with the memory of the depths I had *seen* in the mirror. It was a mixture of pure longing for those depths plus an absolute fear of their chilling solitude.

Don Juan remarked that in the life of warriors it was extremely natural to be sad for no overt reason. Seers say that the luminous egg, as a field of energy, senses its final destination whenever the boundaries of the known are broken. A mere glimpse of the eternity outside the cocoon is enough to disrupt the coziness of our inventory. The resulting melancholy is sometimes so intense that it can bring about death.

He said that the best way to get rid of melancholy is to make fun of it. He commented in a mocking tone that my first attention was doing everything to restore the order that had been disrupted by my contact with the ally. Since there was no way of restoring it by rational means, my first attention was doing it by focusing all its power on sadness.

I told him that the fact remained the melancholy was real. Indulging in it, moping around, being gloomy, were not part of the feeling of aloneness that I had felt upon remembering those depths.

"Something is finally getting through to you," he said. "You're right. There is nothing more lonely than eternity. And nothing is more cozy for us than to be a human being. This indeed is another contradiction— how can man keep the bonds of his humanness and still venture gladly and purposefully into the absolute loneliness of eternity? Whenever you resolve this riddle, you'll be ready for the definitive journey."

I knew then with total certainty the reason for my sadness. It was a recurrent feeling with me, one that I would always forget until I again realized the same thing: the puniness of humanity against the immensity of that thing-in-itself which I had *seen* reflected in the mirror.

"Human beings are truly nothing, don Juan," I said.

"I know exactly what you're thinking," he said.

"Sure, we're nothing, but that's exactly what makes it the ultimate challenge, that we nothings could actually face the loneliness of eternity."

He abruptly changed the subject, leaving me with my mouth open, my next question unsaid. He began to discuss our bout with the ally. He said that first of all, the struggle with the ally had been no joke. It had not really been a matter of life or death, but it had not been a picnic either.

"I chose that technique," he went on, "because my benefactor showed it to me. When I asked him to give me an example of the old seers' techniques, he nearly split a gut laughing; my request reminded him so much of his own experience. His benefactor, the nagual Elias, had also given him a harsh demonstration of the same technique."

Don Juan said that as he had made the frame for his mirror out of wood, he should have asked me to do the same, but he wanted to know what would happen if the frame was sturdier than his or his benefactor's. Both of their frames broke, and both times the ally came out.

He explained that during his own bout the ally ripped the frame apart. He and his benefactor were left holding two pieces of wood while the mirror sank and the ally climbed out of it.

His benefactor knew what kind of trouble to expect. In the reflection of mirrors, allies are not really frightening because one *sees* only a shape, a mass of sorts. But when they are out, besides being truly fearsome-looking things, they are a pain in the neck. He remarked that once the allies get out of their level it is very difficult for them to go back. The same prevails for man. If seers venture into a level of those creatures, chances are they are never heard of again.

"My mirror was shattered with the ally's force," he said. "There was no more window and the ally couldn't go back, so it came after me. It actually ran after me, rolling on itself. I scrambled on all fours at top speed, screaming with terror. I went up and down hills like a possessed man. The ally was inches away from me the whole time."

Don Juan said that his benefactor ran after him, but he was too old and could not move fast enough; he had the good sense, however, to tell don Juan to back-track, and in that way was able to take measures to get rid of the ally. He shouted that he was going to build a fire and that don Juan should run in circles until everything was ready. He went ahead to gather dry branches while don Juan ran around a hill, driven mad with fear.

Don Juan confessed that the thought had occurred to him, as he ran around in circles, that his benefactor was actually enjoying the whole thing. He knew that his benefactor was a warrior capable of finding delight in any conceivable situation. Why not also in this one? For a moment he got so angry at his benefactor that the ally stopped chasing him, and don Juan, in no uncertain terms, accused his benefactor of malice. His benefactor didn't answer, but made a gesture of gen-uine horror as he looked past don Juan at the ally, which was looming over the two of them. Don Juan forgot his anger and began running around in circles again.

"My benefactor was indeed a devilish old man," don Juan said, laughing. "He had learned to laugh internally. It wouldn't show on his face, so he could pretend to be weeping or raging when he was really laughing. That day, as the ally chased me in circles, my benefactor stood there and defended himself from my accusations. I only heard bits of his long speech every time I ran by him. When he was through with that, I heard bits of another long explanation: that he had to gather a great deal of wood, that the ally was big, that the fire had to be as big as the ally itself, that the maneuver might not work.

99

"Only my maddening fear kept me going. Finally he must have realized that I was about to drop dead from exhaustion; he built the fire and with the flames he shielded me from the ally."

Don Juan said that they stayed by the fire for the entire night. The worst time for him was when his benefactor had to go away to look for more dry branches and left him alone. He was so afraid that he promised to God that he was going to leave the path of knowledge and become a farmer.

"In the morning, after I had exhausted all my energy, the ally managed to shove me into the fire, and I was badly burned," don Juan added.

"What happened to the ally?" I asked.

"My benefactor never told me what happened to it," he replied. "But I have the feeling that it is still running around aimlessly, trying to find its way back."

"And what happened to your promise to God?"

"My benefactor said not to worry, that it had been a good promise, but that I didn't know yet that there is no one to hear such promises, because there is no God. All there is is the Eagle's emanations, and there is no way to make promises to them."

"What would have happened if the ally had caught you?" I asked.

"I might have died of fright," he said. "If I had known what was entailed in being caught I would've let it catch me. At that time I was a reckless man. Once an ally catches you, you either have a heart attack and die or you wrestle with it. Then after a moment of thrashing around in sham ferocity, the ally's energy wanes. There is nothing that an ally can do to us, or vice versa. We are separated by an abyss.

"The ancient seers believed that at the moment the ally's energy dwindles the ally surrenders its power to man. Power, my eye! The old seers had allies coming out of their ears and their allies' power didn't mean a thing."

Don Juan explained that once again it had been up to the new seers to straighten out this confusion. They had found that the only thing that counts is impeccability, that is, freed energy. There were indeed some among the ancient seers who were saved by their allies, but that had had nothing to do with the allies' power to fend off anything; rather, it was the impeccability of the men that had permitted them to use the energy of those other forms of life.

The new seers also found out the most important thing yet about the allies: what makes them useless or usable to man. Useless allies, of which there are staggering numbers, are those that have emanations inside them for which we have no match inside ourselves. They are so different from us as to be thoroughly unusable. Other allies, which are remarkably few in number, are akin to us, meaning that they possess occasional emanations that match ours.

"How is that kind utilized by man?" I asked.

"We should use another word instead of 'utilize,' " he replied. "I'd say that what takes place between seers and allies of this kind is a fair exchange of energy."

"How does the exchange take place?" I asked.

"Through their matching emanations," he said. "Those emanations are, naturally, on the left-side awareness of man; the side that the average man never uses. For this reason, allies are totally barred from the world of the right-side awareness, or the side of rationality."

He said that the matching emanations give both a common ground. Then, with familiarity, a deeper link is established, which allows both forms of life to profit. Seers seek the allies' ethereal quality; they make fabulous scouts and guardians. Allies seek the greater energy field of man, and with it they can even materialize themselves.

He assured me that experienced seers play those

shared emanations until they bring them into total focus; the exchange takes place at that time. The ancient seers did not understand this process, and they developed complex techniques of gazing in order to descend into the depths that I had *seen* in the mirror.

"The old seers had a very elaborate tool to help them in their descent," he went on. "It was a rope of special twine that they tied around their waist. It had a soft butt soaked in resin which fitted into the navel itself, like a plug. The seers had an assistant or a number of them who held them by the rope while they were lost in their gazing. Naturally, to gaze directly into the reflection of a deep, clear pond or lake is infinitely more overwhelming and dangerous than what we did with the mirror."

"But did they actually descend bodily?" I asked.

"You'd be surprised what men are capable of, especially if they control awareness," he replied. "The old seers were aberrant. In their excursions to the depths they found marvels. It was routine for them to encounter allies.

"Of course, by now you realize that to say the depths is a figure of speech. There are no depths, there is only the handling of awareness. Yet the old seers never made that realization."

I told don Juan that from what he had said about his experience with the ally, plus my own subjective impression on feeling the ally's thrashing force in the water, I had concluded that allies are very aggressive.

"Not really," he said. "It is not that they don't have enough energy to be aggressive, but rather that they have a different kind of energy. They are more like an electric current. Organic beings are more like heat waves."

"But why did it chase you for such a long time?" I asked.

"That's no mystery," he said. "They are attracted to emotions. Animal fear is what attracts them the most; it releases the kind of energy that suits them. The emanations inside them are rallied by animal fear. Since my fear was relentless the ally went after it, or rather, my fear hooked the ally and didn't let it go.''

He said that it was the old seers who found out that allies enjoy animal fear more than anything else. They even went to the extreme of purposely feeding it to their allies by actually scaring people to death. The old seers were convinced that the allies had human feelings, but the new seers *saw* it differently. They *saw* that allies are attracted to the energy released by emotions; love is equally effective, as well as hatred, or sadness.

Don Juan added that if he had felt love for that ally, the ally would have come after him anyway, although the chase would have had a different mood. I asked him whether the ally would have stopped going after him if he had controlled his fear. He answered that controlling fear was a trick of the old seers. They learned to control it to the point of being able to parcel it out. They hooked their allies with their own fear and by gradually doling it out, like food, they actually held the allies in bondage.

"Those old seers were terrifying men," don Juan continued. "I shouldn't use the past tense—they are terrifying even today. Their bid is to dominate, to master everybody and everything."

"Even today, don Juan?" I asked, trying to get him to explain further.

He changed the subject by commenting that I had missed the opportunity of being really scared beyond measure. He said that doubtless the way I had sealed the frame of the mirror with tar had prevented the water from seeping behind the glass. He counted that as the deciding factor that had kept the ally from smashing the mirror.

"Too bad," he said. "You might even have liked that ally. By the way, it was not the same one that came the day before. The second one was perfectly akin to you."

"Don't you have some allies yourself, don Juan?" I asked.

"As you know, I have my benefactor's allies," he said. "I can't say that I have the same feeling for them that my benefactor did. He was a serene but thoroughly passionate man, who lavishly gave away everything he possessed, including his energy. He loved his allies. To him it was no sweat to allow the allies to use his energy and materialize themselves. There was one in particular that could even take a grotesque human form."

Don Juan went on to say that since he was not partial to allies, he had never given me a real taste of them, as his benefactor had done to him while he was still recovering from the wound in his chest. It all began with the thought that his benefactor was a strange man. Having barely escaped from the clutches of the petty tyrant, don Juan suspected that he had fallen into another trap. His intention was to wait a few days to get his strength back and then run away when the old man was not home. But the old man must have read his thoughts, because one day, in a confidential tone, he whispered to don Juan that he ought to get well as quickly as possible so that the two of them could escape from his captor and tormentor. Then, shaking with fear and impotence, the old man flung the door open and a monstrous fish-faced man came into the room, as if he had been listening behind the door. He was a grayish-green, had only one huge unblinking eye, and was as big as a door. Don Juan said that he was so surprised and terrified that he passed out, and it took him years to get out from under the spell of that fright.

"Are your allies useful to you, don Juan?" I asked.

"That's a very difficult thing to decide," he said.

"In some way, I love the allies my benefactor gave me. They are capable of giving back inconceivable affection. But they are incomprehensible to me. They were given to me for companionship in case I am ever stranded alone in that immensity that is the Eagle's emanations."

7

The Assemblage Point

Don Juan discontinued his explanation of the mastery of awareness for several months after my bout with the allies. One day he started it again. A strange event triggered it.

Don Juan was in northern Mexico. It was late afternoon. I had just arrived at the house he kept there, and he immediately had me shift into heightened awareness. And I had instantly remembered that don Juan always came back to Sonora as means of renewal. He had explained that a nagual, being a leader who has tremendous responsibilities, has to have a physical point of reference, a place where an amenable confluence of energies occurs. The Sonoran desert was such a place for him.

On entering into heightened awareness, I had noticed that there was another person hiding in the semi-darkness inside the house. I asked don Juan if Genaro was with him. He replied that he was alone, that what I had noticed was one of his allies, the one that guarded the house.

Don Juan then made a strange gesture. He contorted his face as if he were surprised or terrified. And instantly the frightening shape of a strange man appeared at the door of the room where we were. The presence of the strange man scared me so much that I actually felt dizzy. And before I could recuperate from my fright, the man lurched at me with a chilling ferocity. As he grabbed my forearms, I felt a jolt of something quite like a discharge of an electric current.

I was speechless, caught in a terror I could not dispel. Don Juan was smiling at me. I mumbled and groaned, trying to voice a plea for help, while I felt an even greater jolt.

The man tightened his grip and tried to throw me backward on the ground. Don Juan, with no hurry in his voice, urged me to pull myself together and not fight my fear, but roll with it. "Be afraid without being terrified," he said. Don Juan came to my side and, without intervening in my struggle, whispered in my ear that I should put all my concentration on the midpoint of my body.

Over the years, he had insisted that I measure my body to the hundredth of an inch and establish its exact midpoint, lengthwise as well as in width. He had always said that such a point is a true center of energy in all of us.

As soon as I had focused my attention on that midpoint, the man let go of me. At that instant I became aware that what I had thought was a human being was something that only looked like one. The moment it lost its human shape to me, the ally became an amorphous blob of opaque light. It moved away. I went after it, moved by a great force that made me follow that opaque light.

Don Juan stopped me. He gently walked me to the porch of his house and made me sit down on a sturdy crate he used as a bench.

I was terribly disturbed by the experience, but even more disturbed by the fact that my paralyzing fear had disappeared so fast and so completely.

I commented on my abrupt change of mood. Don

Juan said that there was nothing strange about my volatile change, and that fear did not exist as soon as the glow of awareness moved beyond a certain threshold inside man's cocoon.

He then began his explanation. He briefly outlined the truths about awareness he had discussed: that there is no objective world, but only a universe of energy fields which seers call the Eagle's emanations. That human beings are made of the Eagle's emanations and are in essence bubbles of luminescent energy; each of us is wrapped in a cocoon that encloses a small portion of these emanations. That awareness is achieved by the constant pressure that the emanations outside our cocoons, which are called emanations at large, exert on those inside our cocoons. That awareness gives rise to perception, which happens when the emanations inside our cocoons align themselves with the corresponding emanations at large.

"The next truth is that perception takes place," he went on, "because there is in each of us an agent called the assemblage point that selects internal and external emanations for alignment. The particular alignment that we perceive as the world is the product of the specific spot where our assemblage point is located on our cocoon."

He repeated this several times, allowing me time to grasp it. Then he said that in order to corroborate the truths about awareness, I needed energy.

"I've mentioned to you," he continued, "that dealing with petty tyrants helps seers accomplish a sophisticated maneuver: that maneuver is to move their assemblage points."

He said that for me to have perceived an ally meant that I had moved my assemblage point away from its customary position. In other words, my glow of awareness had moved beyond a certain threshold, also erasing my fear. And all this had happened because I had enough surplus energy.

Later that night, after we had returned from a trip into the surrounding mountains, which had been part of his teachings for the right side, don Juan had me shift again into heightened awareness and then continued his explanation. He told me that in order to discuss the nature of the assemblage point, he had to start with a discussion of the first attention.

He said that the new seers looked into the unnoticed ways in which the first attention functions, and as they tried to explain them to others, they devised an order for the truths about awareness. He assured me that not every seer is given to explaining. For instance, his benefactor, the nagual Julian, could not have cared less about explanations. But the nagual Julian's benefactor, the nagual Elias, whom don Juan was fortunate enough to meet, did care. Between the nagual Elias's detailed, lengthy explanations, the nagual Julian's scanty ones, and his own personal *seeing*, don Juan came to understand and to corroborate those truths.

Don Juan explained that in order for our first attention to bring into focus the world that we perceive, it has to emphasize certain emanations selected from the narrow band of emanations where man's awareness is located. The discarded emanations are still within our reach but remain dormant, unknown to us for the duration of our lives.

The new seers call the emphasized emanations the right side, normal awareness, the tonal, this world, the known, the first attention. The average man calls it reality, rationality, common sense.

The emphasized emanations compose a large portion of man's band of awareness, but a very small piece of the total spectrum of emanations present inside the cocoon of man. The disregarded emanations within man's band are thought of as a sort of preamble to the unknown, the unknown proper consisting of the bulk of emanations which are not part of the human band and which are never emphasized. Seers call them the left-side awareness, the nagual, the other world, the unknown, the second attention.

"This process of emphasizing certain emanations," don Juan went on, "was discovered and practiced by the old seers. They realized that a nagual man or a nagual woman, by the fact that they have extra strength, can push the emphasis away from the usual emanations and make it shift to neighboring ones. That push is known as the nagual's blow."

Don Juan said that the shift was utilized by the old seers in practical ways to keep their apprentices in bondage. With that blow they made their apprentices enter into a state of heightened, keenest, most impressionable awareness; while they were helplessly pliable, the old seers taught them aberrant techniques that made the apprentices into sinister men, just like their teachers.

The new seers employ the same technique, but instead of using it for sordid purposes, they use it to guide their apprentices to learn about man's possibilities.

Don Juan explained that the nagual's blow has to be delivered on a precise spot, on the assemblage point, which varies minutely from person to person. Also, the blow has to be delivered by a nagual who *sees*. He assured me that it is equally useless to have the strength of a nagual and not *see*, as it is to *see* and not have the strength of a nagual. In either case the results are just blows. A seer could strike on the precise spot over and over without the strength to move awareness, and a non-*seeing* nagual would not be able to strike the precise spot.

He also said that the old seers discovered that the assemblage point is not in the physical body, but in the luminous shell, in the cocoon itself. The nagual identifies that spot by its intense luminosity and pushes it, rather than striking it. The force of the push creates a dent in the cocoon and it is felt like a blow to the right shoulder blade, a blow that knocks all the air out of the lungs.

"Are there different types of dents?" I asked.

"There are only two types," he responded. "One is a concavity and the other is a crevice; each has a distinct effect. The concavity is a temporary feature and produces a temporary shift—but the crevice is a profound and permanent feature of the cocoon and produces a permanent shift."

He explained that usually a luminous cocoon hardened by self-reflection is not affected at all by the nagual's blow. Sometimes, however, the cocoon of man is very pliable and the smallest force creates a bowl-like dent ranging in size from a small depression to one that is a third the size of the total cocoon; or it creates a crevice that may run across the width of the egglike shell, or along its length, making the cocoon look as if it has curled in on itself.

Some luminous shells, after being dented, go back to their original shape instantly. Others remain dented for hours or even days at a time, but they revert back by themselves. Still others get a firm, impervious dent that requires another blow from the nagual on a bordering area to restore the original shape of the luminous cocoon. And a few never lose their indentation once they get it. No matter how many blows they get from a nagual they never revert back to their egglike shapes.

Don Juan further said that the dent acts on the first attention by displacing the glow of awareness. The dent presses the emanations inside the luminous shell, and the seers witness how the first attention shifts its emphasis under the force of that pressure. The dent, by displacing the Eagle's emanations inside the cocoon, makes the glow of awareness fall on other emanations from areas that are ordinarily inaccessible to the first attention.

I asked him if the glow of awareness is *seen* only on the surface of the luminous cocoon. He did not answer me right away. He seemed to immerse himself in thought. After perhaps ten minutes he answered my question; he said that normally the glow of awareness is *seen* on the surface of the cocoon of all sentient beings. After man develops attention, however, the glow of awareness acquires depth. In other words, it is transmitted from the surface of the cocoon to quite a number of emanations inside the cocoon.

"The old seers knew what they were doing when they handled awareness," he went on. "They realized that by creating a dent in the cocoon of man, they could force the glow of awareness, since it is already glowing on the emanations inside the cocoon, to spread to other neighboring ones."

'You make it all sound as if it's a physical affair," I said. "How can dents be made in something that is just a glow?"

"In some inexplicable way, it is a matter of a glow that creates a dent in another glow," he replied. "Your flaw is to remain glued to the inventory of reason. Reason doesn't deal with man as energy. Reason deals with instruments that create energy, but it has never seriously occurred to reason that we are better than instruments: we are organisms that create energy. We are a bubble of energy. It isn't farfetched, then, that a bubble of energy would make a dent in another bubble of energy."

He said that the glow of awareness created by the dent should rightfully be called temporary heightened attention, because it emphasizes emanations that are so proximal to the habitual ones that the change is minimal, yet the shift produces a greater capacity to understand and to concentrate and, above all, a greater capacity to forget. Seers knew exactly how to use this upshift in the scale of quality. They *saw* that only the emanations surrounding those we use daily suddenly become bright after the nagual's blow. The more distant ones remain unmoved, which meant to them that while being in a state of heightened attention, human beings could work as if they were in the world of everyday life. The need of a nagual man and a nagual woman became paramount to them, because that state lasts only for as long as the depression remains, after which the experiences are immediately forgotten.

"Why does one have to forget?" I asked.

"Because the emanations that account for greater clarity cease to be emphasized once warriors are out of heightened awareness," he replied. "Without that emphasis whatever they experience or witness vanishes."

Don Juan said that one of the tasks the new seers had devised for their students was to force them to remember, that is, to reemphasize by themselves, at a later time, those emanations used during states of heightened awareness.

He reminded me that Genaro was always recommending to me that I learn to write with the tip of my finger instead of a pencil so as not to accumulate notes. Don Juan said that what Genaro had actually meant was that while I was in states of heightened awareness I should utilize some unused emanations for storage of dialogue and experience, and someday recall it all by reemphasizing the emanations that were used.

He went on to explain that a state of heightened awareness is *seen* not only as a glow that goes deeper inside the egglike shape of human beings, but also as a more intense glow on the surface of the cocoon. Yet it is nothing in comparison to the glow produced by a state of total awareness, which is *seen* as a burst of incandescence in the entire luminous egg. It is an explosion of light of such a magnitude that the boundaries of the shell are diffused and the inside emanations extend themselves beyond anything imaginable.

"Are those special cases, don Juan?"

"Certainly. They happen only to seers. No other men or any other living creatures brighten up like that. Seers who deliberately attain total awareness are a sight to behold. That is the moment when they burn from within. The fire from within consumes them. And in full awareness they fuse themselves to the emanations at large, and glide into eternity."

After a few days in Sonora I drove don Juan back to the town in the southern part of Mexico where he and his party of warriors lived.

The next day was hot and hazy. I felt lazy and somehow annoyed. In midafternoon, there was a most unpleasant quietude in that town. Don Juan and I were sitting on the comfortable chairs in the big room. I told him that life in rural Mexico was not my cup of tea. I disliked the feeling I had that the silence of that town was forced. The only noise I ever heard was the sound of children's voices yelling in the distance. I was never able to find out whether they were playing or yelling in pain.

"When you're here, you're always in a state of heightened awareness," don Juan said. "That makes a great difference. But no matter what, you should be getting used to living in a town like this. Someday you will live in one."

"Why should I have to live in a town like this, don Juan?"

"I've explained to you that the new seers aim to be free. And freedom has the most devastating implications. Among them is the implication that warriors must purposely seek change. Your predilection is to live the way you do. You stimulate your reason by running through your inventory and pitting it against your friends' inventories. Those maneuvers leave you very little time to examine yourself and your fate. You will have to give up all that. Likewise, if all you knew were the dead calm of this town, you'd have to seek, sooner or later, the other side of the coin."

"Is that what you're doing here, don Juan?"

"Our case is a little bit different, because we are at the end of our trail. We are not seeking anything. What all of us do here is something comprehensible only to a warrior. We go from day to day doing nothing. We are waiting. I will not tire of repeating this: we know that we are waiting and we know what we are waiting for. We are waiting for freedom!

"And now that you know that," he added with a grin, "let's get back to our discussion of awareness."

Usually, when we were in that room we were never interrupted by anyone and don Juan would always decide on the length of our discussions. But this time there was a polite knock on the door and Genaro walked in and sat down. I had not seen Genaro since the day after we had run out of his house in a great hurry. I embraced him.

"Genaro has something to tell you," don Juan said. "I've told you that he is the master of awareness. Now I can tell you what all that means. He can make the assemblage point move deeper into the luminous egg after that point has been jolted out of its position by the nagual's blow."

He explained that Genaro had pushed my assemblage point countless times after I had attained heightened awareness. The day we had gone to the gigantic flat rock to talk, Genaro had made my assemblage point move dramatically into the left side—so dramatically, in fact, that it had been a bit dangerous.

Don Juan stopped talking and seemed to be ready to give Genaro the spotlight. He nodded as if to signal Genaro to say something. Genaro stood up and came to my side.

"Flame is very important," he said softly. "Do you

remember that day when I made you look at the reflection of the sunlight on a piece of quartz, when we were sitting on that big flat rock?"

When Genaro mentioned it I remembered. On that day just after don Juan had stopped talking, Genaro had pointed to the refraction of light as it went through a piece of polished quartz that he had taken out of his pocket and placed on the flat rock. The shine of the quartz had immediately caught my attention. The next thing I knew, I was crouching on the flat rock as don Juan stood by with a worried look on his face.

I was about to tell Genaro what I had remembered when he began to talk. He put his mouth to my ear and pointed to one of the two gasoline lamps in the room.

"Look at the flame," he said. "There is no heat in it. It's pure flame. Pure flame can take you to the depths of the unknown."

As he talked, I began to feel a strange pressure; it was a physical heaviness. My ears were buzzing; my eyes teared to the point that I could hardly make out the shape of the furniture. My vision seemed to be totally out of focus. Although my eyes were open, I could not see the intense light of the gasoline lamps. Everything around me was dark. There were streaks of chartreuse phosphorescence that illuminated dark, moving clouds. Then, as abruptly as it had faded away, my eyesight returned.

I could not make out where I was. I seemed to be floating like a balloon. I was alone. I had a pang of terror, and my reason rushed in to construct an explanation that made sense to me at that moment: Genaro had hypnotized me, using the flame of the gasoline lamp. I felt almost satisfied. I quietly floated, trying not to worry; I thought that a way to avoid worrying was to concentrate on the stages that I would have to go through to wake up.

The first thing I noticed was that I was not myself.

I could not really look at anything because I had nothing to look with. When I tried to examine my body I realized that I could only be aware and yet it was as if I were looking down into infinite space. There were portentous clouds of brilliant light and masses of blackness; both were in motion. I clearly *saw* a ripple of amber glow that was coming at me, like an enormous, slow ocean wave. I knew then that I was like a buoy floating in space and that the wave was going to overtake me and carry me. I accepted it as unavoidable. But just before it hit me something thoroughly unexpected happened—a wind blew me out of the wave's path.

The force of that wind carried me with tremendous speed. I went through an immense tunnel of intense colored lights. My vision blurred completely and then I felt that I was waking up, that I had been having a dream, a hypnotic dream brought about by Genaro. In the next instant I was back in the room with don Juan and Genaro.

I slept most of the following day. In the late afternoon, don Juan and I again sat down to talk. Genaro had been with me earlier but had refused to comment on my experience.

"Genaro again pushed your assemblage point last night," don Juan said. "But perhaps the shove was too forceful."

I eagerly told don Juan the content of my vision. He smiled, obviously bored.

"Your assemblage point moved away from its normal position," he said. "And that made you perceive emanations that are not ordinarily perceived. Sounds like nothing, doesn't it? And yet it is a supreme accomplishment that the new seers strive to elucidate."

He explained that human beings repeatedly choose the same emanations for perceiving because of two reasons. First, and most important, because we have been taught that those emanations are perceivable, and second because our assemblage points select and prepare those emanations for being used.

"Every living being has an assemblage point," he went on, "which selects emanations for emphasis. Seers can *see* whether sentient beings share the same view of the world, by *seeing* if the emanations their assemblage points have selected are the same."

He affirmed that one of the most important break-throughs for the new seers was to find that the spot where that point is located on the cocoon of all living creatures is not a permanent feature, but is established on that specific spot by habit. Hence the tremendous stress the new seers put on new actions, on new prac-ticalities. They want desperately to arrive at new usages, new habits.

"The nagual's blow is of great importance," he went on, "because it makes that point move. It alters its location. Sometimes it even creates a permanent crevice there. The assemblage point is totally dis-lodged, and awareness changes dramatically. But what is a matter of even greater importance is the proper understanding of the truths about awareness in order to realize that that point can be moved from within. The unfortunate truth is that human beings always lose by default. They simply don't know about their possibilities."

"How can one accomplish that change from within?" I asked.

"The new seers say that realization is the tech-nique," he said. "They say that, first of all, one must become aware that the world we perceive is the result of our assemblage points' being located on a specific spot on the cocoon. Once that is understood, the as-semblage point can move almost at will, as a conse-quence of new habits."

I did not quite understand what he meant by habits. I asked him to clarify his point.

"The assemblage point of man appears around a definite area of the cocoon, because the Eagle commands it," he said. "But the precise spot is determined by habit, by repetitious acts. First we learn that it can be placed there and then we ourselves command it to be there. Our command becomes the Eagle's command and that point is fixated at that spot. Consider this very carefully; our command becomes the Eagle's command. The old seers paid dearly for that finding. We'll come back to that later on."

He stated once again that the old seers had concentrated exclusively on developing thousands of the most complex techniques of sorcery. He added that what they never realized was that their intricate devices, as bizarre as they were, had no other value than being the means to break the fixation of their assemblage points and make them move.

I asked him to explain what he had said.

"I've mentioned to you that sorcery is something like entering a dead-end street," he replied. "What I meant was that sorcery practices have no intrinsic value. Their worth is indirect, for their real function is to make the assemblage point shift by making the first attention release its control on that point.

"The new seers realized the true role those sorcery practices played and decided to go directly into the process of making their assemblage points shift, avoiding all the other nonsense of rituals and incantations. Yet rituals and incantations are indeed necessary at one time in every warrior's life. I personally have initiated you in all kinds of sorcery procedures, but only for purposes of luring your first attention away from the power of self-absorption, which keeps your assemblage point rigidly fixed."

He added that the obsessive entanglement of the first attention in self-absorption or reason is a powerful binding force, and that ritual behavior, because it is repetitive, forces the first attention to free some energy from watching the inventory, as a consequence of which the assemblage point loses its rigidity.

"What happens to the persons whose assemblage points lose rigidity?" I asked.

"If they're not warriors, they think they're losing their minds," he said, smiling. "Just as you thought you were going crazy at one time. If they're warriors, they know they've gone crazy, but they patiently wait. You see, to be healthy and sane means that the assemblage point is immovable. When it shifts, it literally means that one is deranged."

He said that two options are opened to warriors whose assemblage points have shifted. One is to acknowledge being ill and to behave in deranged ways, reacting emotionally to the strange worlds that their shifts force them to witness; the other is to remain impassive, untouched, knowing that the assemblage point always returns to its original position.

"What if the assemblage point doesn't return to its original position?" I asked.

"Then those people are lost," he said. "They are either incurably crazy, because their assemblage points could never assemble the world as we know it, or they are peerless seers who have begun their movement toward the unknown."

"What determines whether it is one or the other?"

"Energy! Impeccability! Impeccable warriors don't lose their marbles. They remain untouched. I've said to you many times that impeccable warriors may *see* horrifying worlds and yet the next moment they are telling a joke, laughing with their friends or with strangers."

I said to him then what I had told him many times before, that what made me think I was ill was a series of disruptive sensorial experiences that I had had as aftereffects of ingesting hallucinogenic plants. I went through states of total space and time discordance, very annoying lapses of mental concentration, actual visions or hallucinations of places and people I would be staring at as if they really existed. I could not help thinking that I was losing my mind.

"By all ordinary measures, you were indeed losing your mind," he said, "but in the seers' view, if you had lost it, you wouldn't have lost much. The mind, for a seer, is nothing but the self-reflection of the inventory of man. If you lose that self-reflection, but don't lose your underpinnings, you actually live an infinitely stronger life than if you had kept it."

He remarked that my flaw was my emotional reaction, which prevented me from realizing that the oddity of my sensorial experiences was determined by the depth to which my assemblage point had moved into man's band of emanations.

I told him that I couldn't understand what he was explaining because the configuration that he had called man's band of emanations was something incomprehensible to me. I had pictured it to be like a ribbon placed on the surface of a ball.

He said that calling it a band was misleading, and that he was going to use an analogy to illustrate what he meant. He explained that the luminous shape of man is like a ball of jack cheese with a thick disk of darker cheese injected into it. He looked at me and chuckled. He knew that I did not like cheese.

He made a diagram on a small blackboard. He drew an egglike shape and divided it in four longitudinal sections, saying that he would immediately erase the division lines because he had drawn them only to give me an idea where the band was located in the cocoon of man. He then drew a thick band at the line between the first and second sections and erased the division lines. He explained that the band was like a disk of cheddar cheese that had been inserted into the ball of jack cheese.

"Now if that ball of jack cheese were transparent," he went on, "you would have the perfect replica of man's cocoon. The cheddar cheese goes all the way inside the ball of jack cheese. It's a disk that goes from the surface on one side to the surface on the other side.

"The assemblage point of man is located high up, three-fourths of the way toward the top of the egg on the surface of the cocoon. When a nagual presses on that point of intense luminosity, the point moves into the disk of the cheddar cheese. Heightened awareness comes about when the intense glow of the assemblage point lights up dormant emanations way inside the disk of cheddar cheese. To *see* the glow of the assemblage point moving inside that disk gives the feeling that it is shifting toward the left on the surface of the cocoon."

He repeated his analogy three or four times, but I did not understand it and he had to explain it further. He said that the transparency of the luminous egg creates the impression of a movement toward the left, when in fact every movement of the assemblage point is in depth, into the center of the luminous egg along the thickness of man's band.

I remarked that what he was saying made it sound as if seers would be using their eyes when they *see* the assemblage point move.

"Man is not the unknowable," he said. "Man's luminosity can be *seen* almost as if one were using the eyes alone."

He further explained that the old seers had *seen* the movement of the assemblage point but it never occurred to them that it was a movement in depth; instead they followed their *seeing* and coined the phrase "shift to the left," which the new seers retained although they knew that it was erroneous to call it a shift to the left.

He also said that in the course of my activity with him he had made my assemblage point move countless times, as was the case at that very moment. Since the shift of the assemblage point was always in depth, I had never lost my sense of identity, in spite of the fact that I was always using emanations I had never used before.

"When the nagual pushes that point," he went on, "the point ends up any which way along man's band, but it absolutely doesn't matter where, because wherever it ends up is always virgin ground.

"The grand test that the new seers developed for their warrior-apprentices is to retrace the journey that their assemblage points took under the influence of the nagual. This retracing, when it is completed, is called regaining the totality of oneself."

He went on to say that the contention of the new seers is that in the course of our growth, once the glow of awareness focuses on man's band of emanations and selects some of them for emphasis, it enters into a vicious circle. The more it emphasizes certain emanations, the more stable the assemblage point gets to be. This is equivalent to saying that our command becomes the Eagle's command. It goes without saying that when our awareness develops into first attention the command is so strong that to break that circle and make the assemblage point shift is a genuine triumph.

Don Juan said that the assemblage point is also responsible for making the first attention perceive in terms of clusters. An example of a cluster of emanations that receive emphasis together is the human body as we perceive it. Another part of our total being, our luminous cocoon, never receives emphasis and is relegated to oblivion; for the effect of the assemblage point is not only to make us perceive clusters of emanations, but also to make us disregard emanations.

When I pressed hard for an explanation of clustering he replied that the assemblage point radiates a glow that groups together bundles of encased emanations. These bundles then become aligned, as bundles, with the emanations at large. Clustering is carried out even when seers deal with the emanations that are never used. Whenever they are emphasized, we perceive them just as we perceive the clusters of the first attention.

"One of the greatest moments the new seers had," he continued, "was when they found out that the unknown is merely the emanations discarded by the first attention. It's a huge affair, but an affair, mind you, where clustering can be done. The unknowable, on the other hand, is an eternity where our assemblage point has no way of clustering anything."

He explained that the assemblage point is like a luminous magnet that picks emanations and groups them together wherever it moves within the bounds of man's band of emanations. This discovery was the glory of the new seers, for it put the unknown in a new light. The new seers noticed that some of the obsessive visions of seers, the ones that were almost impossible to conceive, coincided with a shift of the assemblage point to the region of man's band which is diametrically opposed to where it is ordinarily located.

"Those were visions of the dark side of man," he asserted.

"Why do you call it the dark side of man?" I asked.

"Because it is somber and foreboding," he said. "It's not only the unknown, but the who-cares-to-know-it."

"How about the emanations that are inside the cocoon but out of the bounds of man's band?" I asked. "Can they be perceived?"

"Yes, but in really indescribable ways," he said. "They're not the human unknown, as is the case with the unused emanations in the band of man, but the nearly immeasurable unknown where human traits do not figure at all. It is really an area of such an overpowering vastness that the best of seers would be hard put to describe it."

I insisted once more that it seemed to me that the mystery is obviously within us.

"The mystery is outside us," he said. "Inside us we have only emanations trying to break the cocoon. And this fact aberrates us, one way or another, whether we're average men or warriors. Only the new seers get around this. They struggle to *see*. And by means of the shifts of their assemblage points, they get to realize that the mystery is perceiving. Not so much what we perceive, but what makes us perceive.

"I've mentioned to you that the new seers believe that our senses are capable of detecting anything. They believe this because they *see* that the position of the assemblage point is what dictates what our senses perceive.

"If the assemblage point aligns emanations inside the cocoon in a position different from its normal one, the human senses perceive in inconceivable ways."

8

The Position of the Assemblage Point

The next time don Juan resumed his explanation of the mastery of awareness we were again in his house in southern Mexico. That house was actually owned by all the members of the nagual's party, but Silvio Manuel officiated as the owner and everyone openly referred to it as Silvio Manuel's house, although I, for some inexplicable reason, had gotten used to calling it don Juan's house.

Don Juan, Genaro, and I had returned to the house from a trip to the mountains. That day, as we relaxed after the long drive and ate a late lunch, I asked don Juan the reason for the curious deception. He assured me that no deception was involved, and that to call it Silvio Manuel's house was an exercise in the art of *stalking* to be performed by all the members of the nagual's party under any circumstances, even in the privacy of their own thoughts. For any of them to insist on thinking about the house in any other terms was tantamount to denying their links to the nagual's party.

I protested that he had never told me that. I did not want to cause any dissension with my habits.

"Don't worry about it," he said, smiling at me and

patting my back. "You can call this house whatever you want. The nagual has authority. The nagual woman, for instance, calls it the house of shadows."

Our conversation was interrupted, and I did not see him until he sent for me to come to the back patio a couple of hours later.

He and Genaro were strolling around at the far end of the corridor; I could see them moving their hands in what seemed to be an animated conversation.

It was a clear sunny day. The midafternoon sun shone directly on some of the flower pots that hung from the eaves of the roof around the corridor and projected their shadows on the north and east walls of the patio. The combination of intense yellow sunlight, the massive black shadows of the pots, and the lovely, delicate, bare shadows of the frail flowering plants that grew in them was stunning. Someone with a keen eye for balance and order had pruned those plants to create such an exquisite effect.

"The nagual woman has done that," don Juan said as if reading my thoughts. "She gazes at these shadows in the afternoons."

The thought of her gazing at shadows in the afternoons had a swift and devastating effect on me. The intense yellow light of that hour, the quietness of that town, and the affection that I felt for the nagual woman conjured up for me in one instant all the solitude of the warriors' endless path.

Don Juan had defined the scope of that path when he said to me that the new seers are the warriors of total freedom, that their only search is the ultimate liberation that comes when they attain total awareness. I understood with unimpaired clarity, as I looked at those haunting shadows on the wall, what it meant to the nagual woman when she said that to read poems out loud was the only release that her spirit had.

I remember that the day before she had read something to me, there in the patio, but I had not quite understood her urgency, her longing. It was a poem by Juan Ramón Jiménez, "Hora Inmensa," which she told me synthesized for her the solitude of warriors who live to escape to total freedom.

> *Only a bell and a bird break the stillness . . .*
> *It seems that the two talk with the setting sun.*
> *Golden colored silence, the afternoon is made of crystals.*
> *A roving purity sways the cool trees,*
> *and beyond all that,*
> *a transparent river dreams that trampling over pearls*
> *it breaks loose*
> *and flows into infinity.*

Don Juan and Genaro came to my side and looked at me with an expression of surprise.

"What are we really doing, don Juan?" I asked. "Is it possible that warriors are only preparing themselves for death?"

"No way," he said, gently patting my shoulder. "Warriors prepare themselves to be aware, and full awareness comes to them only when there is no more self-importance left in them. Only when they are nothing do they become everything."

We were quiet for a moment. Then don Juan asked me if I was in the throes of self-pity. I did not answer because I was not sure.

"You're not sorry that you're here, are you?" don Juan asked with a faint smile.

"He's certainly not," Genaro assured him. Then he seemed to have a moment of doubt. He scratched his head, then looked at me and arched his brows. "Maybe you are," he said. "Are you?"

"He's certainly not," don Juan assured Genaro this time. He went through the same gestures of scratching

128

his head and arching his brows. "Maybe you are," he said. "Are you?"

"He's certainly not!" Genaro boomed, and both of them exploded into uncontrolled laughter.

When they had calmed down, don Juan said that self-importance is the motivating force for every attack of melancholy. He added that warriors are entitled to have profound states of sadness, but that sadness is there only to make them laugh.

"Genaro has something to show you which is more exciting than all the self-pity you can muster up," don Juan continued. "It has to do with the position of the assemblage point."

Genaro immediately began to walk around the corridor, arching his back and lifting his thighs to his chest.

"The nagual Julian showed him how to walk that way," don Juan said in a whisper. "It's called the gait of power. Genaro knows several gaits of power. Watch him fixedly."

Genaro's movements were indeed mesmeric. I found myself following his gait, first with my eyes and then irresistibly with my feet. I imitated his gait. We walked once around the patio and stopped.

While walking, I had noticed the extraordinary lucidity that each step brought to me. When we stopped, I was in a state of keen alertness. I could hear every sound; I could detect every change in the light or in the shadows around me. I became enthralled with a feeling of urgency, of impending action. I felt extraordinarily aggressive, muscular, daring. At that moment I saw an enormous span of flat land in front of me; right behind me I saw a forest. Huge trees were lined up as straight as a wall. The forest was dark and green; the plain was sunny and yellow.

My breathing was deep and strangely accelerated, but not in an abnormal way. Yet it was the rhythm of my breathing that was forcing me to trot on the spot. I wanted to take off running, or rather my body wanted to, but just as I was taking off something stopped me.

Don Juan and Genaro were suddenly by my side. We walked down the corridor with Genaro to my right. He nudged me with his shoulder. I felt the weight of his body on me. He gently shoved me to the left and we angled off straight for the east wall of the patio. For a moment I had the weird impression that we were going to go through the wall, and I even braced myself for the impact, but we stopped right in front of the wall.

While my face was still against the wall, they both examined me with great care. I knew what they were searching for; they wanted to make sure that I had shifted my assemblage point. I knew that I had because my mood had changed. They obviously knew it too. They gently took me by the arms and walked in silence with me to the other side of the corridor, to a dark passageway, a narrow hall that connected the patio with the rest of the house. We stopped there. Don Juan and Genaro moved a few feet away from me.

I was left facing the side of the house that was in dark shadows. I looked into an empty dark room. I had a sense of physical weariness. I felt languid, indifferent, and yet I experienced a sense of spiritual strength. I realized then that I had lost something. There was no strength in my body. I could hardly stand. My legs finally gave in and I sat down and then I lay down on my side. While I lay there, I had the most wonderful, fulfilling thoughts of love for God, for goodness.

Then all at once I was in front of the main altar of a church. The bas-reliefs covered with gold leaf glittered with the light of thousands of candles. I saw the dark figures of men and women carrying an enormous crucifix mounted on a huge palanquin. I moved out of their way and stepped outside the church. I saw a multitude of people, a sea of candles, coming toward me. I felt elated. I ran to join them. I was moved by profound love. I wanted to be with them, to pray to the Lord. I was only a few feet away from the mass of people when something swished me away.

The next instant, I was with don Juan and Genaro. They flanked me as we walked lazily around the patio.

While we were having lunch the next day, don Juan said that Genaro had pushed my assemblage point with his gait of power, and that he had been able to do that because I had been in a state of inner silence. He explained that the articulation point of everything seers do is something he had talked about since the day we met: stopping the internal dialogue. He stressed over and over that the internal dialogue is what keeps the assemblage point fixed to its original position.

"Once silence is attained, everything is possible," he said.

I told him I was very conscious of the fact that in general I had stopped talking to myself, but did not know how I had done it. If asked to explain the procedure I would not know what to say.

"The explanation is simplicity itself," he said. "You *willed* it, and thus you set a new *intent*, a new command. Then your command became the Eagle's command.

"This is one of the most extraordinary things that the new seers found out: that our command can become the Eagle's command. The internal dialogue stops in the same way it begins: by an act of *will*. After all, we are forced to start talking to ourselves by those who teach us. As they teach us, they engage their *will*

131

and we engage ours, both without knowing it. As we learn to talk to ourselves, we learn to handle *will*. We *will* ourselves to talk to ourselves. The way to stop talking to ourselves is to use exactly the same method: we must *will* it, we must *intend* it.''

We were silent for a few minutes. I asked him to whom he was referring when he said that we had teachers who taught us to talk to ourselves.

''I was talking about what happens to human beings when they are infants,'' he replied, ''a time when they are taught by everyone around them to repeat an endless dialogue about themselves. The dialogue becomes internalized, and that force alone keeps the assemblage point fixed.

''The new seers say that infants have hundreds of teachers who teach them exactly where to place their assemblage point.''

He said that seers *see* that infants have no fixed assemblage point at first. Their encased emanations are in a state of great turmoil, and their assemblage points shift everywhere in the band of man, giving children a great capacity to focus on emanations that later will be thoroughly disregarded. Then as they grow, the older humans around them, through their considerable power over them, force the children's assemblage points to become more steady by means of an increasingly complex internal dialogue. The internal dialogue is a process that constantly strengthens the position of the assemblage point, because that position is an arbitrary one and needs steady reinforcement.

''The fact of the matter is that many children *see*,'' he went on. ''Most of those who *see* are considered to be oddballs and every effort is made to correct them, to make them solidify the position of their assemblage points.''

''But would it be possible to encourage children to

keep their assemblage points more fluid?" I asked.

"Only if they live among the new seers," he said. "Otherwise they would get entrapped, as the old seers did, in the intricacies of the silent side of man. And, believe me, that's worse than being caught in the clutches of rationality."

Don Juan went on to express his profound admiration for the human capacity to impart order to the chaos of the Eagle's emanations. He maintained that every one of us, in his own right, is a masterful magician and that our magic is to keep our assemblage point unwaveringly fixed.

"The force of the emanations at large," he went on, "makes our assemblage point select certain emanations and cluster them for alignment and perception. That's the command of the Eagle, but all the meaning that we give to what we perceive is our command, our gift of magic."

He said that in the light of what he had explained, what Genaro had made me do the day before was something extraordinarily complex and yet very simple. It was complex because it required a tremendous discipline on everybody's part; it required that the internal dialogue be stopped, that a state of heightened awareness be reached, and that someone walk away with one's assemblage point. The explanation behind all these complex procedures was very simple; the new seers say that since the exact position of the assemblage point is an arbitrary position chosen for us by our ancestors, it can move with a relatively small effort; once it moves, it forces new alignments of emanations, thus new perceptions.

"I used to give you power plants in order to make your assemblage point move," don Juan continued. "Power plants have that effect; but hunger, tiredness, fever, and other things like that can have a similar effect. The flaw of the average man is that he thinks the result of a shift is purely mental. It isn't, as you yourself can attest."

He explained that my assemblage point had shifted scores of times in the past, just as it had shifted the day before, and that most of the time the worlds it had assembled had been so close to the world of everyday life as to be virtually phantom worlds. He emphatically added that visions of that kind are automatically rejected by the new seers.

"Those visions are the product of man's inventory," he went on. "They are of no value for warriors in search of total freedom, because they are produced by a lateral shift of the assemblage point."

He stopped talking and looked at me. I knew that by "lateral shift" he had meant a shift of the point from one side to the other along the width of man's band of emanations instead of a shift in depth. I asked him if I was right.

"That's exactly what I meant," he said. "On both edges of man's band of emanations there is a strange storage of refuse, an incalculable pile of human junk. It's a very morbid, sinister storehouse. It had great value for the old seers but not for us.

"One of the easiest things one can do is to fall into it. Yesterday Genaro and I wanted to give you a quick example of that lateral shift; that was why we walked your assemblage point, but any person can reach that storehouse by simply stopping his internal dialogue. If the shift is minimal, the results are explained as fantasies of the mind. If the shift is considerable, the results are called hallucinations."

I asked him to explain the act of walking the assemblage point. He said that once warriors have attained inner silence by stopping their internal dialogue, the sound of the gait of power, more than the sight of it, is what traps their assemblage points. The rhythm of muffled steps instantly catches the alignment force of the emanations inside the cocoon, which has been disconnected by inner silence.

"That force hooks itself immediately to the edges of the band," he went on. "On the right edge we find endless visions of physical activity, violence, killing, sensuality. On the left edge we find spirituality, religion, God. Genaro and I walked your assemblage point to both edges, so as to give you a complete view of that human junk pile."

Don Juan restated, as if on second thought, that one of the most mysterious aspects of the seers' knowledge is the incredible effects of inner silence. He said that once inner silence is attained, the bonds that tie the assemblage point to the particular spot where it is placed begin to break and the assemblage point is free to move.

He said that the movement ordinarily is toward the left, that such a directional preference is a natural reaction of most human beings, but that there are seers who can direct that movement to positions below the customary spot where the point is located. The new seers call that shift "the shift below."

"Seers also suffer accidental shifts below," he went on. "The assemblage point doesn't remain there long, and that's fortunate, because that is the place of the beast. To go below is counter to our interest, although the easiest thing to do."

Don Juan also said that among the many errors of judgment the old seers had committed, one of the most grievous was moving their assemblage points to the immeasurable area below, which made them experts at adopting animal forms. They chose different animals as their point of reference and called those animals their nagual. They believed that by moving their assemblage points to specific spots they would acquire the characteristics of the animal of their choice, its strength or wisdom or cunning or agility or ferocity.

Don Juan assured me that there are many dreadful

examples of such practices even among the seers of our day. The relative facility with which the assemblage point of man moves toward any lower position poses a great temptation to seers, especially to those whose inclination leans toward that end. It is the duty of a nagual, therefore, to test his warriors.

He told me then that he had put me to the test by moving my assemblage point to a position below, while I was under the influence of a power plant. He then guided my assemblage point until I could isolate the crows' band of emanations, which resulted in my changing into a crow.

I again asked don Juan the question I had asked him dozens of times. I wanted to know whether I had physically turned into a crow or had merely thought and felt like one. He explained that a shift of the assemblage point to the area below always results in a total transformation. He added that if the assemblage point moves beyond a crucial threshold, the world vanishes; it ceases to be what it is to us at man's level.

He conceded that my transformation was indeed horrifying by any standards. My reaction to that experience proved to him that I had no leanings toward that direction. Had it not been that way, I would have had to employ enormous energy in order to fight off a tendency to remain in that area below, which some seers find most comfortable.

He further said that an unwitting downshift occurs periodically to every seer, but that such a downshift becomes less and less frequent as their assemblage points move farther toward the left. Every time it occurs, however, the power of a seer undergoing it diminishes considerably. It is a drawback that takes time and great effort to correct.

"Those lapses make seers extremely morose and narrow-minded," he continued, "and in certain cases, extremely rational."

"How can seers avoid those downshifts?" I asked.

"It all depends on the warrior," he said. "Some of them are naturally inclined to indulge in their quirks—yourself, for instance. They are the ones who are hard hit. For those like you, I recommend a twenty-four-hour vigil of everything they do. Disciplined men or women are less prone to that kind of shift; for those I would recommend a twenty-three-hour vigil."

He looked at me with shiny eyes and laughed.

"Female seers have downshifts more often than males," he said. "But they are also capable of bouncing out of that position with no effort at all, while males linger dangerously in it."

He also said that women seers have an extraordinary capacity to make their assemblage points hold on to any position in the area below. Men cannot. Men have sobriety and purpose, but very little talent; that is the reason why a nagual must have eight women seers in his party. Women give the impulse to cross the immeasurable vastness of the unknown. Together with that natural capacity, or as a consequence of it, women have a most fierce intensity. They can, therefore, reproduce an animal form with flare, ease, and a matchless ferocity.

"If you think about scary things," he continued, "about something unnamable lurking in the darkness, you're thinking, without knowing it, about a woman seer holding a position in the immeasurable area below. True horror lies right there. If you ever find an aberrant woman seer, run for the hills!"

I asked him whether other organisms were capable of shifting their assemblage points.

"Their points can shift," he said, "but the shift is not a voluntary thing with them."

"Is the assemblage point of other organisms also trained to appear where it does?" I asked.

"Every newborn organism is trained, one way or

137

another," he replied. "We may not understand how their training is done—after all, we don't even understand how it is done to us—but seers see that the newborn are coaxed to do what their kind does. That's exactly what happens to human infants: seers *see* their assemblage points shifting every which way and then they *see* how the presence of adults fastens each point to one spot. The same happens to every other organism."

Don Juan seemed to reflect for a moment and then added that there was indeed one unique effect that man's assemblage point has. He pointed to a tree outside.

"When we, as serious adult human beings, look at a tree," he said, "our assemblage points align an infinite number of emanations and achieve a miracle. Our assemblage points make us perceive a cluster of emanations that we call tree."

He explained that the assemblage point not only effects the alignment needed for perception, but also obliterates the alignment of certain emanations in order to arrive at a greater refinement of perception, a skimming, a tricky human construct with no parallel.

He said that the new seers had observed that only human beings were capable of further clustering the clusters of emanations. He used the Spanish word for skimming, *desnate*, to describe the act of collecting the most palatable cream off the top of a container of boiled milk after it cools. Likewise, in terms of perception, man's assemblage point takes some part of the emanations already selected for alignment and makes a more palatable construct with it.

"The skimmings of men," don Juan continued, "are more real than what other creatures perceive. That is our pitfall. They are so real to us that we forget we have constructed them by commanding our assemblage points to appear where they do. We forget they are real to us only because it is our command to perceive them as real. We have the power to skim the top off the alignments, but we don't have the power to protect ourselves from our own commands. That has to be learned. To give our skimmings a free hand, as we do, is an error of judgment for which we pay as dearly as the old seers paid for theirs.''

9

The Shift Below

Don Juan and Genaro made their yearly trip to the northern part of Mexico, to the Sonoran desert, to look for medicinal plants. One of the seers of the nagual's party, Vicente Medrano, the herbalist among them, used those plants to make medicines.

I had joined don Juan and Genaro in Sonora, at the last stage of their journey, just in time to drive them south, back to their home.

The day before we started on our drive, don Juan abruptly continued his explanation of the mastery of awareness. We were resting in the shade of some tall bushes in the foothills of the mountains. It was late afternoon, almost dark. Each of us carried a large burlap sack filled with plants. As soon as we had put them down, Genaro lay down on the ground and fell asleep, using his folded jacket as a pillow.

Don Juan spoke to me in a low voice, as if he didn't want to wake up Genaro. He said that by now he had explained most of the truths about awareness, and that there was only one truth left to discuss. The last truth, he assured me, was the best of the old seers' findings, although they never knew that themselves. Its tremendous value was only recognized, ages later, by the new seers.

"I've explained to you that man has an assemblage point," he went on, "and that that assemblage point aligns emanations for perception. We've also discussed that that point moves from its fixed position. Now, the last truth is that once that assemblage point moves beyond a certain limit, it can assemble worlds entirely different from the world we know."

Still in a whisper, he said that certain geographical areas not only help that precarious movement of the assemblage point, but also select specific directions for that movement. For instance, the Sonoran desert helps the assemblage point move downward from its customary position, to the place of the beast.

"That's why there are true sorcerers in Sonora," he continued. "Especially sorceresses. You already know one, la Catalina. In the past, I have arranged bouts between the two of you. I wanted to make your assemblage point shift, and la Catalina, with her sorcery antics, jolted it loose."

Don Juan explained that the chilling experiences I had had with la Catalina had been part of a prearranged agreement between the two of them.

"What would you think if we invited her to join us?" Genaro asked me in a loud voice, as he sat up.

The abruptness of his question and the strange sound of his voice plunged me into instant terror.

Don Juan laughed and shook me by the arms. He assured me that there was no need for alarm. He said that la Catalina was like a cousin or an aunt to us. She was part of our world, although she did not quite follow our quests. She was infinitely closer to the ancient seers.

Genaro smiled and winked at me.

"I understand that you've got hot pants for her," he said to me. "She herself confessed to me that every time you have had a confrontation with her, the greater your fright, the hotter your pants."

Don Juan and Genaro laughed to near hysteria.

I had to admit that somehow I had always found la Catalina to be a very scary but at the same time an extremely appealing woman. What impressed me the most about her was her exuding energy.

"She has so much energy saved," don Juan commented, "that you didn't have to be in heightened awareness for her to move your assemblage point all the way to the depths of the left side."

Don Juan said again that la Catalina was very closely related to us, because she belonged to the nagual Julian's party. He explained that usually the nagual and all the members of his party leave the world together, but that there are instances when they leave either in smaller groups or one by one. The nagual Julian and his party were an example of the latter. Although he had left the world nearly forty years ago, la Catalina was still here.

He reminded me about something he mentioned to me before, that the nagual Julian's party consisted of a group of three thoroughly inconsequential men and eight superb women. Don Juan had always maintained that such a disparity was one of the reasons why the members of the nagual Julian's party left the world one by one.

He said that la Catalina had been attached to one of the superb women seers of the nagual Julian's party, who taught her extraordinary maneuvers to shift her assemblage point to the area below. That seer was one of the last to leave the world. She lived to an extremely old age, and since both she and la Catalina were originally from Sonora, they returned, in her advanced years, to the desert and lived together until the seer left the world. In the years they spent together, la Catalina became her most dedicated helper and disciple, a disciple who was willing to learn the extravagant ways the old seers knew to make the assemblage point shift.

I asked don Juan if la Catalina's knowledge was inherently different from his own.

"We are exactly the same," he replied. "She's more like Silvio Manuel or Genaro; she is really the female version of them, but, of course, being a woman she's infinitely more aggressive and dangerous than both of them."

Genaro assented with a nod of his head. "Infinitely more," he said and winked again.

"Is she attached to your party?" I asked don Juan.

"I said that she's like a cousin or an aunt to us," he replied. "I meant she belongs to the older generation, although she's younger than all of us. She is the last of that group. She is rarely in contact with us. She doesn't quite like us. We are too stiff for her, because she's used to the nagual Julian's touch. She prefers the high adventure of the unknown to the quest for freedom."

"What is the difference between the two?" I asked don Juan.

"In the last part of my explanation of the truths about awareness," he replied, "we are going to discuss that difference slowly and thoroughly. What's important for you to know, at this moment, is that you're jealously guarding weird secrets in your left-side awareness; that is why la Catalina and you like each other."

I insisted again that it was not that I liked her, it was rather that I admired her great strength.

Don Juan and Genaro laughed and patted me as if they knew something I did not.

"She likes you because she knows what you're like," Genaro said and smacked his lips. "She knew the nagual Julian very well."

Both of them gave me a long look that made me feel embarrassed.

"What are you driving at?" I asked Genaro in a belligerent tone.

He grinned at me and moved his eyebrows up and down in a comical gesture. But he kept quiet.

Don Juan spoke and broke the silence.

"There are very strange points in common between the nagual Julian and you," he said. "Genaro is just trying to figure out if you're aware of it."

I asked both of them how on earth I would be aware of something so farfetched.

"La Catalina thinks you are," Genaro said. "She says so because she knew the nagual Julian better than any of us here."

I commented that I couldn't believe that she knew the nagual Julian, since he had left the world nearly forty years ago.

"La Catalina is no spring chicken," Genaro said. "She just looks young; that's part of her knowledge. Just as it was part of the nagual Julian's knowledge. You've seen her only when she looks young. If you see her when she looks old, she'll scare the living daylights out of you."

"What la Catalina does," don Juan interrupted, "can be explained only in terms of the three masteries: the mastery of awareness, the mastery of *stalking*, and the mastery of *intent*.

"But today, we are going to examine what she does only in light of the last truth about awareness: the truth that says that the assemblage point can assemble worlds different from our own after it moves from its original position."

Don Juan signaled me to get up. Genaro also stood up. I automatically grabbed the burlap sack filled with medicinal plants. Genaro stopped me as I was about to put it on my shoulders.

"Leave the sack alone," he said, smiling. "We have to take a little hike up the hill and meet la Catalina."

"Where is she?" I asked.

"Up there," Genaro said, pointing to the top of a small hill. "If you stare with your eyes half-closed, you'll *see* her as a very dark spot against the green shrubbery."

I strained to see the dark spot, but I couldn't see anything.

"Why don't you walk up there?" don Juan suggested to me.

I felt dizzy and sick to my stomach. Don Juan urged me with a movement of his hand to go up, but I didn't dare move. Finally, Genaro took me by the arm and both of us climbed toward the top of the hill. When we got there, I realized that don Juan had come up right behind us. The three of us reached the top at the same time.

Don Juan very calmly began to talk to Genaro. He asked him if he remembered the many times the nagual Julian was about to choke both of them to death, because they indulged in their fears.

Genaro turned to me and assured me that the nagual Julian had been a ruthless teacher. He and his own teacher, the nagual Elias, who was still in the world then, used to push everyone's assemblage points beyond a crucial limit and let them fend for themselves.

"I once told you that the nagual Julian recommended us not to waste our sexual energy," Genaro went on. "He meant that for the assemblage point to shift, one needs energy. If one doesn't have it, the nagual's blow is not the blow of freedom, but the blow of death."

"Without enough energy," don Juan said, "the force of alignment is crushing. You have to have energy to sustain the pressure of alignments which never take place under ordinary circumstances."

Genaro said that the nagual Julian was an inspiring teacher. He always found ways to teach and at the same time entertain himself. One of his favorite teaching devices was to catch them unawares once or twice, in their normal awareness, and make their assemblage points shift. From then on, all he had to do to have their undivided attention was to threaten them with an unexpected nagual's blow.

"The nagual Julian was really an unforgettable man," don Juan said. "He had a great touch with people. He would do the worst things in the world, but done by him they were great. Done by anyone else, they would have been crude and callous.

"The nagual Elias, on the other hand, had no touch, but he was indeed a great, great teacher."

"The nagual Elias was very much like the nagual Juan Matus," Genaro said to me. "They got along very fine. And the nagual Elias taught him everything without ever raising his voice, or playing tricks on him.

"But the nagual Julian was quite different," Genaro went on, giving me a friendly shove. "I'd say that he jealously guarded strange secrets in his left side, just like you. Wouldn't you say so?" he asked don Juan.

Don Juan did not answer, but nodded affirmatively. He seemed to be holding back his laughter.

"He had a playful nature," don Juan said, and both of them broke into a great laughter.

The fact that they were obviously alluding to something they knew made me feel even more threatened.

Don Juan matter-of-factly said that they were referring to the bizarre sorcery techniques that the nagual Julian had learned in the course of his life. Genaro added that the nagual Julian had a unique teacher besides the nagual Elias. A teacher who had liked him immensely and had taught him novel and complex ways of moving his assemblage point. As a result of this, the nagual Julian was extraordinarily eccentric in his behavior.

"Who was that teacher, don Juan?" I asked.

Don Juan and Genaro looked at each other and giggled like two children.

"That is a very tough question to answer," don Juan replied. "All I can say is that he was the teacher that deviated the course of our line. He taught us many things, good and bad, but among the worst, he taught us what the old seers did. So, some of us got trapped. The nagual Julian was one of them, and so is la Catalina. We only hope that you won't follow them."

I immediately began to protest. Don Juan interrupted me. He said that I did not know what I was protesting.

As don Juan spoke, I became terribly angry with him and Genaro. Suddenly, I was raging, yelling at them at the top of my voice. My reaction was so out of tone with me that it scared me. It was as if I were someone else. I stopped and looked at them for help.

Genaro had his hands on don Juan's shoulders as if he needed support. Both of them were laughing uncontrollably.

I became so despondent I was nearly in tears. Don Juan came to my side. He reassuringly put his hand on my shoulder. He said that the Sonoran desert, for reasons incomprehensible to him, fostered definite belligerence in man or any other organism.

"People may say that it's because the air is too dry here," he continued, "or because it's too hot. Seers would say that there is a particular confluence of the Eagle's emanations here, which, as I've already said, helps the assemblage point to shift below.

"Be that as it may, warriors are in the world to train themselves to be unbiased witnesses, so as to understand the mystery of ourselves and relish the exultation of finding what we really are. This is the highest of the new seers' goals. And not every warrior attains it. We believe that the nagual Julian didn't attain it. He was waylaid, and so was la Catalina."

He further said that to be a peerless nagual, one has to love freedom, and one has to have supreme detachment. He explained that what makes the warrior's path so very dangerous is that it is the opposite of the life situation of modern man. He said that modern man has left the realm of the unknown and the mysterious, and has settled down in the realm of the functional. He has turned his back to the world of the foreboding and the exulting and has welcomed the world of boredom.

"To be given a chance to go back again to the mystery of the world," don Juan continued, "is sometimes too much for warriors, and they succumb; they are waylaid by what I've called the high adventure of the unknown. They forget the quest for freedom; they forget to be unbiased witnesses. They sink into the unknown and love it."

"And you think I'm like that, don't you?" I asked don Juan.

"We don't think, we know," Genaro replied. "And la Catalina knows better than anyone else."

"Why would she know it?" I demanded.

"Because she's like you," Genaro replied, pronouncing his words with a comical intonation.

I was about to get into a heated argument again when don Juan interrupted me.

"There's no need to get so worked up," he said to me. "You are what you are. The fight for freedom is harder for some. You are one of them.

"In order to be unbiased witnesses," he went on, "we begin by understanding that the fixation or the movement of the assemblage point is all there is to us and the world we witness, whatever that world might be.

"The new seers say that when we were taught to talk to ourselves, we were taught the means to dull ourselves in order to keep the assemblage point fixed on one spot."

Genaro clapped his hands noisily and let out a piercing whistle that imitated the whistle of a football coach.

"Let's get that assemblage point moving!" he yelled. "Up, up, up! Move, move, move!"

We were all still laughing when the bushes by my right side were suddenly stirred. Don Juan and Genaro immediately sat down with the left leg tucked under the seat. The right leg, with the knee up, was like a shield in front of them. Don Juan signaled me to do the same. He raised his brows and made a gesture of resignation at the corner of his mouth.

"Sorcerers have their own quirks," he said in a whisper. "When the assemblage point moves to the regions below its normal position, the vision of sorcerers becomes limited. If they see you standing, they'll attack you."

"The nagual Julian kept me once for two days in this warrior's position," Genaro whispered to me. "I even had to urinate while I sat in this position."

"And defecate," don Juan added.

"Right," Genaro said. And then he whispered to me, as if on second thought, "I hope you did your kaka earlier. If your bowels aren't empty when la Catalina shows up, you'll shit in your pants, unless I show you how to take them off. If you have to shit in this position, you've got to get your pants off."

He began to show me how to maneuver out of my trousers. He did it in a most serious and concerned manner. All my concentration was focused on his movements. It was only when I had gotten out of my pants that I became aware that don Juan was roaring with laughter. I realized that Genaro was again poking fun at me. I was about to stand up to put on my pants, when don Juan stopped me. He was laughing so hard that he could hardly articulate his words. He told me to stay put, that Genaro did things only half in fun,

149

and that la Catalina was really there behind the bushes.

His tone of urgency, in the midst of laughter, got to me. I froze on the spot. A moment later a rustle in the bushes sent me into such a panic that I forgot about my pants. I looked at Genaro. He was again wearing his pants. He shrugged his shoulders.

"I'm sorry," he whispered. "I didn't have time to show you how to put them back on without getting up."

I did not have time to get angry or to join them in their mirth. Suddenly, right in front of me, the bushes separated and a most horrendous creature came out. It was so outlandish I was no longer afraid. I was spellbound. Whatever was in front of me was not a human being; it was something not even remotely resembling one. It was more like a reptile. Or a bulky grotesque insect. Or even a hairy, ultimately repulsive bird. Its body was dark and had coarse reddish hair. I could not see any legs, just the ugly enormous head. The nose was flat and the nostrils were two enormous lateral holes. It had something like a beak with teeth. Horrifying as that thing was, its eyes were magnificent. They were like two mesmeric pools of inconceivable clarity. They had knowledge. They were not human eyes, or bird eyes, or any kind of eyes I had ever seen.

The creature moved toward my left, rustling the bushes. As I moved my head to follow it, I noticed that don Juan and Genaro seemed to be as spellbound by its presence as I was. It occurred to me that they had never seen anything like that either.

In an instant, the creature had moved completely out of sight. But a moment later there was a growl and its gigantic shape again loomed in front of us.

I was fascinated and at the same time worried by the fact that I was not in the least afraid of that grotesque creature. It was as if my early panic had been experienced by someone else.

I felt, at one moment, that I was beginning to stand up. Against my volition, my legs straightened up and I found myself standing up, facing the creature. I vaguely felt that I was taking off my jacket, my shirt, and my shoes. Then I was naked. The muscles of my legs tensed with a tremendously powerful contraction. I jumped up and down with colossal agility, and then the creature and I raced toward some ineffable greenness in the distance.

The creature raced ahead of me, coiling on itself, like a serpent. But then I caught up with it. As we speeded together, I became aware of something I already knew—the creature was really la Catalina. All of a sudden, la Catalina, in the flesh, was next to me. We moved effortlessly. It was as if we were stationary, only posed in a bodily gesture of movement and speed, while the scenery around us was being moved, giving the impression of enormous acceleration.

Our racing stopped as suddenly as it had started, and then I was alone with la Catalina in a different world. There was not a single recognizable feature in it. There was an intense glare and heat coming from what seemed to be the ground, a ground covered with huge rocks. Or at least they seemed to be rocks. They had the color of sandstone, but they had no weight; they were like chunks of sponge tissue. I could send them hurling around by only leaning on them.

I became so fascinated with my strength that I was oblivious to anything else. I had assessed, in whatever way, that the chunks of seemingly weightless material opposed resistance to me. It was my superior strength that sent them hurling around.

I tried to grab them with my hands, and I realized that my entire body had changed. La Catalina was looking at me. She was again the grotesque creature she had been before, and so was I. I could not see myself, but I knew that both of us were exactly alike.

An indescribable joy possessed me, as if joy were some force that came from outside me. La Catalina and I cavorted, and twisted, and played until I had no more thoughts, or feelings, or human awareness in any degree. Yet, I was definitely aware. My awareness was a vague knowledge that gave me confidence; it was a limitless trust, a physical certainty of my existence, not in the sense of a human feeling of individuality, but in the sense of a presence that was everything.

Then, everything came again into human focus all at once. La Catalina was holding my hand. We were walking on the desert floor among the desert shrubs. I had the immediate and painful realization that the desert rocks and hard clumps of dirt were horribly injurious to my bare feet.

We came to a spot clear of vegetation. Don Juan and Genaro were there. I sat down and put on my clothes.

My experience with la Catalina delayed our trip back to the south of Mexico. It had unhinged me in some indescribable way. In my normal state of awareness, I became disassociated. It was as if I had lost a point of reference. I had become despondent. I told don Juan that I had even lost my desire to live.

We were sitting around in the ramada of don Juan's house. My car was loaded with sacks and we were ready to leave, but my feeling of despair got the best of me and I began to weep.

Don Juan and Genaro laughed until their eyes were tearing. The more desperate I felt, the greater was their enjoyment. Finally, don Juan had me shift into heightened awareness and explained that their laughter was not unkindness on their part, or the result of a weird sense of humor, but the genuine expression of happiness at seeing me advance in the path of knowledge.

"I'll tell you what the nagual Juliān used to say to us when we got to where you are," don Juan went on. "That way, you'll know that you're not alone. What's happening to you happens to anyone who stores enough energy to catch a glimpse of the unknown."

He said that the nagual Julian used to tell them that they had been evicted from the homes where they had lived all their lives. A result of having saved energy had been the disruption of their cozy but utterly limiting and boring nest in the world of everyday life. Their depression, the nagual Julian told them, was not so much the sadness of having lost their nest, but the annoyance of having to look for new quarters.

"The new quarters," don Juan went on, "are not as cozy. But they are infinitely more roomy.

"Your eviction notice came in the form of a great depression, a loss of the desire to live, just as it happened to us. When you told us that you didn't want to live, we couldn't help laughing."

"What's going to happen to me now?" I asked.

"Using the vernacular, you got to get another pad," don Juan replied.

Don Juan and Genaro again entered into a state of great euphoria. Every one of their statements and remarks made them laugh hysterically.

"It's all very simple," don Juan said. "Your new level of energy will create a new spot to house your assemblage point. And the warriors' dialogue you carry on with us every time we get together will solidify that new position."

Genaro adopted a serious look and in a booming voice he asked me, "Did you shit today?"

He urged me with a movement of his head to answer. "Did you, did you?" he demanded. "Let's get going with our warriors' dialogue."

When their laughter had subsided, Genaro said that

I had to be aware of a drawback, the fact that from time to time the assemblage point returns to its original position. He told me that in his own case, the normal position of his assemblage point had forced him to see people as threatening and often terrifying beings. To his utter amazement, one day he realized that he had changed. He was considerably more daring and had successfully dealt with a situation that would have ordinarily thrown him into chaos and fear.

"I found myself making love," Genaro continued, and he winked at me. "Usually I was afraid to death of women. But one day I found myself in bed with a most ferocious woman. It was so unlike me that when I realized what I was doing I nearly had a heart attack. The jolt made my assemblage point return to its miserable normal position and I had to run out of the house, shaking like a scared rabbit.

"You'd better watch out for the recoil of the assemblage point," Genaro added, and they were laughing again.

"The position of the assemblage point on man's cocoon," don Juan explained, "is maintained by the internal dialogue, and because of that, it is a flimsy position at best. That's why men and women lose their minds so easily, especially those whose internal dialogue is repetitious, boring, and without any depth.

"The new seers say that the more resilient human beings are those whose internal dialogue is more fluid and varied."

He said that the position of the warrior's assemblage point is infinitely stronger, because as soon as the assemblage point begins to move in the cocoon, it creates a dimple in the luminosity, a dimple that houses the assemblage point from then on.

"That's the reason why we can't say that warriors lose their minds," don Juan went on. "If they lose anything, they lose their dimple."

Don Juan and Genaro found that statement so hilarious that they rolled on the floor laughing.

I asked don Juan to explain my experience with la Catalina. And both of them again howled with laughter.

"Women are definitely more bizarre than men," don Juan finally said. "The fact that they have an extra opening between their legs makes them fall prey to strange influences. Strange, powerful forces possess them through that opening. That's the only way I can understand their quirks."

He kept silent for a while, and I asked what he meant by that.

"La Catalina came to us as a giant worm," he replied.

Don Juan's expression when he said that, and Genaro's explosion of laughter, took me into sheer mirth. I laughed until I was nearly sick.

Don Juan said that la Catalina's skill was so extraordinary that she could do anything she wanted in the realm of the beast. Her unparalleled display had been motivated by her affinity with me. The final result of all that, he said, was that la Catalina pulled my assemblage point with her.

"What did you two do as worms?" Genaro asked and slapped me on the back.

Don Juan seemed to be close to choking with laughter.

"That's why I've said that women are more bizarre than men," he commented at last.

"I don't agree with you," Genaro said to don Juan. "The nagual Julian didn't have an extra hole between his legs and he was more weird than la Catalina. I believe she learned the worm bit from him. He used to do that to her."

Don Juan jumped up and down, like a child who is trying to keep from wetting his pants.

When he had regained a measure of calm, don Juan

said that the nagual Julian had a knack for creating and exploiting the most bizarre situations. He also said that la Catalina had given me a superb example of the shift below. She had let me see her as the being whose form she had adopted by moving her assemblage point, and she had then helped me move mine to the same position that gave her her monstrous appearance.

"The other teacher that the nagual Julian had," don Juan went on, "taught him how to get to specific spots in that immensity of the area below. None of us could follow him there, but all the members of his party did, especially la Catalina and the woman seer who taught her."

Don Juan further said that a shift below entailed a view, not of another world proper, but of our same world of everyday life seen from a different perspective. He added that in order for me to *see* another world I had to perceive another great band of the Eagle's emanations.

He then brought his explanation to an end. He said that he had no time to elaborate on the subject of the great bands of emanations, because we had to be on our way. I wanted to stay a bit longer and keep on talking, but he argued that he would need a good deal of time to explain that topic and I would need fresh concentration.

10
Great Bands of Emanations

Days later, in his house in southern Mexico, don Juan continued with his explanation. He took me to the big room. It was early evening. The room was in darkness. I wanted to light the gasoline lanterns, but don Juan would not let me. He said that I had to let the sound of his voice move my assemblage point so that it would glow on the emanations of total concentration and total recall.

He then told me that we were going to talk about the great bands of emanations. He called it another key discovery that the old seers made, but that, in their aberration, they relegated to oblivion until it was rescued by the new seers.

"The Eagle's emanations are always grouped in clusters," he went on. "The old seers called those clusters the great bands of emanations. They aren't really bands, but the name stuck.

"For instance, there is an immeasurable cluster that produces organic beings. The emanations of that organic band have a sort of fluffiness. They are transparent and have a unique light of their own, a peculiar energy. They are aware, they jump. That's the reason why all organic beings are filled with a peculiar consuming energy. The other bands are darker, less fluffy. Some of them have no light at all, but a quality of opaqueness.''

"Do you mean, don Juan, that all organic beings have the same kind of emanations inside their cocoons?" I asked.

"No. I don't mean that. It isn't really that simple, although organic beings belong to the same great band. Think of it as an enormously wide band of luminous filaments, luminous strings with no end. Organic beings are bubbles that grow around a group of luminous filaments. Imagine that in this band of organic life some bubbles are formed around the luminous filaments in the center of the band, others are formed close to the edges; the band is wide enough to accommodate every kind of organic being with room to spare. In such an arrangement, bubbles that are close to the edges of the band miss altogether the emanations that are in the center of the band, which are shared only by bubbles that are aligned with the center. By the same token, bubbles in the center miss the emanations from the edges.

"As you can understand, organic beings share the emanations of one band; yet seers *see* that within that organic band beings are as different as they can be.''

"Are there many of these great bands?" I asked.

"As many as infinity itself," he replied. "Seers have found out, however, that in the earth there are only forty-eight such bands.''

"What is the meaning of that, don Juan?"

"For seers it means that there are forty-eight types of organizations on the earth, forty-eight types of clusters or structures. Organic life is one of them.''

"Does that mean that there are forty-seven types of inorganic life?"

"No, not at all. The old seers counted seven bands that produced inorganic bubbles of awareness. In other words, there are forty bands that produce bubbles without awareness; those are bands that generate only organization.

"Think of the great bands as being like trees. All of them bear fruit; they produce containers filled with emanations; yet only eight of those trees bear edible fruit, that is, bubbles of awareness. Seven have sour fruit, but edible nonetheless, and one has the most juicy, luscious fruit there is."

He laughed and said that in his analogy he had taken the point of view of the Eagle, for whom the most delectable morsels are the organic bubbles of awareness.

"What makes those eight bands produce awareness?" I asked.

"The Eagle bestows awareness through its emanations," he replied.

His answer made me argue with him. I told him that to say that the Eagle bestows awareness through its emanations is like what a religious man would say about God, that God bestows life through love. It does not mean anything.

"The two statements are not made from the same point of view," he patiently said. "And yet I think they mean the same thing. The difference is that seers *see* how the Eagle bestows awareness through its emanations and religious men don't *see* how God bestows life through his love."

He said that the way the Eagle bestows awareness is by means of three giant bundles of emanations that run through eight great bands. These bundles are quite peculiar, because they make seers feel a hue. One bundle gives the feeling of being beige-pink, something like the glow of pink-colored street lamps; another gives the feeling of being peach, like buff neon lights; and the third bundle gives the feeling of being amber, like clear honey.

"So, it is a matter of *seeing* a hue when seers *see* that the Eagle bestows awareness through its emanations," he went on. "Religious men don't *see* God's love, but if they would *see* it, they would know that it is either pink, peach, or amber.

"Man, for example, is attached to the amber bundle, but so are other beings."

I wanted to know which beings shared those emanations with man.

"Details like that you will have to find out for yourself through your own *seeing*," he said. "There is no point in my telling you which ones; you will only be making another inventory. Suffice it to say that finding that out for yourself will be one of the most exciting things you'll ever do."

"Do the pink and peach bundles also show in man?" I asked.

"Never. Those bundles belong to other living beings," he replied.

I was about to ask a question, but with a forceful movement of his hand, he signaled me to stop. He then became immersed in thought. We were enveloped in complete silence for a long time.

"I've told you that the glow of awareness in man has different colors," he finally said. "What I didn't tell you then, because we hadn't gotten to that point yet, was that they are not colors but casts of amber."

He said that the amber bundle of awareness has an infinitude of subtle variants, which always denote differences in quality of awareness. Pink and pale-green amber are the most common casts. Blue amber is more unusual, but pure amber is by far the most rare.

"What determines the particular casts of amber?"

"Seers say that the amount of energy that one saves and stores determines the cast. Countless numbers of warriors have begun with an ordinary pink amber cast and have finished with the purest of all ambers. Genaro and Silvio Manuel are examples of that."

"What forms of life belong to the pink and the peach bundles of awareness?" I asked.

"The three bundles with all their casts crisscross the eight bands," he replied. "In the organic band, the pink bundle belongs mainly to plants, the peach band belongs to insects, and the amber band belongs to man and other animals.

"The same situation is prevalent in the inorganic bands. The three bundles of awareness produce specific kinds of inorganic beings in each of the seven great bands."

I asked him to elaborate on the kinds of inorganic beings that existed.

"That is another thing that you must *see* for yourself," he said. "The seven bands and what they produce are indeed inaccessible to human reason, but not to human *seeing*."

I told him that I could not quite grasp his explanation of the great bands, because his description had forced me to imagine them as independent bundles of strings, or even as flat bands, like conveyor belts.

He explained that the great bands are neither flat nor round, but indescribably clustered together, like a pile of hay, which is held together in midair by the force of the hand that pitched it. Thus, there is no order to the emanations; to say that there is a central part or that there are edges is misleading, but necessary to understanding.

Continuing, he explained that inorganic beings produced by the seven other bands of awareness are characterized by having a container that has no motion; it is rather a formless receptacle with a low degree of luminosity. It does not look like the cocoon of organic beings. It lacks the tautness, the inflated quality that makes organic beings look like luminous balls bursting with energy.

Don Juan said that the only similarity between inorganic and organic beings is that all of them have the awareness-bestowing pink or peach or amber emanations.

"Those emanations, under certain circumstances," he continued, "make possible the most fascinating communication between the beings of those eight great bands."

He said that usually the organic beings, with their greater fields of energy, are the initiators of communication with inorganic beings, but a subtle and sophisticated follow-up is always the province of the inorganic beings. Once the barrier is broken, inorganic beings change and become what seers call allies. From that moment inorganic beings can anticipate the seer's most subtle thoughts or moods or fears.

"The old seers became mesmerized by such devotion from their allies," he went on. "Stories are that the old seers could make their allies do anything they wanted. That was one of the reasons they believed in their own invulnerability. They got fooled by their self-importance. The allies have power only if the seer who *sees* them is the paragon of impeccability; and those old seers just weren't."

"Are there as many inorganic beings as there are living organisms?" I asked.

He said that inorganic beings are not as plentiful as organic ones, but that this is offset by the greater number of bands of inorganic awareness. Also, the differences among the inorganic beings themselves are more vast than the differences among organisms, because organisms belong to only one band while inorganic beings belong to seven bands.

"Besides, inorganic beings live infinitely longer than organisms," he continued. "This matter is what prompted the old seers to concentrate their *seeing* on the allies, for reasons I will tell you about later on."

He said that the old seers also came to realize that it is the high energy of organisms and the subsequent high development of their awareness that make them delectable morsels for the Eagle. In the old seers' view, gluttony was the reason the Eagle produced as many organisms as possible.

He explained next that the product of the other forty great bands is not awareness at all, but a configuration of inanimate energy. The old seers chose to call whatever is produced by those bands, vessels. While cocoons and containers are fields of energetic awareness, which accounts for their independent luminosity, vessels are rigid receptacles that hold emanations without being fields of energetic awareness. Their luminosity comes only from the energy of the encased emanations.

"You must bear in mind that everything on the earth is encased," he continued. "Whatever we perceive is made up of portions of cocoons or vessels with emanations. Ordinarily, we don't perceive the containers of inorganic beings at all."

He looked at me, waiting for a sign of comprehension. When he realized I was not going to oblige him, he continued explaining.

"The total world is made of the forty-eight bands," he said. "The world that our assemblage point assembles for our normal perception is made up of two bands; one is the organic band, the other is a band that has only structure, but no awareness. The other forty-six great bands are not part of the world we normally perceive."

He paused again for pertinent questions. I had none.

"There are other complete worlds that our assemblage points can assemble," he went on. "The old seers counted seven such worlds, one for each band of awareness. I'll add that two of those worlds, besides the world of everyday life, are easy to assemble; the other five are something else."

When we again sat down to talk, don Juan immediately began to talk about my experience with la Catalina. He said that a shift of the assemblage point to the

163

area below its customary position allows the seer a detailed and narrow view of the world we know. So detailed is that view that it seems to be an entirely different world. It is a mesmerizing view that has a tremendous appeal, especially for those seers who have an adventurous but somehow indolent and lazy spirit.

"The change of perspective is very pleasant," don Juan went on. "Minimal effort is required, and the results are staggering. If a seer is driven by quick gain, there is no better maneuver than the shift below. The only problem is that in those positions of the assemblage point, seers are plagued by death, which happens even more brutally and more quickly than in man's position.

"The nagual Julian thought it was a great place for cavorting, but that's all."

He said that a true change of worlds happens only when the assemblage point moves into man's band, deep enough to reach a crucial threshold, at which stage the assemblage point can use another of the great bands.

"How does it use it?" I asked.

He shrugged his shoulders. "It's a matter of energy," he said. "The force of alignment hooks another band, provided that the seer has enough energy. Our normal energy allows our assemblage points to use the force of alignment of one great band of emanations. And we perceive the world we know. But if we have a surplus of energy, we can use the force of alignment of other great bands, and consequently we perceive other worlds."

Don Juan abruptly changed the subject and began to talk about plants.

"This may seem like an oddity to you," he said, "but trees, for instance, are closer to man than ants. I've told you that trees and man can develop a great relationship; that's so because they share emanations."

"How big are their cocoons?" I asked.

"The cocoon of a giant tree is not much larger than the tree itself. The interesting part is that some tiny plants have a cocoon almost as big as a man's body and three times its width. Those are power plants. They share the largest amount of emanations with man, not the emanations of awareness, but other emanations in general.

"Another thing unique about plants is that their luminosities have different casts. They are pinkish in general, because their awareness is pink. Poisonous plants are a pale yellow pink and medicinal plants are a bright violet pink. The only ones that are white pink are power plants; some are murky white, others are brilliant white.

"But the real difference between plants and other organic beings is the location of their assemblage points. Plants have it on the lower part of their cocoon, while other organic beings have it on the upper part of their cocoon."

"What about the inorganic beings?" I asked. "Where do they have their assemblage points?"

"Some have it on the lower part of their containers," he said. "Those are thoroughly alien to man, but akin to plants. Others have it anywhere on the upper part of their containers. Those are close to man and other organic creatures."

He added that the old seers were convinced that plants have the most intense communication with inorganic beings. They believed that the lower the assemblage point, the easier for plants to break the barrier of perception; very large trees and very small plants have their assemblage points extremely low in their cocoon. Because of this, a great number of the old seers' sorcery techniques were means to harness the awareness of trees and small plants in order to use

165

them as guides to descend to what they called the deepest levels of the dark regions.

"You understand, of course," don Juan went on, "that when they thought they were descending to the depths, they were, in fact, pushing their assemblage points to assemble other perceivable worlds with those seven great bands.

"They taxed their awareness to the limit and assembled worlds with five great bands that are accessible to seers only if they undergo a dangerous transformation."

"But did the old seers succeed in assembling those worlds?" I asked.

"They did," he said. "In their aberration they believed it was worth their while to break all the barriers of perception, even if they had to become trees to do that."

11

Stalking, Intent, and the Dreaming Position

The next day, in the early evening again, don Juan came to the room where I was talking with Genaro. He took me by the arm and walked me through the house to the back patio. It was already fairly dark. We started to walk around in the corridor that encircled the patio.

As we walked, don Juan told me that he wanted to warn me once again that it is very easy in the path of knowledge to get lost in intricacies and morbidity. He said that seers are up against great enemies that can destroy their purpose, muddle their aims, and make them weak; enemies created by the warriors' path itself together with the sense of indolence, laziness, and self-importance that are integral parts of the daily world.

He remarked that the mistakes the ancient seers made as a result of indolence, laziness, and self-importance were so enormous and so grave that the new seers had no option but to scorn and reject their own tradition.

"The most important thing the new seers needed," don Juan continued, "was practical steps in order to make their assemblage points shift. Since they had none, they began by developing a keen interest in *seeing* the glow of awareness, and as a result they worked out three sets of techniques that became their cornerstone.''

Don Juan said that with these three sets, the new seers accomplished a most extraordinary and difficult feat. They succeeded in systematically making the assemblage point shift away from its customary position. He acknowledged that the old seers had also accomplished that feat, but by means of capricious, idiosyncratic maneuvers.

He explained that what the new seers *saw* in the glow of awareness resulted in the sequence in which they arranged the old seers' truths about awareness. This is known as the mastery of awareness. From that, they developed the three sets of techniques. The first is the mastery of *stalking*, the second is the mastery of *intent*, and the third is the mastery of *dreaming*. He maintained that he had taught me these three sets from the very first day we met.

He told me that he had taught me the mastery of awareness in two ways, just as the new seers recommend. In his teachings for the right side, which he had done in normal awareness, he accomplished two goals: he taught me the warriors' way, and he loosened my assemblage point from its original position. In his teachings for the left side, which he had done in heightened awareness, he also accomplished two goals: he had made my assemblage point shift to as many positions as I was capable of sustaining, and he had given me a long series of explanations.

Don Juan stopped talking and stared at me fixedly. There was an awkward silence; then he started to talk about *stalking*. He said that it had very humble and fortuitous origins. It started from an observation the new seers made that when warriors steadily behave in ways not customary for them, the unused emanations inside their cocoons begin to glow. And their assemblage points shift in a mild, harmonious, barely noticeable fashion.

Stimulated by this observation, the new seers began to practice the systematic control of their behavior. They called this practice the art of *stalking*. Don Juan remarked that the name, although objectionable, was appropriate, because *stalking* entailed a specific kind of behavior with people, behavior that could be categorized as surreptitious.

The new seers, armed with this technique, tackled the known in a sober and fruitful way. By continual practice, they made their assemblage points move steadily.

"*Stalking* is one of the two greatest accomplishments of the new seers," he said. "The new seers decided that it should be taught to a modern-day nagual when his assemblage point has moved quite deep into the left side. The reason for this decision is that a nagual must learn the principles of *stalking* without the encumbrance of the human inventory. After all, the nagual is the leader of a group, and to lead them he has to act quickly without first having to think about it.

"Other warriors can learn *stalking* in their normal awareness, although it is advisable that they do it in heightened awareness—not so much because of the value of heightened awareness, but because it imbues *stalking* with a mystery that it doesn't really have; *stalking* is merely behavior with people."

He said that I could now understand that shifting the assemblage point was the reason why the new seers placed such a high value on the interaction with petty tyrants. Petty tyrants forced seers to use the principles of *stalking* and, in doing so, helped seers to move their assemblage points.

I asked him if the old seers knew anything at all about the principles of *stalking*.

"*Stalking* belongs exclusively to the new seers," he said, smiling. "They are the only seers who had to deal with people. The old ones were so wrapped up in their sense of power that they didn't even know that people existed, until people started clobbering them on the head. But you already know all this."

Don Juan said next that the mastery of *intent* together with the mastery of *stalking* are the new seers' two masterpieces, which mark the arrival of the modern-day seers. He explained that in their efforts to gain an advantage over their oppressors the new seers pursued every possibility. They knew that their predecessors had accomplished extraordinary feats by manipulating a mysterious and miraculous force, which they could only describe as power. The new seers had very little information about that force, so they were obliged to examine it systematically through *seeing*. Their efforts were amply rewarded when they discovered that the energy of alignment is that force.

They began by *seeing* how the glow of awareness increases in size and intensity as the emanations inside the cocoon are aligned with the emanations at large. They used that observation as a springboard, just as they had done with *stalking*, and went on to develop a complex series of techniques to handle that alignment of emanations.

At first they referred to those techniques as the mastery of alignment. Then they realized that what was involved was much more than alignment; what was involved was the energy that comes out of the alignment of emanations. They called that energy *will*.

Will became the second basis. The new seers understood it as a blind, impersonal, ceaseless burst of energy that makes us behave in the ways we do. *Will* accounts for our perception of the world of ordinary affairs, and indirectly, through the force of that perception, it accounts for the placement of the assemblage point in its customary position.

Don Juan said that the new seers examined how the perception of the world of everyday life takes place and *saw* the effects of *will*. They *saw* that alignment is ceaselessly renewed in order to imbue perception with continuity. To renew alignment every time with the freshness that it needs to make up a living world, the burst of energy that comes out of those very alignments is automatically rerouted to reinforce some choice alignments.

This new observation served the new seers as another springboard that helped them reach the third basis of the set. They called it *intent,* and they described it as the purposeful guiding of *will,* the energy of alignment.

"Silvio Manuel, Genaro, and Vicente were pushed by the nagual Julian to learn those three aspects of the seers' knowledge," he went on. "Genaro is the master of handling awareness, Vicente is the master of *stalking,* and Silvio Manuel is the master of *intent.*

"We are now doing a final explanation of the mastery of awareness; this is why Genaro is helping you."

Don Juan talked to the female apprentices for a long time. The women listened with serious expressions on their faces. I felt sure he was giving them detailed instructions about difficult procedures, judging from the women's fierce concentration.

I had been barred from their meeting, but I had watched them as they talked in the front room of Genaro's house. I sat at the kitchen table, waiting until they were through.

Then the women got up to leave, but before they did, they came to the kitchen with don Juan. He sat down facing me while the women talked to me with awkward formality. They actually embraced me. All of them were unusually friendly, even talkative. They said that they were going to join the male apprentices, who had gone with Genaro hours earlier. Genaro was going to show all of them his *dreaming body*.

As soon as the women left, don Juan quite abruptly resumed his explanation. He said that as time passed and the new seers established their practices, they realized that under the prevailing conditions of life, *stalking* only moved the assemblage points minimally. For maximum effect, *stalking* needed an ideal setting; it needed petty tyrants in positions of great authority and power. It became increasingly difficult for the new seers to place themselves in such situations; the task of improvising them or seeking them out became an unbearable burden.

The new seers deemed it imperative to *see* the Eagle's emanations in order to find a more suitable way to move the assemblage point. As they tried to *see* the emanations they were faced with a very serious problem. They found out that there is no way to *see* them without running a mortal risk, and yet they had to *see* them. That was the time when they used the old seers' technique of *dreaming* as a shield to protect themselves from the deadly blow of the Eagle's emanations. And in doing so, they realized that *dreaming* was in itself the most effective way to move the assemblage point.

"One of the strictest commands of the new seers," don Juan continued, "was that warriors have to learn *dreaming* while they are in their normal state of awareness. Following that command, I began teaching you *dreaming* almost from the first day we met."

"Why do the new seers command that *dreaming* has to be taught in normal awareness?" I asked.

"Because *dreaming* is so dangerous and dreamers so vulnerable," he said. "It is dangerous because it has inconceivable power; it makes *dreamers* vulnerable because it leaves them at the mercy of the incomprehensible force of alignment.

"The new seers realized that in our normal state of awareness, we have countless defenses that can safeguard us against the force of unused emanations that suddenly become aligned in *dreaming*."

Don Juan explained that *dreaming,* like *stalking,* began with a simple observation. The old seers became aware that in dreams the assemblage point shifts slightly to the left side in a most natural manner. That point indeed relaxes when man sleeps and all kinds of unused emanations begin to glow.

The old seers became immediately intrigued with that observation and began to work with that natural shift until they were able to control it. They called that control *dreaming,* or the art of handling the *dreaming body*.

He remarked that there is hardly a way of describing the immensity of their knowledge about *dreaming*. Very little of it, however, was of any use to the new seers. So when the time of reconstruction came, the new seers took for themselves only the bare essentials of *dreaming* to aid them in *seeing* the Eagle's emanations and to help them move their assemblage points.

He said that seers, old and new, understand *dreaming* as being the control of the natural shift that the assemblage point undergoes in sleep. He stressed that to control that shift does not mean in any way to direct it, but to keep the assemblage point fixed at the position where it naturally moves in sleep, a most difficult maneuver that took the old seers enormous effort and concentration to accomplish.

Don Juan explained that *dreamers* have to strike a very subtle balance, for dreams cannot be interfered with, nor can they be commanded by the conscious effort of the *dreamer,* and yet the shift of the assemblage point must obey the *dreamer's* command—a contradiction that cannot be rationalized but must be resolved in practice.

173

After observing *dreamers* while they slept, the old seers hit upon the solution of letting dreams follow their natural course. They had *seen* that in some dreams, the assemblage point of the *dreamer* would drift considerably deeper into the left side than in other dreams. This observation posed to them the question of whether the content of the dream makes the assemblage point move, or the movement of the assemblage point by itself produces the content of the dream by activating unused emanations.

They soon realized that the shifting of the assemblage point into the left side is what produces dreams. The farther the movement, the more vivid and bizarre the dream. Inevitably, they attempted to command their dreams, aiming to make their assemblage points move deeply into the left side. Upon trying it, they discovered that when dreams are consciously or semiconsciously manipulated, the assemblage point immediately returns to its usual place. Since what they wanted was for that point to move, they reached the unavoidable conclusion that interfering with dreams was interfering with the natural shift of the assemblage point.

Don Juan said that from there the old seers went on to develop their astounding knowledge on the subject —a knowledge which had a tremendous bearing on what the new seers aspired to do with *dreaming*, but was of little use to them in its original form.

He told me that thus far I had understood *dreaming* as being the control of dreams, and that every one of the exercises he had given me to perform, such as finding my hands in my dreams, was not, although it might seem to be, aimed at teaching me to command my dreams. Those exercises were designed to keep my assemblage point fixed at the place where it had moved in my sleep. It is here that the *dreamers* have to strike a subtle balance. All they can direct is the fixation of their assemblage points. Seers are like fishermen equipped with a line that casts itself wherever it may; the only thing they can do is keep the line anchored at the place where it sinks.

"Wherever the assemblage point moves in dreams is called the *dreaming position*," he went on. "The old seers became so expert at keeping their *dreaming position* that they were even able to wake up while their assemblage points were anchored there.

"The old seers called that state the *dreaming body*, because they controlled it to the extreme of creating a temporary new body every time they woke up at a new *dreaming position*.

"I have to make it clear to you that *dreaming* has a terrible drawback," he went on. "It belongs to the old seers. It's tainted with their mood. I've been very careful in guiding you through it, but still there is no way to make sure."

"What are you warning me about, don Juan?" I asked.

"I'm warning you about the pitfalls of *dreaming*, which are truly stupendous," he replied. "In *dreaming*, there is really no way of directing the movement of the assemblage point; the only thing that dictates that shift is the inner strength or weakness of *dreamers*. Right there we have the first pitfall."

He said that at first the new seers were hesitant to use *dreaming*. It was their belief that *dreaming*, instead of fortifying, made warriors weak, compulsive, capricious. The old seers were all like that. In order to offset the nefarious effect of *dreaming*, since they had no other option but to use it, the new seers developed a complex and rich system of behavior called the warriors' way, or the warriors' path.

With that system, the new seers fortified themselves and acquired the internal strength they needed to guide the shift of the assemblage point in dreams. Don

Juan stressed that the strength that he was talking about was not conviction alone. No one could have had stronger convictions than the old seers, and yet they were weak to the core. Internal strength meant a sense of equanimity, almost of indifference, a feeling of being at ease, but, above all, it meant a natural and profound bent for examination, for understanding. The new seers called all these traits of character sobriety.

"The conviction that the new seers have," he continued, "is that a life of impeccability by itself leads unavoidably to a sense of sobriety, and this in turn leads to the movement of the assemblage point.

"I've said that the new seers believed that the assemblage point can be moved from within. They went one step further and maintained that impeccable men need no one to guide them, that by themselves, through saving their energy, they can do everything that seers do. All they need is a minimal chance, just to be cognizant of the possibilities that seers have unraveled."

I told him that we were back in the same position we had been in in my normal state of awareness. I was still convinced that impeccability or saving energy was something so vague that it could be interpreted by anyone in whatever whimsical way he wanted.

I wanted to say more to build my argument, but a strange feeling overtook me. It was an actual physical sensation that I was rushing through something. And then I rebuffed my own argument. I knew without any doubt whatsoever that don Juan was right. All that is required is impeccability, energy, and that begins with a single act that has to be deliberate, precise, and sustained. If that act is repeated long enough, one acquires a sense of unbending intent, which can be applied to anything else. If that is accomplished the road is clear. One thing will lead to another until the warrior realizes his full potential.

When I told don Juan what I had just realized, he laughed with apparent delight and exclaimed that this was indeed a godsent example of the strength that he was talking about. He explained that my assemblage point had shifted, and that it had been moved by sobriety to a position that fostered understanding. It could have as well been moved by capriciousness to a position that only enhances self-importance, as had been the case many times before.

"Let's talk now about the *dreaming body*," he went on. "The old seers concentrated all their efforts on exploring and exploiting the *dreaming body*. And they succeeded in using it as a more practical body, which is tantamount to saying they recreated themselves in increasingly weird ways."

Don Juan maintained that it is common knowledge among the new seers that flocks of the old sorcerers never came back after waking up at a *dreaming position* of their liking. He said that chances are they all died in those inconceivable worlds, or they may still be alive today in who knows what kind of contorted shape or manner.

He stopped and looked at me and broke into a great laugh.

"You're dying to ask me what the old seers did with the *dreaming body,* aren't you?" he asked, and urged me with a movement of his chin to ask the question.

Don Juan stated that Genaro, being the indisputable master of awareness, had shown me the *dreaming body* many times while I was in a state of normal awareness. The effect that Genaro was after with his demonstrations was to make my assemblage point move, not from a position of heightened awareness, but from its normal setting.

Don Juan told me then, as if he were letting a secret be known, that Genaro was waiting for us in some fields near the house to show me his *dreaming body*.

He repeated over and over that I was now in the perfect state of awareness to *see* and understand what the *dreaming body* really is. Then he had me get up, and we walked through the front room to reach the door to the outside. As I was about to open the door, I noticed that someone was lying on the pile of floor mats that the apprentices used as beds. I thought that one of the apprentices must have returned to the house while don Juan and I were talking in the kitchen.

I went up to him, and then I realized that it was Genaro. He was sound asleep, snoring peacefully, lying face down.

"Wake him up," don Juan said to me. "We've got to be going. He must be dead tired."

I gently shook Genaro. He slowly turned around, made the sounds of someone waking up from a deep slumber. He stretched his arms, and then he opened his eyes. I screamed involuntarily and jumped back.

Genaro's eyes were not human eyes at all. They were two points of intense amber light. The jolt of my fright had been so intense that I became dizzy. Don Juan tapped my back and restored my equilibrium.

Genaro stood up and smiled at me. His features were rigid. He moved as if he were drunk or physically impaired. He walked by me and headed directly for the wall. I winced at the imminent crash, but he went through the wall as if it were not there at all. He came back into the room through the kitchen doorway. And then, as I looked in true horror, Genaro walked on the walls, with his body parallel to the ground, and on the ceiling, with his head upside down.

I fell backwards as I tried to follow his movements. From that position I didn't see Genaro anymore; instead I was looking at a blob of light that moved on the ceiling above me and on the walls, circling the room. It was as if someone with a giant flashlight was shining the beam on the ceiling and the walls. The beam of light was finally turned off. It disappeared from view by vanishing against a wall.

Don Juan remarked that my animal fright was always out of measure, that I had to struggle to bring it under control, but that all in all, I had behaved very well. I had *seen* Genaro's *dreaming body* as it really is, a blob of light.

I asked him how he was so sure I had done that. He replied that he had *seen* my assemblage point first move toward its normal setting in order to compensate for my fright, then move deeper into the left, beyond the point where there are no doubts.

"At that position there is only one thing one can *see:* blobs of energy," he went on. "But from heightened awareness to that other point deeper into the left side, it is only a short hop. The real feat is to make the assemblage point shift from its normal setting to the point of no doubt."

He added that we still had an appointment with Genaro's *dreaming body* in the fields around the house, while I was in normal awareness.

When we were back in Silvio Manuel's house, don Juan said that Genaro's proficiency with the *dreaming body* was a very minor affair compared with what the old seers did with it.

"You'll *see* that very soon," he said with an ominous tone, then laughed.

I questioned him about it with mounting fear, and that only evoked more laughter. He finally stopped and said that he was going to talk about the way the new seers got to the *dreaming body* and the way they used it.

"The old seers were after a perfect replica of the body," he continued, "and they nearly succeeded in getting one. The only thing they never could copy was the eyes. Instead of eyes, the *dreaming body* has just the glow of awareness. You never realized that before, when Genaro used to show you his *dreaming body*.

"The new seers could not care less about a perfect replica of the body; in fact, they are not even interested in copying the body at all. But they have kept just the name *dreaming body* to mean a feeling, a surge of energy that is transported by the movement of the assemblage point to any place in this world, or to any place in the seven worlds available to man."

Don Juan then outlined the procedure for getting to the *dreaming body*. He said that it starts with an initial act, which by the fact of being sustained breeds unbending intent. Unbending intent leads to internal silence, and internal silence to the inner strength needed to make the assemblage point shift in dreams to suitable positions.

He called this sequence the groundwork. The development of control comes after the groundwork has been completed; it consists of systematically maintaining the *dreaming position* by doggedly holding on to the vision of the dream. Steady practice results in a great facility to hold new *dreaming positions* with new dreams, not so much because one gains deliberate control with practice, but because every time this control is exercised the inner strength gets fortified. Fortified inner strength in turn makes the assemblage point shift into *dreaming positions*, which are more and more suitable to fostering sobriety; in other words, dreams by themselves become more and more manageable, even orderly.

"The development of *dreamers* is indirect," he went on. "That's why the new seers believed we can do *dreaming* by ourselves, alone. Since *dreaming* uses a natural, built-in shift of the assemblage point, we should need no one to help us.

"What we badly need is sobriety, and no one can give it to us or help us get it except ourselves. Without it, the shift of the assemblage point is chaotic, as our ordinary dreams are chaotic.

"So, all in all, the procedure to get to the *dreaming body* is impeccability in our daily life."

Don Juan explained that once sobriety is acquired and the *dreaming positions* become increasingly stronger, the next step is to wake up at any *dreaming position*. He remarked that the maneuver, although made to sound simple, was really a very complex affair—so complex that it requires not only sobriety but all the attributes of warriorship as well, especially *intent*.

I asked him how *intent* helps seers wake up at a *dreaming position*. He replied that *intent*, being the most sophisticated control of the force of alignment, is what maintains, through the *dreamer*'s sobriety, the alignment of whatever emanations have been lit up by the movement of the assemblage point.

Don Juan said that there is one more formidable pitfall of *dreaming*: the very strength of the *dreaming body*. For example, it is very easy for the *dreaming body* to gaze at the Eagle's emanations uninterruptedly for long periods of time, but it is also very easy in the end for the *dreaming body* to be totally consumed by them. Seers who gazed at the Eagle's emanations without their *dreaming bodies* died, and those who gazed at them with their *dreaming bodies* burned with the fire from within. The new seers solved the problem by *seeing* in teams. While one seer gazed at the emanations, others stood by ready to end the *seeing*.

"How did the new seers *see* in teams?" I asked.

"They *dreamed together*," he replied. "As you yourself know, it's perfectly possible for a group of seers to activate the same unused emanations. And in this case also, there are no known steps, it just happens; there is no technique to follow."

He added that in *dreaming together*, something in

us takes the lead and suddenly we find ourselves sharing the same view with other *dreamers*. What happens is that our human condition makes us focus the glow of awareness automatically on the same emanations that other human beings are using; we adjust the position of our assemblage points to fit the others around us. We do that on the right side, in our ordinary perception, and we also do it on the left side, while *dreaming together*.

12

The Nagual Julian

There was a strange excitement in the house. All the seers of don Juan's party seemed to be so elated that they were actually absentminded, a thing that I had never witnessed before. Their usual high level of energy appeared to have increased. I became very apprehensive. I asked don Juan about it. He took me to the back patio. We walked in silence for a moment. He said that the time was getting closer for all of them to leave. He was pressing his explanation in order to finish it in time.

"How do you know that you are closer to leaving?" I asked.

"It is an internal knowledge," he said. "You'll know it someday yourself. You see, the nagual Julian made my assemblage point shift countless times, just as I have made yours shift. Then he left me the task of realigning all those emanations which he had helped me align through these shifts. That is the task that every nagual is left to do.

"At any rate, the job of realigning all those emanations paves the way for the peculiar maneuver of lighting up all the emanations inside the cocoon. I have nearly done that. I am about to reach my maximum.

Since I am the nagual, once I do light up all the emanations inside my cocoon we will all be gone in an instant."

I felt I should be sad and weep, but something in me was so overjoyed to hear that the nagual Juan Matus was about to be free that I jumped and yelled with sheer delight. I knew that sooner or later I would reach another state of awareness and I would weep with sadness. But that day I was filled with happiness and optimism.

I told don Juan how I felt. He laughed and patted my back.

"Remember what I've told you," he said. "Don't count on emotional realizations. Let your assemblage point move first, then years later have the realization."

We walked to the big room and sat down to talk. Don Juan hesitated for a moment. He looked out of the window. From my chair I could see the patio. It was early afternoon; a cloudy day. It looked like rain. Thunderhead clouds were moving in from the west. I liked cloudy days. Don Juan did not. He seemed restless as he tried to find a more comfortable sitting position.

Don Juan began his elucidation by commenting that the difficulty in remembering what takes place in heightened awareness is due to the infinitude of positions that the assemblage point can adopt after being loosened from its normal setting. Facility in remembering everything that takes place in normal awareness, on the other hand, has to do with the fixity of the assemblage point on one spot, the spot where it normally sets.

He told me that he commiserated with me. He suggested that I accept the difficulty of recollecting and acknowledge that I might fail in my task and never be able to realign all the emanations that he had helped me align.

"Think of it this way," he said, smiling. "You may never be able to remember this very conversation that we are having now, which at this moment seems to you so commonplace, so taken for granted.

"This indeed is the mystery of awareness. Human beings reek of that mystery; we reek of darkness, of things which are inexplicable. To regard ourselves in any other terms is madness. So don't demean the mystery of man in you by feeling sorry for yourself or by trying to rationalize it. Demean the stupidity of man in you by understanding it. But don't apologize for either; both are needed.

"One of the great maneuvers of *stalkers* is to pit the mystery against the stupidity in each of us."

He explained that *stalking* practices are not something one can rejoice in; in fact, they are downright objectionable. Knowing this, the new seers realize that it would be against everybody's interest to discuss or practice the principles of *stalking* in normal awareness.

I pointed out to him an incongruity. He had said that there is no way for warriors to act in the world while they are in heightened awareness, and he had also said that *stalking* is simply behaving with people in specific ways. The two statements contradicted each other.

"By not teaching it in normal awareness I was referring only to teaching it to a nagual," he said. "The purpose of *stalking* is twofold: first, to move the assemblage point as steadily and safely as possible, and nothing can do the job as well as *stalking;* second, to imprint its principles at such a deep level that the human inventory is bypassed, as is the natural reaction of refusing and judging something that may be offensive to reason."

I told him that I sincerely doubted I could judge or refuse anything like that. He laughed and said that I could not be an exception, that I would react like

185

everyone else once I heard about the deeds of a master *stalker,* such as his benefactor, the nagual Julian.

"I am not exaggerating when I tell you that the nagual Julian was the most extraordinary *stalker* I have ever met," don Juan said. "You have already heard about his *stalking* skills from everybody else. But I've never told you what he did to me."

I wanted to make it clear to him that I had not heard anything about the nagual Julian from anyone, but just before I voiced my protest a strange feeling of uncertainty swept over me. Don Juan seemed to know instantly what I was feeling. He chuckled with delight.

"You can't remember, because *will* is not available to you yet," he said. "You need a life of impeccability and a great surplus of energy, and then *will* might release those memories.

"I am going to tell you the story of how the nagual Julian behaved with me when I first met him. If you judge him and find his behavior objectionable while you are in heightened awareness, think of how revolted you might be with him in normal awareness."

I protested that he was setting me up. He assured me that all he wanted to do with his story was to illustrate the manner in which *stalkers* operate and the reasons why they do it.

"The nagual Julian was the last of the old-time *stalkers,*" he went on. "He was a *stalker* not so much because of the circumstances of his life but because that was the bent of his character."

Don Juan explained that the new seers *saw* that there are two main groups of human beings: those who care about others and those who do not. In between these two extremes they *saw* an endless mixture of the two. The nagual Julian belonged to the category of men who do not care; don Juan classified himself as belonging to the opposite category.

"But didn't you tell me that the nagual Julian was

generous, that he would give you the shirt off his back?" I asked.

"He certainly was," don Juan replied. "Not only was he generous; he was also utterly charming, winning. He was always deeply and sincerely interested in everybody around him. He was kind and open and gave away everything he had to anyone who needed it, or to anyone he happened to like. He was in turn loved by everyone, because being a master *stalker*, he conveyed to them his true feelings: he didn't give a plugged nickel for any of them."

I did not say anything, but don Juan was aware of my sense of disbelief or even distress at what he was saying. He chuckled and shook his head from side to side.

"That's *stalking*," he said. "You see, I haven't even begun my story of the nagual Julian and you are already annoyed."

He exploded into a giant laugh as I tried to explain what I was feeling.

"The nagual Julian didn't care about anyone," he continued. "That's why he could help people. And he did; he gave them the shirt off his back, because he didn't give a fig about them."

"Do you mean, don Juan, that the only ones who help their fellow men are those who don't give a damn about them?" I asked, truly miffed.

"That's what *stalkers* say," he said with a beaming smile. "The nagual Julian, for instance, was a fabulous curer. He helped thousands and thousands of people, but he never took credit for it. He let people believe that a woman seer of his party was the curer.

"Now, if he had been a man who cared for his fellow men, he would've demanded acknowledgment. Those who care for others care for themselves and demand recognition where recognition is due."

Don Juan said that he, since he belonged to the category of those who care for their fellow men, had never helped anyone: he felt awkward with generosity; he could not even conceive being loved as the nagual Julian was, and he would certainly feel stupid giving anyone the shirt off his back.

"I care so much for my fellow man," he continued, "that I don't do anything for him. I wouldn't know what to do. And I would always have the nagging sense that I was imposing my will on him with my gifts.

"Naturally, I have overcome all these feelings with the warriors' way. Any warrior can be successful with people, as the nagual Julian was, provided he moves his assemblage point to a position where it is immaterial whether people like him, dislike him, or ignore him. But that's not the same."

Don Juan said that when he first became aware of the *stalkers'* principles, as I was then doing, he was as distressed as he could be. The nagual Elias, who was very much like don Juan, explained to him that *stalkers* like the nagual Julian are natural leaders of people. They can help people do anything.

"The nagual Elias said that these warriors can help people to get cured," don Juan went on, "or they can help them to get ill. They can help them to find happiness or they can help them to find sorrow. I suggested to the nagual Elias that instead of saying that these warriors help people, we should say that they affect people. He said that they don't just affect people, but that they actively herd them around."

Don Juan chuckled and looked at me fixedly. There was a mischievous glint in his eyes.

"Strange, isn't it?" he asked. "The way *stalkers* arranged what they *see* about people?"

Then don Juan started his story about the nagual Julian. He said that the nagual Julian spent many, many years waiting for an apprentice nagual. He stumbled on don Juan one day while returning home after a short visit with acquaintances in a nearby village.

He was, in fact, thinking about an apprentice nagual as he walked on the road when he heard a loud gunshot and saw people scrambling in every direction. He ran with them into the bushes by the side of the road and only came out from his hiding place at the sight of a group of people gathered around someone wounded, lying on the ground.

The wounded person was, of course, don Juan, who had been shot by the tyrannical foreman. The nagual Julian *saw* instantly that don Juan was a special man whose cocoon was divided into four sections instead of two; he also realized that don Juan was badly wounded. He knew that he had no time to waste. His wish had been fulfilled, but he had to work fast, before anyone sensed what was going on. He held his head and cried, "They've shot my son!"

He was traveling with one of the female seers of his party, a husky Indian woman, who always officiated publicly as his mean shrewish wife. They were an excellent team of *stalkers*. He cued the woman seer, and she also started weeping and wailing for their son, who was unconscious and bleeding to death. The nagual Julian begged the onlookers not to call the authorities but rather to help him move his son to his house in the city, which was some distance away. He offered money to some strong young men if they would carry his wounded, dying son.

The men carried don Juan to the nagual Julian's house. The nagual was very generous with them and paid them handsomely. The men were so touched by the grieving couple, who had cried all the way to the house, that they refused to take the money, but the nagual Julian insisted that they take it to give his son luck.

For a few days, don Juan did not know what to think about the kind couple who had taken him into their home. He said that to him, the nagual Julian appeared as an almost senile old man. He was not an Indian, but was married to a young, irascible, fat Indian wife, who was as physically strong as she was ill-tempered. Don Juan thought that she was definitely a curer, judging by the way she treated his wound and by the quantities of medicinal plants stashed away in the room where they had put him.

The woman also dominated the old man and made him tend to don Juan's wound every day. They had made a bed for don Juan out of a thick floor mat, and the old man had a terrible time kneeling down to reach him. Don Juan had to fight not to laugh at the comical sight of the frail old man trying his best to bend his knees. Don Juan said that while the old man washed his wound, he would mumble incessantly; he had a vacant look in his eyes; his hands shook, and his body trembled from head to toe.

When he was down on his knees, he could never get up by himself. He would call his wife, yelling in a raspy voice, filled with contained anger. The wife would come into the room and both of them would get into a horrible argument. Often she would walk out, leaving the old man to get up by himself.

Don Juan assured me that he had never felt so sorry for anyone as he felt for that poor, kind old man. Many times he wanted to rise and help him up, but he could hardly move himself. Once the old man spent half an hour cursing and yelling, as he puffed and crawled like a slug, before he dragged himself to the door and painfully lifted himself up to a standing position.

He explained to don Juan that his poor health was due to advanced age, broken bones that had not mended properly, and rheumatism. Don Juan said that the old man raised his eyes toward heaven and confessed to don Juan that he was the most wretched man on earth; he had come to the curer for help and had ended up marrying her and becoming a slave.

"I asked the old man why he didn't leave," don Juan continued. "The old man's eyes widened with fear. He choked on his own saliva trying to hush me and then he went rigid and fell down like a log on the floor, next to my bed, trying to make me stop talking. 'You don't know what you're saying; you don't know what you're saying. Nobody can run away from this place,' the old man kept on repeating with a wild expression in his eyes.

"And I believed him. I was convinced that he was more miserable, more wretched than I had ever been myself. And with every day that passed I became more and more uncomfortable in that house. The food was great and the woman was always out curing people, so I was left with the old man. We talked a lot about my life. I liked to talk to him. I told him that I had no money to pay him for his kindness, but that I would do anything to help him. He told me that he was beyond help, that he was ready to die, but that if I really meant what I said, he would appreciate it if I would marry his wife after he died.

"Right then I knew the old man was nuts. And right then I also knew that I had to run away as soon as possible."

Don Juan said that when he was well enough to walk around unaided, his benefactor gave him a chilling demonstration of his ability as a *stalker*. Without any warning or preamble he put don Juan face to face with an inorganic living being. Sensing that don Juan was planning to run away, he seized the opportunity to scare him with an ally that was somehow able to look like a monstrous man.

"The sight of that ally nearly drove me insane," don Juan continued. "I couldn't believe my eyes, and yet the monster was right in front of me. And the frail old man was next to me whimpering and begging the monster to spare his life. You see, my benefactor was like the old seers; he could dole out his fear, a piece at a time, and the ally was reacting to it. I didn't know that. All I could see with my very own eyes was a horrendous creature advancing on us, ready to tear us apart, limb from limb.

"The moment the ally lurched onto us, hissing like a serpent, I passed out cold. When I came to my senses again, the old man told me that he had made a deal with the creature."

He explained to don Juan that the man had agreed to let both of them live, provided don Juan enter the man's service. Don Juan apprehensively asked what was involved in the service. The old man replied that it would be slavery, but pointed out that don Juan's life had nearly ended a few days back when he had been shot. Had not he and his wife come along to stop the bleeding, don Juan would surely have died, so there was really very little to bargain with, or to bargain for. The monstrous man knew that and had him over a barrel. The old man told don Juan to stop vacillating and accept the deal, because if he refused, the monstrous man, who was listening behind the door, would burst in and kill them both on the spot and be done with it.

"I had enough nerve to ask the frail old man, who was shaking like a leaf, how the man would kill us," don Juan went on. "He said that the monster planned to break all the bones in our bodies, starting with our feet, as we screamed in unspeakable agony, and that it would take at least five days for us to die.

"I accepted that man's conditions instantly. The old man, with tears in his eyes, congratulated me and said that the deal wasn't really that bad. We were going to be more prisoners than slaves of the monstrous man, but we would eat at least twice a day; and since we had life, we could work for our freedom; we could plot, connive, and fight our way out of that hell."

Don Juan smiled and then broke into laughter. He had known beforehand how I would feel about the nagual Julian.

"I told you you'd be upset," he said.

"I really don't understand, don Juan," I said. "What was the point of putting on such an elaborate masquerade?"

"The point is very simple," he said, still smiling. "This is another method of teaching, a very good one. It requires tremendous imagination and tremendous control on the part of the teacher. My method of teaching is closer to what you consider teaching. It requires a tremendous amount of words. I go to the extremes of talking. The nagual Julian went to the extremes of *stalking*."

Don Juan said that there were two methods of teaching among the seers. He was familiar with both of them. He preferred the one that called for explaining everything and letting the other person know the course of action beforehand. It was a system that fostered freedom, choice, and understanding. His benefactor's method, on the other hand, was more coercive and did not allow for choice or understanding. Its great advantage was that it forced warriors to live the seers' concepts directly with no intermediary elucidation.

Don Juan explained that everything his benefactor did to him was a masterpiece of strategy. Every one of the nagual Julian's words and actions was deliberately selected to cause a particular effect. His art was to provide his words and actions with the most suitable context, so that they would have the necessary impact.

"That's the *stalkers'* method," don Juan went on. "It fosters not understanding but total realization. For instance, it took me a lifetime to understand what he had done to me by making me face the ally, although I realized all that without any explanation as I lived that experience.

"I've told you that Genaro, for example, doesn't understand what he does, but his realization of what he is doing is as keen as it can be. That's because his

193

assemblage point was moved by the *stalkers'* method."

He said that if the assemblage point is forced out of its customary setting by the method of explaining everything, as in my case, there is always the need for someone else not only to help in the actual dislodging of the assemblage point, but in dispensing the explanations of what is going on. But if the assemblage point is moved by the *stalkers'* method, as in his own case, or Genaro's, there is only a need for the initial catalytic act that yanks the point from its location.

Don Juan said that when the nagual Julian made him face the monstrous-looking ally his assemblage point moved under the impact of fear. So intense a fright as that caused by the confrontation, coupled with his weak physical condition, was ideal for dislodging his assemblage point.

In order to offset the injurious effects of fright, its impact had to be cushioned, but not minimized. Explaining what was happening would have minimized fear. What the nagual Julian wanted was to make sure that he could use that initial catalytic fright as many times as he needed it, but he also wanted to make sure that he could cushion its devastating impact; that was the reason for his masquerade. The more elaborate and dramatic his stories were, the greater their cushioning effect. If he, himself, seemed to be in the same boat with don Juan, the fright would not be as intense as if don Juan were alone.

"With his penchant for drama," don Juan went on, "my benefactor was able to move my assemblage point enough to imbue me right away with an overpowering feeling for the two basic qualities of warriors: sustained effort and unbending intent. I knew that in order to be free again someday, I would have to work in an orderly and steady fashion and in cooperation with the frail old man, who in my opinion needed my help as much as I needed his. I knew beyond a shadow of a doubt that that was what I wanted to do more than anything else in life."

I did not get to talk to don Juan again until two days later. We were in Oaxaca, strolling in the main square, in the early morning. There were children walking to school, people going to church, a few men sitting on the benches, and taxi drivers waiting for tourists from the main hotel.

"It goes without saying that the most difficult thing in the warriors' path is to make the assemblage point move," don Juan said. "That movement is the completion of the warriors' quest. To go on from there is another quest; it is the seers' quest proper."

He repeated that in the warriors' way, the shift of the assemblage point is everything. The old seers absolutely failed to realize this truth. They thought the movement of the point was like a marker that determined their positions on a scale of worth. They never conceived that it was that very position which determined what they perceived.

"The *stalkers'* method," don Juan went on, "in the hands of a master *stalker* like the nagual Julian, accounts for stupendous shifts of the assemblage point. These are very solid changes; you see, by buttressing the apprentice, the *stalker*-teacher gets the apprentice's full cooperation and full participation. To get anybody's full cooperation and full participation is about the most important outcome of the *stalkers'* method; and the nagual Julian was the best at getting both of them."

Don Juan said that there was no way for him to describe the turmoil that he went through as he found out, little by little, about the richness and the complexity of the nagual Julian's personality and life. As long as don Juan faced a scared, frail old man who seemed helpless, he was fairly at ease, comfortable. But one day, soon after they had made the deal with what don

Juan thought of as a monstrous-looking man, his comfort was shot to pieces when the nagual Julian gave don Juan another unnerving demonstration of his *stalking* skills.

Although don Juan was quite well by then, the nagual Julian still slept in the same room with him in order to nurse him. When he woke up that day, he announced to don Juan that their captor was gone for a couple of days, which meant that he did not have to act like an old man. He confided to don Juan that he only pretended to be old in order to fool the monstrous-looking man.

Without giving don Juan time to think, he jumped up from his mat with incredible agility; he bent over and dunked his head in a pot of water and kept it there for a while. When he straightened up, his hair was jet black, the gray hair had washed away, and don Juan was looking at a man he had never seen before, a man perhaps in his late thirties. He flexed his muscles, breathed deeply, and stretched every part of his body as if he had been too long inside a constricting cage.

"When I saw the nagual Julian as a young man, I thought that he was indeed the devil," don Juan went on. "I closed my eyes and knew that my end was near. The nagual Julian laughed until he was crying."

Don Juan said that the nagual Julian then put him at ease by making him shift back and forth between the right side and the left side awareness.

"For two days the young man pranced around the house," don Juan continued. "He told me stories about his life and jokes that sent me reeling around the room with laughter. But what was even more astounding was the way his wife had changed. She was actually thin and beautiful. I thought she was a completely different woman. I raved about how complete her change was and how beautiful she looked. The young man said that when their captor was away she was actually another woman."

Don Juan laughed and said that his devilish benefactor was telling the truth. The woman was really another seer of the nagual's party.

Don Juan asked the young man why they pretended to be what they were not. The young man looked at don Juan, his eyes filled with tears, and said that the mysteries of the world are indeed unfathomable. He and his young wife had been caught by inexplicable forces and had to protect themselves with that pretense. The reason why he carried on the way he did, as a feeble old man, was that their captor was always peeking in through cracks in the doors. He begged don Juan to forgive him for having fooled him.

Don Juan asked who that monstrous-looking man was. With a deep sigh, the young man confessed that he could not even guess. He told don Juan that although he himself was an educated man, a famous actor from the theater in Mexico City, he was at a loss for explanations. All he knew was that he had come to be treated for the consumption that he had suffered from for many years. He was near death when his relatives brought him to meet the curer. She helped him to get well, and he fell madly in love with the beautiful young Indian and married her. His plans were to take her to the capital so they could get rich with her curing ability.

Before they started on the trip to Mexico City, she warned him that they had to disguise themselves in order to escape a sorcerer. She explained to him that her mother had also been a curer, and had been taught curing by that master sorcerer, who had demanded that she, the daughter, stay with him for life. The young man said that he had refused to ask his wife about that relationship. He only wanted to free her, so he disguised himself as an old man and disguised her as a fat woman.

Their story did not end happily. The horrible man caught them and kept them as prisoners. They did not dare to take off their disguise in front of that nightmarish man, and in his presence they carried on as if they hated each other; but in reality, they pined for each other and lived only for the short times when that man was away.

Don Juan said that the young man embraced him and told him that the room where don Juan was sleeping was the only safe place in the house. Would he please go out and be on the lookout while he made love to his wife?

"The house shook with their passion," don Juan went on, "while I sat by the door feeling guilty for listening and scared to death that the man would come back any minute. And sure enough, I heard him coming into the house. I banged on the door, and when they didn't answer, I walked in. The young woman was asleep naked and the young man was nowhere in sight. I had never seen a beautiful naked woman in my life. I was still very weak. I heard the monstrous man rattling outside. My embarrassment and my fear were so great that I passed out."

The story about the nagual Julian's doings annoyed me no end. I told don Juan that I had failed to understand the value of the nagual Julian's *stalking* skills. Don Juan listened to me without making a single comment and let me ramble on and on.

When we finally sat down on a bench, I was very tired. I did not know what to say when he asked me why his account of the nagual Julian's method of teaching had upset me so much.

"I can't shake off the feeling that he was a prankster," I finally said.

"Pranksters don't teach anything deliberately with their pranks," don Juan retorted. "The nagual Julian played dramas, magical dramas that required a movement of the assemblage point."

"He seems like a very selfish person to me," I insisted.

"He seems like that to you because you are judging," he replied. "You are being a moralist. I went through all that myself. If you feel the way you do on hearing about the nagual Julian, think of the way I must have felt myself living in his house for years. I judged him, I feared him, and I envied him, in that order.

"I also loved him, but my envy was greater than my love. I envied his ease, his mysterious capacity to be young or old at will; I envied his flair and above all his influence on whoever happened to be around. It would drive me up the walls to hear him engage people in the most interesting conversation. He always had something to say; I never did, and I always felt incompetent, left out."

Don Juan's revelations made me feel ill at ease. I wished that he would change the subject, for I did not want to hear that he was like me. In my opinion, he was indeed unequaled. He obviously knew how I felt. He laughed and patted my back.

"What I am trying to do with the story of my envy," he went on, "is to point out to you something of great importance, that the position of the assemblage point dictates how we behave and how we feel.

"My great flaw at that time was that I could not understand this principle. I was raw. I lived through self-importance, just as you do, because that was where my assemblage point was lodged. You see, I hadn't learned yet that the way to move that point is to establish new habits, to *will* it to move. When it did move, it was as if I had just discovered that the only way to deal with peerless warriors like my benefactor is not to have self-importance, so that one can celebrate them unbiasedly."

He said that realizations are of two kinds. One is just pep talk, great outbursts of emotion and nothing more. The other is the product of a shift of the assemblage point; it is not coupled with an emotional outburst but with action. The emotional realizations come years later after warriors have solidified, by usage, the new position of their assemblage points.

"The nagual Julian tirelessly guided all of us to that kind of shift," don Juan went on. "He got from all of us total cooperation and total participation in his bigger-than-life dramas. For instance, with his drama of the young man and his wife and their captor he had my undivided attention and concern. To me the story of the old man who was young was very consistent. I had seen the monstrous-looking man with my very own eyes, which meant that the young man got my undying affiliation."

Don Juan said that the nagual Julian was a magician, a conjurer who could handle the force of *will* to a degree that would be incomprehensible to the average man. His dramas included magical characters summoned by the force of *intent,* like the inorganic being that could adopt a grotesque human form.

"The nagual Julian's power was so impeccable," don Juan went on, "that he could force anyone's assemblage point to shift and align emanations that would make him perceive whatever the nagual Julian wanted. For example, he could look very old or very young for his age, depending on what he wanted to accomplish. And all anyone who knew the nagual could say about his age was that it fluctuated. During the thirty-two years that I knew him he was at times not much older than you are now, and at other times he was so wretchedly old that he could not even walk."

Don Juan said that under his benefactor's guidance, his assemblage point moved unnoticeably and yet profoundly. For instance, out of nowhere one day he realized that he had a fear that on the one hand made no sense to him at all, and on the other made all the sense in the world.

"My fear was that through stupidity I would lose

my chance to be free and I would repeat my father's life.

"There was nothing wrong with my father's life, mind you. He lived and died no better and no worse than most men; the important point is that my assemblage point had moved and I realized one day that my father's life and death hadn't amounted to a hill of beans, either to others or to himself.

"My benefactor told me that my father and mother had lived and died just to have me, and that their own parents had done the same for them. He said that warriors were different in that they shift their assemblage points enough to realize the tremendous price that has been paid for their lives. This shift gives them the respect and awe that their parents never felt for life in general, or for being alive in particular."

Don Juan said that not only was the nagual Julian successful in guiding his apprentices to move their assemblage points, but that he enjoyed himself tremendously while doing it.

"He certainly entertained himself immensely with me," don Juan went on. "When the other seers of my party began to come, years later, even I looked forward to the preposterous situations that he created and developed with each one of them.

"When the nagual Julian left the world, delight went away with him and never came back. Genaro delights us sometimes, but no one can take the nagual Julian's place. His dramas were always bigger than life. I assure you we didn't know what enjoyment was until we saw what he did when some of those dramas backfired on him."

Don Juan rose from his favorite bench. He turned to me. His eyes were brilliant and peaceful.

"If you are ever so dumb as to fail in your task," he said, "you must have at least enough energy to move your assemblage point in order to come to this bench. Sit down here for an instant, free of thoughts and desires; I will try to come here from wherever I am and collect you. I promise you that I will try."

He then broke into a great laugh, as if the scope of his promise was too ludicrous to be believed.

"These words should be said in the late afternoon," he said, still laughing. "Never in the morning. The morning makes one feel optimistic and such words lose their meaning."

13

The Earth's Boost

"Let's walk on the road to Oaxaca," don Juan said to me. "Genaro is waiting for us somewhere along the way."

His request took me by surprise. I had been waiting all day for him to continue his explanation. We left his house and walked in silence through the town to the unpaved highway. We walked leisurely for a long time. Suddenly don Juan began to talk.

"I've been telling you all along about the great findings that the old seers made," he said. "Just as they found out that organic life is not the only life present on earth, they also discovered that the earth itself is a living being."

He waited a moment before continuing. He smiled at me as if inviting me to make a comment. I could not think of anything to say.

"The old seers *saw* that the earth has a cocoon," he went on. "They *saw* that there is a ball encasing the earth, a luminous cocoon that entraps the Eagle's emanations. The earth is a gigantic sentient being subjected to the same forces we are."

He explained that the old seers, on discovering this, became immediately interested in the practical uses of that knowledge. The result of their interest was that the most elaborate categories of their sorcery had to do with the earth. They considered the earth to be the ultimate source of everything we are.

Don Juan reaffirmed that the old seers were not mistaken in this respect, because the earth is indeed our ultimate source.

He didn't say anything else until we met Genaro about a mile up the road. He was waiting for us, sitting on a rock by the side of the road.

He greeted me with great warmth. He said to me that we should climb up to the top of some small rugged mountains covered with hardy vegetation.

"The three of us are going to sit against a rock," don Juan said to me, "and look at the sunlight as it is reflected on the eastern mountains. When the sun goes down behind the western peaks, the earth may let you *see* alignment."

When we reached the top of a mountain, we sat down, as don Juan had said, with our backs against a rock. Don Juan made me sit in between the two of them.

I asked him what he was planning to do. His cryptic statements and his long silences were ominous. I felt terribly apprehensive.

He didn't answer me. He kept on talking as if I had not spoken at all.

"It was the old seers who, on discovering that perception is alignment," he said, "stumbled onto something monumental. The sad part is that their aberrations again kept them from knowing what they had accomplished."

He pointed at the mountain range east of the small valley where the town is located.

"There is enough glitter in those mountains to jolt your assemblage point," he said to me. "Just before the sun goes down behind the western peaks, you will have a few moments to catch all the glitter you need. The magic key that opens the earth's doors is made of internal silence plus anything that shines."

"What exactly should I do, don Juan?" I asked.

Both of them examined me. I thought I saw in their eyes a mixture of curiosity and revulsion.

"Just cut off the internal dialogue," don Juan said to me.

I had an intense pang of anxiety and doubt; I had no confidence that I could do it at will. After an initial moment of nagging frustration, I resigned myself just to relax.

I looked around. I noticed that we were high enough to look down into the long, narrow valley. More than half of it was in the late-afternoon shadows. The sun was still shining on the foothills of the eastern range of mountains, on the other side of the valley; the sunlight made the eroded mountains look ocher, while the more distant bluish peaks had acquired a purple tone.

"You do realize that you've done this before, don't you?" don Juan said to me in a whisper.

I told him that I had not realized anything.

"We've sat here before on other occasions," he insisted, "but that doesn't matter, because this occasion is the one that will count.

"Today, with the help of Genaro, you are going to find the key that unlocks everything. You won't be able to use it as yet, but you'll know what it is and where it is. Seers pay the heaviest prices to know that. You, yourself, have been paying your dues all these years."

He explained that what he called the key to everything was the firsthand knowledge that the earth is a sentient being and as such can give warriors a tremendous boost; it is an impulse that comes from the awareness of the earth itself at the instant in which the emanations inside warriors' cocoons are aligned with the appropriate emanations inside the earth's cocoon.

Since both the earth and man are sentient beings, their emanations coincide, or rather, the earth has all the emanations present in man and all the emanations that are present in all sentient beings, organic and inorganic for that matter. When a moment of alignment takes place, sentient beings use that alignment in a limited way and perceive their world. Warriors can use that alignment either to perceive, like everyone else, or as a boost that allows them to enter unimaginable worlds.

"I've been waiting for you to ask me the only meaningful question you can ask, but you never ask it," he continued. "You are hooked on asking about whether the mystery of it all is inside us. You came close enough, though.

"The unknown is not really inside the cocoon of man in the emanations untouched by awareness, and yet it is there, in a manner of speaking. This is the point you haven't understood. When I told you that we can assemble seven worlds besides the one we know, you took it as being an internal affair, because your total bias is to believe that you are only imagining everything you do with us. Therefore, you have never asked me where the unknown really is. For years I have circled with my hand to point to everything around us and I have told you that the unknown is there. You never made the connection."

Genaro began to laugh, then coughed and stood up. "He still hasn't made the connection," he said to don Juan.

I admitted to them that if there was a connection to be made, I had failed to make it.

Don Juan restated over and over that the portion of emanations inside man's cocoon is in there only for awareness, and that awareness is matching that portion of emanations with the same portion of emanations at large. They are called emanations at large because they are immense; and to say that outside man's cocoon is the unknowable is to say that within the earth's cocoon is the unknowable. However, inside the earth's cocoon is also the unknown, and inside man's cocoon the unknown is the emanations untouched by awareness. When the glow of awareness touches them, they become active and can be aligned with the corresponding emanations at large. Once that happens the unknown is perceived and becomes the known.

"I'm too dumb, don Juan. You have to break it into smaller pieces for me," I said.

"Genaro is going to break it up for you," don Juan retorted.

Genaro stood up and started doing the same gait of power that he had done before, when he circled an enormous flat rock in a corn field by his house, while don Juan had watched in fascination. This time don Juan whispered in my ear that I should try to hear Genaro's movements, especially the movements of his thighs as they went up against his chest every time he stepped.

I followed Genaro's movements with my eyes. In a few seconds I felt that some part of me had gotten trapped in Genaro's legs. The movement of his thighs would not let me go. I felt as if I were walking with him. I was even out of breath. Then I realized that I was actually following Genaro. I was in fact walking with him, away from the place where we had been sitting.

I did not see don Juan, just Genaro walking ahead of me in the same strange manner. We walked for hours and hours. My fatigue was so intense that I got a terrible headache, and suddenly I got sick. Genaro stopped walking and came to my side. There was an intense glare around us, and the light was reflected in Genaro's features. His eyes glowed.

"Don't look at Genaro!" a voice ordered me in my ear. "Look around!"

I obeyed. I thought I was in hell! The shock of seeing the surroundings was so great that I screamed in terror, but there was no sound to my voice. Around me was the most vivid picture of all the descriptions of hell in my Catholic upbringing. I was seeing a reddish world, hot and oppressive, dark and cavernous, with no sky, no light but the malignant reflections of reddish lights that kept on moving around us, at great speed.

Genaro started to walk again, and something pulled me with him. The force that was making me follow Genaro also kept me from looking around. My awareness was glued to Genaro's movements.

I saw Genaro plop down as if he were utterly exhausted. The instant he touched the ground and stretched himself to rest, something was released in me and I was able again to look around. Don Juan was watching me inquisitively. I was standing up facing him. We were at the same place where we had sat down, a wide rocky ledge on top of a small mountain. Genaro was panting and wheezing, and so was I. I was covered with perspiration. My hair was dripping wet. My clothes were soaked, as if I had been dunked in a river.

"My God, what's going on!" I exclaimed in utter seriousness and concern.

The exclamation sounded so silly that don Juan and Genaro started to laugh.

"We're trying to make you understand alignment," Genaro said.

Don Juan gently helped me to sit down. He sat by me.

"Do you remember what happened?" he asked me.

I told him that I did and he insisted that I tell him exactly what I had *seen*. His request was incongruous with what he had told me, that the only value of my

208

experiences was the movement of my assemblage point and not the content of my visions.

He explained that Genaro had tried to help me before in very much the same fashion as he had just done, but that I could never remember anything. He said that Genaro had guided my assemblage point this time, as he had done before, to assemble a world with another of the great bands of emanations.

There was a long silence. I was numb, shocked, yet my awareness was as keen as it had ever been. I thought I had finally understood what alignment was. Something inside me, which I had been activating without knowing how, gave me the certainty that I had comprehended a great truth.

"I think you're beginning to gather your own momentum," don Juan said to me. "Let's go home. You've had enough for one day."

"Oh, come on," Genaro said. "He's stronger than a bull. He's got to be pushed a little further."

"No!" don Juan said emphatically. "We've got to save his strength. He's only got so much of it."

Genaro insisted that we stay. He looked at me and winked.

"Look," he said to me, pointing to the eastern range of mountains. "The sun has hardly moved an inch over those mountains and yet you plodded in hell for hours and hours. Don't you find that overwhelming?"

"Don't scare him unnecessarily!" don Juan protested almost vehemently.

It was then that I *saw* their maneuvers. At that moment the voice of *seeing* told me that don Juan and Genaro were a team of superb *stalkers* playing with me. It was don Juan who always pushed me beyond my limits, but he always let Genaro be the heavy. That day at Genaro's house, when I reached a dangerous state of hysterical fright as Genaro questioned don

Juan whether I should be pushed, and don Juan assured me that Genaro was enjoying himself at my expense, Genaro was actually worrying about me.

My *seeing* was so shocking to me that I began to laugh. Both don Juan and Genaro looked at me with surprise. Then don Juan seemed to realize at once what was going through my mind. He told Genaro, and both of them laughed like children.

"You're coming of age," don Juan said to me. "Right on time; you're neither too stupid nor too bright. Just like me. You're not like me in your aberrations. There you are more like the nagual Julian, except that he was brilliant."

He stood up and stretched his back. He looked at me with the most piercing, ferocious eyes I had ever seen. I stood up.

"A nagual never lets anyone know that he is in charge," he said to me. "A nagual comes and goes without leaving a trace. That freedom is what makes him a nagual."

His eyes glared for an instant, and then they were covered by a cloud of mellowness, kindness, humanness, and they were again don Juan's eyes.

I could hardly keep my balance. I was swooning helplessly. Genaro jumped to my side and helped me to sit down. Both of them sat down flanking me.

"You are going to catch a boost from the earth," don Juan said to me in one ear.

"Think about the nagual's eyes," Genaro said to me in the other.

"The boost will come at the moment you see the glitter on the top of that mountain," don Juan said and pointed to the highest peak on the eastern range.

"You'll never see the nagual's eyes again," Genaro whispered.

"Go with the boost wherever it takes you," don Juan said.

"If you think of the nagual's eyes, you'll realize that there are two sides to a coin," Genaro whispered.

I wanted to think about what both of them were saying, but my thoughts did not obey me. Something was pressing down on me. I felt I was shrinking. I had a sensation of nausea. I saw the evening shadows advancing rapidly up the sides of those eastern mountains. I had the feeling that I was running after them.

"Here we go," Genaro said in my ear.

"Watch the big peak, watch the glitter," don Juan said in my other ear.

There was indeed a point of intense brilliance where don Juan had pointed, on the highest peak of the range. I watched the last ray of sunlight being reflected on it. I felt a hole in the pit of my stomach, just as if I were on a roller coaster.

I felt, rather than heard, a faraway earthquake rumble which abruptly overtook me. The seismic waves were so loud and so enormous that they lost all meaning for me. I was an insignificant microbe being twisted and twirled.

The motion slowed down by degrees. There was one more jolt before everything came to a halt. I tried to look around. I had no point of reference. I seemed to be planted, like a tree. Above me there was a white, shiny, inconceivably big dome. Its presence made me feel elated. I flew toward it, or rather I was ejected like a projectile. I had the sensation of being comfortable, nurtured, secure; the closer I got to the dome, the more intense those feelings became. They finally overwhelmed me and I lost all sense of myself.

The next thing I knew, I was rocking slowly in the air like a leaf that falls. I felt exhausted. A suction force started to pull me. I went through a dark hole and then I was with don Juan and Genaro.

The next day don Juan, Genaro, and I went to Oaxaca. While don Juan and I strolled around the main square, in the later afternoon, he suddenly started to talk about what we had done the day before. He asked me if I had understood what he was referring to when he said that the old seers had stumbled onto something monumental.

I told him that I did, but that I couldn't explain it in words.

"And what do you think was the main thing we wanted you to find out on top of that mountain?" he asked.

"Alignment," a voice said in my ear, at the same time I said it myself.

I turned around in a reflex action and bumped into Genaro, who was just behind me, walking in my tracks. The speed of my movement startled him. He broke into a giggle and then embraced me.

We sat down. Don Juan said that there were very few things that he could say about the boost I had gotten from the earth, that warriors are always alone in such cases, and true realizations come much later, after years of struggle.

I told don Juan that my problem in understanding was magnified by the fact that he and Genaro were doing all the work. I was simply a passive subject who could only react to their maneuvers. I could not for the life of me initiate any action, because I did not know what a proper action should be, nor did I know how to initiate it.

"That's precisely the point," don Juan said. "You are not supposed to know yet. You are going to be left behind, by yourself, to reorganize on your own everything we are doing to you now. This is the task every nagual has to face.

"The nagual Julian did the same thing to me, much more ruthlessly than the way we do it to you. He knew what he was doing; he was a brilliant nagual who was able to reorganize in a few years everything the nagual Elias had taught him. He did, in no time at all, something that would take a lifetime for you or for me. The difference was that all the nagual Julian ever needed was a slight insinuation; his awareness would take it from there and open the only door there is."

"What do you mean, don Juan, by the only door there is?"

"I mean that when man's assemblage point moves beyond a crucial limit, the results are always the same for every man. The techniques to make it move may be as different as they can be, but the results are always the same, meaning that the assemblage point assembles other worlds, aided by the boost from the earth."

"Is the boost from the earth the same for every man, don Juan?"

"Of course. The difficulty for the average man is the internal dialogue. Only when a state of total silence is attained can one use the boost. You will corroborate that truth the day you try to use that boost by yourself."

"I wouldn't recommend that you try it," Genaro said sincerely. "It takes years to become an impeccable warrior. In order to withstand the impact of the earth's boost you must be better than you are now."

"The speed of that boost will dissolve everything about you," don Juan said. "Under its impact we become nothing. Speed and the sense of individual existence don't go together. Yesterday on the mountain, Genaro and I supported you and served as your anchors; otherwise you wouldn't have returned. You'd be like some men who purposely used that boost and went into the unknown and are still roaming in some incomprehensible immensity."

I wanted him to elaborate on that, but he refused. He changed the subject abruptly.

"There's one thing you haven't understood yet about the earth's being a sentient being," he said.

"And Genaro, this awful Genaro, wants to push you until you understand."

Both of them laughed. Genaro playfully shoved me and winked at me as he mouthed the words, "I am awful."

"Genaro is a terrible taskmaster, mean and ruthless," don Juan continued. "He doesn't give a hoot about your fears and pushes you mercilessly. If it wasn't for me . . ."

He was a perfect picture of a good, thoughtful old gentleman. He lowered his eyes and sighed. The two of them broke into roaring laughter.

When they had quieted down, don Juan said that Genaro wanted to show me what I had not understood yet, that the supreme awareness of the earth is what makes it possible for us to change into other great bands of emanations.

"We living beings are perceivers," he said. "And we perceive because some emanations inside man's cocoon become aligned with some emanations outside. Alignment, therefore, is the secret passageway, and the earth's boost is the key.

"Genaro wants you to watch the moment of alignment. Watch him!"

Genaro stood up like a showman and took a bow, then showed us that he had nothing up his sleeves or inside the legs of his pants. He took his shoes off and shook them to show that there was nothing concealed there either.

Don Juan was laughing with total abandon. Genaro moved his hands up and down. The movement created an immediate fixation in me. I sensed that the three of us suddenly got up and walked away from the square, the two of them flanking me.

As we continued walking, I lost my peripheral vision. I did not distinguish any more houses or streets. I did not notice any mountains or any vegetation either. At one moment I realized that I had lost sight of don Juan and Genaro; instead I *saw* two luminous bundles moving up and down beside me.

I felt an instantaneous panic, which I immediately controlled. I had the unusual but well-known sensation that I was myself and yet I was not. I was aware, however, of everything around me by means of a strange and at the same time most familiar capacity. The sight of the world came to me all at once. All of me *saw;* the entirety of what I in my normal consciousness call my body was capable of sensing as if it were an enormous eye that detected everything. What I first detected, after *seeing* the two blobs of light, was a sharp violet-purple world made out of something that looked like colored panels and canopies. Flat, screenlike panels of irregular concentric circles were everywhere.

I felt a great pressure all over me, and then I heard a voice in my ear. I was *seeing*. The voice said that the pressure was due to the act of moving. I was moving together with don Juan and Genaro. I felt a faint jolt, as if I had broken a paper barrier, and I found myself facing a luminescent world. Light radiated from everyplace, but without being glaring. It was as if the sun were about to erupt from behind some white diaphanous clouds. I was looking down into the source of light. It was a beautiful sight. There were no landmasses, just fluffy white clouds and light. And we were walking on the clouds.

Then something imprisoned me again. I moved at the same pace as the two blobs of light by my sides. Gradually they began to lose their brilliance, then became opaque, and finally they were don Juan and Genaro. We were walking on a deserted side street away from the main square. Then we turned back.

"Genaro just helped you to align your emanations with those emanations at large that belong to another band," don Juan said to me. "Alignment has to be a very peaceful, unnoticeable act. No flying away, no great fuss.''

He said that the sobriety needed to let the assemblage point assemble other worlds is something that cannot be improvised. Sobriety has to mature and become a force in itself before warriors can break the barrier of perception with impunity.

We were coming closer to the main square. Genaro had not said a word. He walked in silence, as if absorbed in thought. Just before we came into the square, don Juan said that Genaro wanted to show me one more thing: that the position of the assemblage point is everything, and that the world it makes us perceive is so real that it does not leave room for anything except realness.

"Genaro will let his assemblage point assemble another world just for your benefit," don Juan said to me. "And then you'll realize that as he perceives it, the force of his perception will leave room for nothing else."

Genaro walked ahead of us, and don Juan ordered me to roll my eyes in a counterclockwise direction while I looked at Genaro, to avoid being dragged with him. I obeyed him. Genaro was five or six feet away from me. Suddenly his shape became diffuse and in one instant he was gone like a puff of air.

I thought of the science fiction movies I had seen and wondered whether we are subliminally aware of our possibilities.

"Genaro is separated from us at this moment by the force of perception," don Juan said quietly. "When the assemblage point assembles a world, that world is total. This is the marvel that the old seers stumbled upon and never realized what it was: the awareness of the earth can give us a boost to align other great bands of emanations, and the force of that new alignment makes the world vanish.

"Every time the old seers made a new alignment, they believed they had descended to the depths below or ascended to the heavens above. They never knew that the world disappears like a puff of air when a new total alignment makes us perceive another total world."

14

The Rolling Force

Don Juan was about to start his explanation of the mastery of awareness, but he changed his mind and stood up. We had been sitting in the big room, observing a moment of quiet.

"I want you to try *seeing* the Eagle's emanations," he said. "For that you must first move your assemblage point until you *see* the cocoon of man."

We walked from the house to the center of town. We sat down on an empty, worn park bench in front of the church. It was early afternoon; a sunny, windy day with lots of people milling around.

He repeated, as if he were trying to drill it into me, that alignment is a unique force because it either helps the assemblage point shift, or it keeps it glued to its customary position. The aspect of alignment that keeps the point stationary, he said, is *will;* and the aspect that makes it shift is *intent*. He remarked that one of the most haunting mysteries is how *will*, the impersonal force of alignment, changes into *intent*, the personalized force, which is at the service of each individual.

"The strangest part of this mystery is that the change is so easy to accomplish," he went on. "But what is not so easy is to convince ourselves that it is possible. There, right there, is our safety catch. We have to be convinced. And none of us wants to be.''

He told me then that I was in my keenest state of awareness, and that it was possible for me to *intend* my assemblage point to shift deeper into my left side, to a *dreaming position*. He said that warriors should never attempt *seeing* unless they are aided by *dreaming*. I argued that to fall asleep in public was not one of my fortes. He clarified his statement, saying that to move the assemblage point away from its natural setting and to keep it fixed at a new location is to be asleep; with practice, seers learn to be asleep and yet behave as if nothing is happening to them.

After a moment's pause he added that for purposes of *seeing* the cocoon of man, one has to gaze at people from behind, as they walk away. It is useless to gaze at people face to face, because the front of the egglike cocoon of man has a protective shield, which seers call the front plate. It is an almost impregnable, unyielding shield that protects us throughout our lives against the onslaught of a peculiar force that stems from the emanations themselves.

He also told me not to be surprised if my body was stiff, as though it were frozen; he said that I was going to feel very much like someone standing in the middle of a room looking at the street through a window, and that speed was of the essence, as people were going to move extremely fast by my *seeing* window. He told me then to relax my muscles, shut off my internal dialogue, and let my assemblage point drift away under the spell of inner silence. He urged me to smack myself gently but firmly on my right side, between my hipbone and my ribcage.

I did that three times and I was sound asleep. It was a most peculiar state of sleep. My body was dormant, but I was perfectly aware of everything that was taking place. I could hear don Juan talking to me and I could follow every one of his statements as if I were awake, yet I could not move my body at all.

Don Juan said that a man was going to walk by my *seeing* window and that I should try to *see* him. I unsuccessfully attempted to move my head and then a shiny egglike shape appeared. It was resplendent. I was awed by the sight and before I could recover from my surprise, it was gone. It floated away, bobbing up and down.

Everything had been so sudden and fast that it made me feel frustrated and impatient. I felt that I was beginning to wake up. Don Juan talked to me again and urged me to relax. He said that I had no right and no time to be impatient. Suddenly, another luminous being appeared and moved away. It seemed to be made of a white fluorescent shag.

Don Juan whispered in my ear that if I wanted to, my eyes were capable of slowing down everything they focused on. Then he warned me that another man was coming. I realized at that instant that there were two voices. The one I had just heard was the same one that had admonished me to be patient. That was don Juan's. The other, the one that told me to use my eyes to slow down movement, was the voice of *seeing*.

That afternoon, I *saw* ten luminous beings in slow motion. The voice of *seeing* guided me to witness in them everything don Juan had told me about the glow of awareness. There was a vertical band with a stronger amber glow on the right side of those egglike luminous creatures, perhaps one-tenth of the total volume of the cocoon. The voice said that that was man's band of awareness. The voice pointed out a dot on man's band, a dot with an intense shine; it was high on the oblong shapes, almost on the crest of them, on the surface of the cocoon; the voice said that it was the assemblage point.

When I *saw* each luminous creature in profile, from the point of view of its body, its egglike shape was like a gigantic asymmetrical yoyo that was standing edge-wise, or like an almost round pot that was resting on its side with its lid on. The part that looked like a lid was the front plate; it was perhaps one-fifth the thickness of the total cocoon.

I would have gone on *seeing* those creatures, but don Juan said that I should now gaze at people face to face and sustain my gaze until I had broken the barrier and I was *seeing* the emanations.

I followed his command. Almost instantaneously, I *saw* a most brilliant array of live, compelling fibers of light. It was a dazzling sight that immediately shattered my balance. I fell down on the cement walk on my side. From there, I *saw* the compelling fibers of light multiply themselves. They burst open and myriads of other fibers came out of them. But the fibers, compelling as they were, somehow did not interfere with my ordinary view. There were scores of people going into church. I was no longer *seeing* them. There were quite a few women and men just around the bench. I wanted to focus my eyes on them, but instead I noticed how one of those fibers of light bulged suddenly. It became like a ball of fire that was perhaps seven feet in diameter. It rolled on me. My first impulse was to roll out of its way. Before I could even move a muscle the ball had hit me. I felt it as clearly as if someone had punched me gently in the stomach. An instant later another ball of fire hit me, this time with considerably more strength, and then don Juan whacked me really hard on the cheek with his open hand. I jumped up involuntarily and lost sight of the fibers of light and the balloons that were hitting me.

Don Juan said that I had successfully endured my first brief encounter with the Eagle's emanations, but that a couple of shoves from the tumbler had dangerously opened up my gap. He added that the balls that had hit me were called the rolling force, or the tumbler.

We had returned to his house, although I did not remember how or when. I had spent hours in a sort of semisleeping state. Don Juan and the other seers of his group had given me large amounts of water to drink. They had also submerged me in an ice-cold tub of water for short periods of time.

"Were those fibers I *saw* the Eagle's emanations?" I asked don Juan.

"Yes. But you didn't really *see* them," he replied. "No sooner had you begun to *see* than the tumbler stopped you. If you had remained a moment longer it would have blasted you."

"What exactly is the tumbler?" I asked.

"It is a force from the Eagle's emanations," he said. "A ceaseless force that strikes us every instant of our lives. It is lethal when *seen,* but otherwise we are oblivious to it, in our ordinary lives, because we have protective shields. We have consuming interests that engage all our awareness. We are permanently worried about our station, our possessions. These shields, however, do not keep the tumbler away, they simply keep us from *seeing* it directly, protecting us in this way from getting hurt by the fright of *seeing* the balls of fire hitting us. Shields are a great help and a great hindrance to us. They pacify us and at the same time fool us. They give us a false sense of security."

He warned me that a moment would come in my life when I would be without any shields, uninterruptedly at the mercy of the tumbler. He said that it is an obligatory stage in the life of a warrior, known as losing the human form.

I asked him to explain to me once and for all what the human form is and what it means to lose it.

He replied that seers describe the human form as the compelling force of alignment of the emanations lit by the glow of awareness on the precise spot on which normally man's assemblage point is fixated. It is the force that makes us into persons. Thus, to be a person is to be compelled to affiliate with that force of alignment and consequently to be affiliated with the precise spot where it originates.

By reason of their activities, at a given moment the assemblage points of warriors drift toward the left. It is a permanent move, which results in an uncommon sense of aloofness, or control, or even abandon. That drift of the assemblage point entails a new alignment of emanations. It is the beginning of a series of greater shifts. Seers very aptly called this initial shift losing the human form, because it marks an inexorable movement of the assemblage point away from its original setting, resulting in the irreversible loss of our affiliation to the force that makes us persons.

He asked me then to describe all the details I could remember about the balls of fire. I told him that I had *seen* them so briefly I was not sure I could describe them in detail.

He pointed out that *seeing* is a euphemism for moving the assemblage point, and that if I moved mine a fraction more to the left I would have a clear picture of the balls of fire, a picture which I could interpret then as having remembered them.

I tried to have a clear picture, but I couldn't, so I described what I remembered.

He listened attentively and then urged me to recall if they were balls or circles of fire. I told him I didn't remember.

He explained that those balls of fire are of crucial importance to human beings because they are the expression of a force that pertains to all details of life and death, something that the new seers call the rolling force.

I asked him to clarify what he meant by all the details of life and death.

"The rolling force is the means through which the

Eagle distributes life and awareness for safekeeping," he said. "But it also is the force that, let's say, collects the rent. It makes all living beings die. What you *saw* today was called by the ancient seers the tumbler."

He said that seers describe it as an eternal line of iridescent rings, or balls of fire, that roll onto living beings ceaselessly. Luminous organic beings meet the rolling force head on, until the day when the force proves to be too much for them and the creatures finally collapse. The old seers were mesmerized by *seeing* how the tumbler then tumbles them into the beak of the Eagle to be devoured. That was the reason they called it the tumbler.

"You said that it is a mesmerizing sight. Have you yourself *seen* it rolling human beings?" I asked.

"Certainly I've *seen* it," he replied, and after a pause he added, "You and I *saw* it only a short while ago in Mexico City."

His assertion was so farfetched that I felt obliged to tell him that this time he was wrong. He laughed and reminded me that on that occasion, while both of us were sitting on a bench in the Alameda Park in Mexico City, we had witnessed the death of a man. He said that I had recorded the event in my everyday-life memory as well as in my left-side emanations.

As don Juan spoke to me I had the sensation of something inside me becoming lucid by degrees, and I could visualize with uncanny clarity the whole scene in the park. The man was lying on the grass with three policemen standing by him to keep onlookers away. I distinctly remembered don Juan hitting me on my back to make me change levels of awareness. And then I *saw*. My *seeing* was imperfect. I was unable to shake off the sight of the world of everyday life. What I ended up with was a composite of filaments of the most gorgeous colors superimposed on the buildings and the traffic. The filaments were actually lines of colored light that came from above. They had inner life; they were bright and bursting with energy.

When I looked at the dying man, I *saw* what don Juan was talking about; something that was at once like circles of fire, or iridescent tumbleweeds, was rolling everywhere I focused my eyes. The circles were rolling on people, on don Juan, on me. I felt them in my stomach and became ill.

Don Juan told me to focus my eyes on the dying man. I *saw* him at one moment curling up, just as a sowbug curls itself up upon being touched. The incandescent circles pushed him away, as if they were casting him aside, out of their majestic, inalterable path.

I had not liked the feeling. The circles of fire had not scared me; they were not awesome, or sinister. I did not feel morbid or somber. The circles rather had nauseated me. I'd felt them in the pit of my stomach. It was a revulsion that I'd felt that day.

Remembering them conjured up again the total feeling of discomfort I had experienced on that occasion. As I got ill, don Juan laughed until he was out of breath.

"You're such an exaggerated fellow," he said. "The rolling force is not that bad. It's lovely, in fact. The new seers recommend that we open ourselves to it. The old seers also opened themselves to it, but for reasons and purposes guided mostly by self-importance and obsession.

"The new seers, on the other hand, make friends with it. They become familiar with that force by handling it without any self-importance. The result is staggering in its consequences."

He said that a shift of the assemblage point is all that is needed to open oneself to the rolling force. He added that if the force is *seen* in a deliberate manner, there is minimal danger. A situation that is extremely dangerous, however, is an involuntary shift of the assemblage point owing, perhaps, to physical fatigue, emotional exhaustion, disease, or simply a minor emotional or physical crisis, such as being frightened or being drunk.

"When the assemblage point shifts involuntarily, the rolling force cracks the cocoon," he went on. "I've talked many times about a gap that man has below his navel. It's not really below the navel itself, but in the cocoon, at the height of the navel. The gap is more like a dent, a natural flaw in the otherwise smooth cocoon. It is there where the tumbler hits us ceaselessly and where the cocoon cracks."

He went on to explain that if it is a minor shift of the assemblage point, the crack is very small, the cocoon quickly repairs itself, and people experience what everybody has at one time or another: blotches of color and contorted shapes, which remain even if the eyes are closed.

If the shift is considerable, the crack also is extensive and it takes time for the cocoon to repair itself, as in the case of warriors who purposely use power plants to elicit that shift or people who take drugs and unwittingly do the same. In these cases men feel numb and cold; they have difficulty talking or even thinking; it is as if they have been frozen from inside.

Don Juan said that in cases in which the assemblage point shifts drastically because of the effects of trauma or of a mortal disease, the rolling force produces a crack the length of the cocoon; the cocoon collapses and curls in on itself, and the individual dies.

"Can a voluntary shift also produce a gap of that nature?" I asked.

"Sometimes," he replied. "We're really frail. As the tumbler hits us over and over, death comes to us through the gap. Death is the rolling force. When it finds weakness in the gap of a luminous being it automatically cracks it open and makes it collapse."

"Does every living being have a gap?" I asked.

"Of course," he replied. "If it didn't have one it

wouldn't die. The gaps are different, however, in size and configuration. Man's gap is a bowl-like depression the size of a fist, a very frail vulnerable configuration. The gaps of other organic creatures are very much like man's; some are stronger than ours and others are weaker. But the gap of inorganic beings is really different. It's more like a long thread, a hair of luminosity; consequently, inorganic beings are infinitely more durable than we are.

"There is something hauntingly appealing about the long life of those creatures, and the old seers could not resist being carried away by that appeal."

He said that the same force can produce two effects that are diametrically opposed. The old seers were imprisoned by the rolling force, and the new seers are rewarded for their toils with the gift of freedom. By becoming familiar with the rolling force through the mastery of *intent,* the new seers, at a given moment, open their own cocoons and the force floods them rather than rolling them up like a curled-up sowbug. The final result is their total and instantaneous disintegration.

I asked him a lot of questions about the survival of awareness after the luminous being is consumed by the fire from within. He did not answer. He simply chuckled, shrugged his shoulders, and went on to say that the old seers' obsession with the tumbler blinded them to the other side of that force. The new seers, with their usual thoroughness in refusing tradition, went to the other extreme. They were at first totally averse to focusing their *seeing* on the tumbler; they argued that they needed to understand the force of the emanations at large in its aspect of life-giver and enhancer of awareness.

"They realized that it is infinitely easier to destroy something," don Juan went on, "than it is to build it and maintain it. To roll life away is nothing compared to giving it and nourishing it. Of course, the new seers were wrong on this count, but in due course they corrected their mistake.''

''How were they wrong, don Juan?''

''It's an error to isolate anything for *seeing*. At the beginning, the new seers did exactly the opposite from what their predecessors did. They focused with equal attention on the other side of the tumbler. What happened to them was as terrible as, if not worse than, what happened to the old seers. They died stupid deaths, just as the average man does. They didn't have the mystery or the malignancy of the ancient seers, nor had they the quest for freedom of the seers of today.

''Those first new seers served everybody. Because they were focusing their *seeing* on the life-giving side of the emanations, they were filled with love and kindness. But that didn't keep them from being tumbled. They were vulnerable, just as were the old seers who were filled with morbidity.''

He said that for the modern-day new seers, to be left stranded after a life of discipline and toil, just like men who have never had a purposeful moment in their lives, was intolerable.

Don Juan said that these new seers realized, after they had readopted their tradition, that the old seers' knowledge of the rolling force had been complete; at one point the old seers had concluded that there were, in effect, two different aspects of the same force. The tumbling aspect relates exclusively to destruction and death. The circular aspect, on the other hand, is what maintains life and awareness, fulfillment and purpose. They had chosen, however, to deal exclusively with the tumbling aspect.

''Gazing in teams, the new seers were able to *see* the separation between the tumbling and the circular aspects,'' he explained. ''They *saw* that both forces are fused, but are not the same. The circular force comes to us just before the tumbling force; they are so close to each other that they seem the same.

"The reason it's called the circular force is that it comes in rings, threadlike hoops of iridescence—a very delicate affair indeed. And just like the tumbling force, it strikes all living beings ceaselessly, but for a different purpose. It strikes them to give them strength, direction, awareness; to give them life.

"What the new seers discovered is that the balance of the two forces in every living being is a very delicate one," he continued. "If at any given time an individual feels that the tumbling force strikes harder than the circular one, that means the balance is upset; the tumbling force strikes harder and harder from then on, until it cracks the living being's gap and makes it die."

He added that out of what I had called balls of fire comes an iridescent hoop exactly the size of living beings, whether men, trees, microbes, or allies.

"Are there different-size circles?" I asked.

"Don't take me so literally," he protested. "There are no circles to speak of, just a circular force that gives seers, who are *dreaming* it, the feeling of rings. And there are no different sizes either. It's one indivisible force that fits all living beings, organic and inorganic."

"Why did the old seers focus on the tumbling aspect?" I asked.

"Because they believed that their lives depended on *seeing* it," he replied. "They were sure that their *seeing* was going to give them answers to age-old questions. You see, they figured that if they unraveled the secrets of the rolling force they would be invulnerable and immortal. The sad part is that in one way or another, they did unravel the secrets and yet they were neither invulnerable nor immortal.

"The new seers changed it all by realizing that there

is no way to aspire to immortality as long as man has a cocoon."

Don Juan explained that the old seers apparently never realized that the human cocoon is a receptacle and cannot sustain the onslaught of the rolling force forever. In spite of all the knowledge that they had accumulated, they were in the end certainly no better, and perhaps much worse, off than the average man.

"In what way were they left worse off than the average man?" I asked.

"Their tremendous knowledge forced them to take it for granted that their choices were infallible," he said. "So they chose to live at any cost."

Don Juan looked at me and smiled. With his theatrical pause he was telling me something I could not fathom.

"They chose to live," he repeated. "Just as they chose to become trees in order to assemble worlds with those nearly unreachable great bands."

"What do you mean by that, don Juan?"

"I mean that they used the rolling force to shift their assemblage points to unimaginable *dreaming positions,* instead of letting it roll them to the beak of the Eagle to be devoured."

15

The Death Defiers

I arrived at Genaro's house around 2:00 P.M. Don Juan
and I became involved in conversation, and then don
Juan made me shift into heightened awareness.

"Here we are again, the three of us, just as we were
the day we went to that flat rock," don Juan said.
"And tonight we're going to make another trip to that
area.

"You have enough knowledge now to draw very
serious conclusions about that place and its effects on
awareness."

"What is it with that place, don Juan?"

"Tonight you're going to find out some gruesome
facts that the old seers collected about the rolling
force; and you're going to *see* what I meant when I
told you that the old seers chose to live at any cost."

Don Juan turned to Genaro, who was about to fall
asleep. He nudged him.

"Wouldn't you say, Genaro, that the old seers were
dreadful men?" don Juan asked.

"Absolutely," Genaro said in a crisp tone and then
seemed to succumb to fatigue.

He began to nod noticeably. In an instant he was

sound asleep, his head resting on his chest with his chin tucked in. He snored.

I wanted to laugh out loud. But then I noticed that Genaro was staring at me, as if he were sleeping with his eyes open.

"They were such dreadful men that they even defied death," Genaro added between snores.

"Aren't you curious to know how those gruesome men defied death?" don Juan asked me.

He seemed to be urging me to ask for an example of their gruesomeness. He paused and looked at me with what I thought was a glint of expectation in his eyes.

"You're waiting for me to ask for an example, aren't you?" I said.

"This is a great moment," he said, patting me on the back and laughing. "My benefactor had me on the edge of my seat at this point. I asked him to give me an example, and he did; now I'm going to give you one whether you ask for it or not."

"What are you going to do?" I asked, so frightened that my stomach was tied in knots and my voice cracked.

It took quite a while for don Juan to stop laughing. Every time he started to speak, he'd get an attack of coughing laughter.

"As Genaro told you, the old seers were dreadful men," he said, rubbing his eyes. "There was something they tried to avoid at all costs: they didn't want to die. You may say that the average man doesn't want to die either, but the advantage that the old seers had over the average man was that they had the concentration and the discipline to *intend* things away; and they actually *intended* death away."

He paused and looked at me with raised eyebrows. He said that I was falling behind, that I was not asking my usual questions. I remarked that it was plain to me that he was leading me to ask if the old seers had succeeded in *intending* death away, but he himself had

232

already told me that their knowledge about the tumbler had not saved them from dying.

"They succeeded in *intending* death away," he said, pronouncing his words with extra care. "But they still had to die."

"How did they *intend* death away?" I asked.

"They observed their allies," he said, "and *seeing* that they were living beings with a much greater resilience to the rolling force, the seers patterned themselves on their allies."

The old seers realized, don Juan explained, that only organic beings have a gap that resembles a bowl. Its size and shape and its brittleness make it the ideal configuration to hasten the cracking and collapsing of the luminous shell under the onslaughts of the tumbling force. The allies, on the other hand, who have only a line for a gap, present such a small surface to the rolling force as to be practically immortal. Their cocoons can sustain the onslaughts of the tumbler indefinitely, because hairline gaps offer no ideal configuration to it.

"The old seers developed the most bizarre techniques for closing their gaps," don Juan continued. "They were essentially correct in assuming that a hairline gap is more durable than a bowl-like one."

"Are those techniques still in existence?" I asked.

"No, they are not," he said. "But some of the seers who practiced them are."

For reasons unknown to me, his statement caused a reaction of sheer terror in me. My breathing was altered instantly, and I couldn't control its rapid pace.

"They're still alive to this day, isn't that so, Genaro?" don Juan asked.

"Absolutely," Genaro muttered from an apparent state of deep sleep.

I asked don Juan if he knew the reason for my being so frightened. He reminded me about a previous occasion in that very room when they had asked me if I had noticed the weird creatures that had come in the moment Genaro opened the door.

"That day your assemblage point went very deep into the left side and assembled a frightening world," he went on. "But I have already said that to you; what you don't remember is that you went directly to a very remote world and scared yourself pissless there."

Don Juan turned to Genaro, who was snoring peacefully with his legs stretched out in front of him.

"Wasn't he scared pissless, Genaro?" he asked.

"Absolutely pissless," Genaro muttered, and don Juan laughed.

"I want you to know that we don't blame you for being scared," don Juan continued. "We, ourselves, are revolted by some of the actions of the old seers. I'm sure that you have realized by now that what you can't remember about that night is that you *saw* the old seers who are still alive."

I wanted to protest that I had realized nothing, but I could not voice my words. I had to clear my throat over and over before I could articulate a word. Genaro had stood up and was gently patting my upper back, by my neck, as if I were choking.

"You have a frog in your throat," he said.

I thanked him in a high squeaky voice.

"No, I think you have a chicken there," he added and sat down to sleep.

Don Juan said that the new seers had rebelled against all the bizarre practices of the old seers and declared them not only useless but injurious to our total being. They even went so far as to ban those techniques from whatever was taught to new warriors; and for generations there was no mention of those practices at all.

It was in the early part of the eighteenth century that the nagual Sebastian, a member of don Juan's direct line of naguals, rediscovered the existence of those techniques.

"How did he rediscover them?" I asked.

"He was a superb *stalker*, and because of his impeccability he got a chance to learn marvels," don Juan replied.

He said that one day as the nagual Sebastian was about to start his daily routines—he was the sexton at the cathedral in the city where he lived—he found a middle-aged Indian man who seemed to be in a quandary at the door of the church.

The nagual Sebastian went to the man's side and asked him if he needed help. "I need a bit of energy to close my gap," the man said to him in a loud clear voice. "Would you give me some of your energy?"

Don Juan said that according to the story, the nagual Sebastian was dumbfounded. He did not know what the man was talking about. He offered to take the Indian to see the parish priest. The man lost his patience and angrily accused the nagual Sebastian of stalling. "I need your energy because you're a nagual," he said. "Let's go quietly."

The nagual Sebastian succumbed to the magnetic power of the stranger and meekly went with him into the mountains. He was gone for many days. When he came back he not only had a new outlook about the ancient seers, but detailed knowledge of their techniques. The stranger was an ancient Toltec. One of the last survivors.

"The nagual Sebastian found out marvels about the old seers," don Juan went on. "He was the one who first knew how grotesque and aberrant they really were. Before him, that knowledge was only hearsay.

"One night my benefactor and the nagual Elias gave me a sample of those aberrations. They really showed it to Genaro and me together, so it's only proper that we both show you the same sample."

I wanted to talk in order to stall; I needed time to calm down, to think things out. But before I could say anything, don Juan and Genaro were practically dragging me out of the house. They headed for the same eroded hills we had visited before.

We stopped at the bottom of a large barren hill. Don Juan pointed toward some distant mountains to the south, and said that between the place where we stood and a natural cut in one of those mountains, a cut that looked like an open mouth, there were at least seven sites where the ancient seers had focused all the power of their awareness.

Don Juan said that those seers had not only been knowledgeable and daring but downright successful. He added that his benefactor had showed him and Genaro a site where the old seers, driven by their love for life, had buried themselves alive and actually *intended* the rolling force away.

"There is nothing that would catch the eye in those places," he went on. "The old seers were careful not to leave marks. It is just a landscape. One has to *see* to know where those places are."

He said that he did not want to walk to the faraway sites, but would take me to the one that was nearest. I insisted on knowing what we were after. He said that we were going to *see* the buried seers, and that for that we had to stay until it got dark under the cover of some green bushes. He pointed them out; they were perhaps half a mile away, up a steep slope.

We reached the patch of bushes and sat down as comfortably as we could. He began then to explain in a very low voice that in order to get energy from the earth, ancient seers used to bury themselves for periods of time, depending on what they wanted to accomplish. The more difficult their task, the longer their burial period.

Don Juan stood up and in a melodramatic way showed me a spot a few yards from where we were.

"Two old seers are buried there," he said. "They buried themselves about two thousand years ago to escape death, not in the spirit of running away from it but in the spirit of defying it."

Don Juan asked Genaro to show me the exact spot where the old seers were buried. I turned to look at Genaro and realized that he was sitting by my side sound asleep again. But to my utter amazement, he jumped up and barked like a dog and ran on all fours to the spot don Juan was pointing out. There he ran around the place in a perfect mime of a small dog.

I found his performance hilarious. Don Juan was nearly on the ground laughing.

"Genaro has shown you something extraordinary," don Juan said, after Genaro had returned to where we were and had gone back to sleep. "He has shown you something about the assemblage point and *dreaming*. He's *dreaming* now, but he can act as if he were fully awake and he can hear everything you say. From that position he can do more than if he were awake."

He was silent for a moment as if assessing what to say next. Genaro snored rhythmically.

Don Juan remarked how easy it was for him to find flaws with what the old seers had done, yet, in all fairness, he never tired of repeating how wonderful their accomplishments were. He said that they understood the earth to perfection. Not only did they discover and use the boost from the earth, but they also discovered that if they remained buried, their assemblage points aligned emanations that were ordinarily inaccessible, and that such an alignment engaged the earth's strange, inexplicable capacity to deflect the ceaseless strikes of the rolling force. Consequently, they developed the most astounding and complex techniques for burying themselves for extremely long periods of time without any detriment to themselves. In their fight against death, they learned how to elongate those periods to cover millennia.

It was a cloudy day, and night fell quickly. In no time at all, everything was in darkness. Don Juan stood up and guided me and the sleepwalker Genaro to an enormous flat oval rock that had caught my eye the moment we got to that place. It was similar to the flat rock we had visited before, but bigger. It occurred to me that the rock, enormous as it was, had deliberately been placed there.

"This is another site," don Juan said. "This huge rock was placed here as a trap, to attract people. Soon you'll know why."

I felt a shiver run through my body. I thought I was going to faint. I knew that I was definitely overreacting and wanted to say something about it, but don Juan kept on talking in a hoarse whisper. He said that Genaro, since he was *dreaming,* had enough control over his assemblage point to move it until he could reach the specific emanations that would wake up whatever was around that rock. He recommended that I try to move my assemblage point, and follow Genaro's. He said that I could do it, first by setting up my unbending intent to move it, and second by letting the context of the situation dictate where it should move.

After a moment's thought he whispered in my ear not to worry about procedures, because most of the really unusual things that happen to seers, or to the average man for that matter, happen by themselves, with only the intervention of *intent.*

He was silent for a moment and then added that the danger for me was going to be the buried seers' inevitable attempt to scare me to death. He exhorted me to keep myself calm and not to succumb to fear, but follow Genaro's movements.

I fought desperately not to be sick. Don Juan patted me on the back and said that I was an old pro at playing an innocent bystander. He assured me that I was not consciously refusing to let my assemblage point move, but that every human being does it automatically.

"Something is going to scare the living daylights out

238

of you," he whispered. "Don't give up, because if you do, you'll die and the old vultures around here are going to feast on your energy."

"Let's get out of here," I pleaded. "I really don't give a damn about getting an example of the old seers' grotesqueness."

"It's too late," Genaro said, fully awake now, standing by my side. "Even if we try to get away, the two seers and their allies on the other spot will cut you down. They have already made a circle around us. There are as many as sixteen awarenesses focused on you right now."

"Who are they?" I whispered in Genaro's ear.

"The four seers and their court," he replied. "They've been aware of us since we got here."

I wanted to turn tail and run for dear life, but don Juan held my arm and pointed to the sky. I noticed that a remarkable change in visibility had taken place. Instead of the pitch-black darkness that had prevailed, there was a pleasant dawn twilight. I made a quick assessment of the cardinal points. The sky was definitely lighter toward the east.

I felt a strange pressure around my head. My ears were buzzing. I felt cold and feverish at the same time. I was scared as I had never been before, but what bothered me was a nagging sensation of defeat, of being a coward. I felt nauseated and miserable.

Don Juan whispered in my ear. He said that I had to be on the alert, that the onslaught of the old seers would be felt by all three of us at any moment.

"You can grab on to me if you want to," Genaro said in a fast whisper as if something were prodding him.

I hesitated for an instant. I did not want don Juan to believe that I was so scared I needed to hold on to Genaro.

"Here they come!" Genaro said in a loud whisper.

The world turned upside down instantaneously for

me when something gripped me by my left ankle. I felt the coldness of death on my entire body. I knew I had stepped on an iron clamp, maybe a bear trap. That all flashed through my mind before I let out a piercing scream, as intense as my fright.

Don Juan and Genaro laughed out loud. They were flanking me no more than three feet away, but I was so terrified I did not even notice them.

"Sing! Sing for dear life!" I heard don Juan ordering me under his breath.

I tried to pull my foot loose. I felt then a sting, as if needles were piercing my skin. Don Juan insisted over and over that I sing. He and Genaro started to sing a popular song. Genaro spoke the lyrics as he looked at me from hardly two inches away. They sang off-key in raspy voices, getting so completely out of breath and so high out of the range of their voices that I ended up laughing.

"Sing, or you're going to perish," don Juan said to me.

"Let's make a trio," Genaro said, "We'll sing a bolero."

I joined them in an off-key trio. We sang for quite a while at the top of our voices, like drunkards. I felt that the iron grip on my leg was gradually letting go of me. I had not dared to look down at my ankle. At one moment I did and I realized then that there was no trap clutching me. A dark, headlike shape was biting me!

Only a supreme effort kept me from fainting. I felt I was getting sick and automatically tried to bend over, but somebody with superhuman strength grabbed me painlessly by the elbows and the nape of my neck and did not let me move. I got sick all over my clothes.

My revulsion was so complete that I began to fall in a faint. Don Juan sprinkled my face with some water from the small gourd he always carried when we went into the mountains. The water slid under my collar.

The coldness restored my physical balance, but it did not affect the force that was holding me by my elbows and neck.

"I think you are going too far with your fright," don Juan said loudly and in such a matter-of-fact tone that he created an immediate feeling of order.

"Let's sing again," he added. "Let's sing a song with substance—I don't want any more boleros."

I silently thanked him for his sobriety and for his grand style. I was so moved as I heard them singing "La Valentina" that I began to weep.

> *"Because of my passion, they say*
> *that ill fortune is on my way.*
> *It doesn't matter*
> *that it might be the devil himself.*
> *I do know how to die*
>
> *Valentina, Valentina.*
> *I throw myself in your way.*
> *If I am going to die tomorrow,*
> *why not, once and for all, today?"*

All of my being staggered under the impact of that inconceivable juxtaposition of values. Never had a song meant so much to me. As I heard them sing those lyrics, which I ordinarily considered reeking with cheap sentimentalism, I thought I understood the ethos of the warrior. Don Juan had drilled into me that warriors live with death at their side, and from the knowledge that death is with them they draw the courage to face anything. Don Juan had said that the worst that could happen to us is that we have to die, and since that is already our unalterable fate, we are free; those who have lost everything no longer have anything to fear.

I walked to don Juan and Genaro and embraced

them to express my boundless gratitude and admiration for them.

Then I realized that nothing was holding me any longer. Without a word don Juan took my arm and guided me to sit on the flat rock.

"The show is just about to begin now," Genaro said in a jovial tone as he tried to find a comfortable position to sit. "You've just paid your admission ticket. It's all over your chest."

He looked at me, and both of them began to laugh.

"Don't sit too close to me," Genaro said. "I don't appreciate pukers. But don't go too far, either. The old seers are not yet through with their tricks."

I moved as close to them as politeness permitted. I was concerned about my state for an instant, and then all my qualms became nonsense, for I noticed that some people were coming toward us. I could not make out their shapes clearly but I distinguished a mass of human figures moving in the semidarkness. They did not carry lanterns or flashlights with them, which at that hour they would still have needed. Somehow that detail worried me. I did not want to focus on it and I deliberately began to think rationally. I figured that we must have attracted attention with our loud singing and they were coming to investigate. Don Juan tapped me on the shoulder. He pointed with a movement of his chin to the men in front of the group of others.

"Those four are the old seers," he said. "The rest are their allies."

Before I could remark that they were just local peasants, I heard a swishing sound right behind me. I quickly turned around in a state of total alarm. My movement was so sudden that don Juan's warning came too late.

"Don't turn around!" I heard him yell.

His words were only background; they did not mean anything to me. On turning around, I saw that three grotesquely deformed men had climbed up on the rock right behind me; they were crawling toward me, with their mouths open in a nightmarish grimace and their arms outstretched to grab me.

I intended to scream at the top of my lungs, but what came out was an agonizing croak, as if something were obstructing my windpipe. I automatically rolled out of their reach and onto the ground.

As I stood up, don Juan jumped to my side, at the very same moment that a horde of men, led by those don Juan had pointed out, descended on me like vultures. They were actually squeaking like bats or rats. I yelled in terror. This time I was able to let out a piercing cry.

Don Juan, as nimbly as an athlete in top form, pulled me out of their clutches onto the rock. He told me in a stern voice not to turn around to look, no matter how scared I was. He said that the allies cannot push at all, but that they certainly could scare me and make me fall to the ground. On the ground, however, the allies could hold anybody down. If I were to fall on the ground by the place where the seers were buried, I would be at their mercy. They would rip me apart while their allies held me. He added that he had not told me all that before because he had hoped I would be forced to *see* and understand it by myself. His decision had nearly cost me my life.

The sensation that the grotesque men were just behind me was nearly unbearable. Don Juan forcefully ordered me to keep calm and focus my attention on four men at the head of a crowd of perhaps ten or twelve. The instant I focused my eyes on them, as if on cue, they all advanced to the edge of the flat rock. They stopped there and began hissing like serpents. They walked back and forth. Their movement seemed to be synchronized. It was so consistent and orderly that it seemed to be mechanical. It was as if they were following a repetitive pattern, aimed at mesmerizing me.

"Don't gaze at them, dear," Genaro said to me as if he were talking to a child.

The laughter that followed was as hysterical as my fear. I laughed so hard that the sound reverberated on the surrounding hills.

The men stopped at once and seemed to be perplexed. I could distinguish the shapes of their heads bobbing up and down as if they were talking, deliberating among themselves. Then one of them jumped onto the rock.

"Watch out! That one is a seer!" Genaro exclaimed.

"What are we going to do?" I shouted.

"We could start singing again," don Juan replied matter-of-factly.

My fear reached its apex then. I began to jump up and down and to roar like an animal. The man jumped down to the ground.

"Don't pay any more attention to those clowns," don Juan said. "Let's talk as usual."

He said that we had gone there for my enlightenment, and that I was failing miserably. I had to reorganize myself. The first thing to do was to realize that my assemblage point had moved and was now making obscure emanations glow. To carry the feelings from my usual state of awareness into the world I had assembled was indeed a travesty, for fear is only prevalent among the emanations of daily life.

I told him that if my assemblage point had shifted as he was saying it had, I had news for him. My fear was infinitely greater and more devastating than anything I had ever experienced in my daily life.

"You're wrong," he said. "Your first attention is confused and doesn't want to give up control, that's all. I have the feeling that you could walk right up to those creatures and face them and they wouldn't do a thing to you."

I insisted that I was definitely in no condition to test such a preposterous thing as that.

He laughed at me. He said that sooner or later I had to cure myself of my madness, and that to take the initiative and face up to those four seers was infinitely less preposterous than the idea that I was seeing them at all. He said that to him madness was to be confronted by men who had been buried for two thousand years and were still alive, and not to think that that was the epitome of preposterousness.

I heard everything he said with clarity, but I was not really paying attention to him. I was terrified of the men around the rock. They seemed to be preparing to jump us, to jump me really. They were fixed on me. My right arm began to shake as if I were stricken by some muscular disorder. Then I became aware that the light in the sky had changed. I had not noticed before that it was already dawn. The strange thing was that an uncontrollable urge made me stand up and run to the group of men.

I had at that moment two completely different feelings about the same event. The minor one was of sheer terror. The other, the major one, was of total indifference. I could not have cared less.

When I reached the group I realized that don Juan was right; they were not really men. Only four of them had any resemblance to men, but they were not men either; they were strange creatures with huge yellow eyes. The others were just shapes that were propelled by the four that resembled men.

I felt extraordinarily sad for those creatures with yellow eyes. I tried to touch them, but I could not find them. Some sort of wind scooped them away.

I looked for don Juan and Genaro. They were not there. It was pitch-black again. I called out their names over and over again. I thrashed around in darkness for a few minutes. Don Juan came to my side and startled me. I did not see Genaro.

"Let's go home," he said. "We have a long walk."

Don Juan commented on how well I had performed at the site of the buried seers, especially during the last part of our encounter with them. He said that a shift of the assemblage point is marked by a change in light. In the daytime, light becomes very dark; at night, darkness becomes twilight. He added that I had performed two shifts by myself, aided only by animal fright. The only thing he found objectionable was my indulging in fear, especially after I had realized that warriors have nothing to fear.

"How do you know I had realized that?" I asked.

"Because you were free. When fear disappears all the ties that bind us dissolve," he said. "An ally was gripping your foot because it was attracted by your animal terror."

I told him how sorry I was for not being able to uphold my realizations.

"Don't concern yourself with that." He laughed. "You know that such realizations are a dime a dozen; they don't amount to anything in the life of warriors, because they are canceled out as the assemblage point shifts.

"What Genaro and I wanted to do was to make you shift very deeply. This time Genaro was there simply to entice the old seers. He did it once already, and you went so far into the left side that it will take quite a while for you to remember it. Your fright tonight was just as intense as it was that first time when the seers and their allies followed you to this very room, but your sturdy first attention wouldn't let you be aware of them."

"Explain to me what happened at the site of the seers," I asked.

"The allies came out to *see* you," he replied. "Since they have very low energy, they always need

246

the help of men. The four seers have collected twelve allies.

"The countryside in Mexico and also certain cities are dangerous. What happened to you can happen to any man or woman. If they bump into that tomb, they may even *see* the seers and their allies, if they are pliable enough to let their fear make their assemblage points shift; but one thing is for sure: they can die of fright."

"But do you honestly believe that those Toltec seers are still alive?" I asked.

He laughed and shook his head in disbelief.

"It's time for you to shift that assemblage point of yours just a bit," he said. "I can't talk to you when you are in your idiot's stage."

He smacked me with the palm of his hand on three spots: right on the crest of my right hipbone, on the center of my back below my shoulder blades, and on the upper part of my right pectoral muscle.

My ears immediately began to buzz. A trickle of blood ran out of my right nostril, and something inside me became unplugged. It was as if some flow of energy had been blocked and suddenly began to move again.

"What were those seers and their allies after?" I asked.

"Nothing," he replied. "We were the ones who were after them. The seers, of course, had already noticed your field of energy the first time you *saw* them; when you came back, they were set to feast on you."

"You claim that they are alive, don Juan," I said. "You must mean that they are alive as allies are alive, is that so?"

"That's exactly right," he said. "They cannot possibly be alive as you and I are. That would be preposterous."

He went on to explain that the ancient seers' concern with death made them look into the most bizarre possibilities. The ones who opted for the allies' pattern had in mind, doubtless, a desire for a haven. And they found it, at a fixed position in one of the seven bands of inorganic awareness. The seers felt that they were relatively safe there. After all, they were separated from the daily world by a nearly insurmountable barrier, the barrier of perception set by the assemblage point.

"When the four seers *saw* that you could shift your assemblage point they took off like bats out of hell," he said and laughed.

"Do you mean that I assembled one of the seven worlds?" I asked.

"No, you didn't," he replied. "But you have done it before, when the seers and their allies chased you. That day you went all the way to their world. The problem is that you love to act stupid, so you can't remember it at all.

"I'm sure that it is the nagual's presence," he continued, "that sometimes makes people act dumb. When the nagual Julian was still around, I was dumber than I am now. I am convinced that when I'm no longer here, you'll be capable of remembering everything."

Don Juan explained that since he needed to show me the death defiers, he and Genaro had lured them to the outskirts of our world. What I had done at first was a deep lateral shift, which allowed me to *see* them as people, but at the end I had correctly made the shift that allowed me to *see* the death defiers and their allies as they are.

Very early the next morning, at Silvio Manuel's house, don Juan called me to the big room to discuss the events of the previous night. I felt exhausted and wanted to rest, to sleep, but don Juan was pressed for time. He immediately started his explanation. He said that the old seers had found out a way to utilize the rolling force and be propelled by it. Instead of succumbing to the onslaughts of the tumbler they rode with it and let it move their assemblage points to the confines of human possibilities.

Don Juan expressed unbiased admiration for such an accomplishment. He admitted that nothing else could give the assemblage point the boost that the tumbler gives.

I asked him about the difference between the earth's boost and the tumbler's boost. He explained that the earth's boost is the force of alignment of only the amber emanations. It is a boost that heightens awareness to unthinkable degrees. To the new seers it is a blast of unlimited consciousness, which they call total freedom.

He said that the tumbler's boost, on the other hand, is the force of death. Under the impact of the tumbler, the assemblage point moves to new, unpredictable positions. Thus, the old seers were always alone in their journeys, although the enterprise they were involved in was always communal. The company of other seers on their journeys was fortuitous and usually meant struggle for supremacy.

I confessed to don Juan that the concerns of the old seers, whatever they may have been, were worse than morbid horror tales to me. He laughed uproariously. He seemed to be enjoying himself.

"You have to admit, no matter how disgusted you feel, that those devils were very daring," he went on. "I never liked them myself, as you know, but I can't help admiring them. Their love for life is truly beyond me."

"How can that be love for life, don Juan? It's something nauseating," I said.

"What else could push a man to those extremes if it is not love for life?" he asked. "They loved life so intensely that they were not willing to give it up.

That's the way I have *seen* it. My benefactor *saw* something else. He believed that they were afraid to die, which is not the same as loving life. I say that they were afraid to die because they loved life and because they had *seen* marvels, and not because they were greedy little monsters. No. They were aberrant because nobody ever challenged them and they were spoiled like rotten children, but their daring was impeccable and so was their courage.

"Would you venture into the unknown out of greed? No way. Greed works only in the world of ordinary affairs. To venture into that terrifying loneliness one must have something greater than greed. Love, one needs love for life, for intrigue, for mystery. One needs unquenching curiosity and guts galore. So don't give me this nonsense about your being revolted. It's embarrassing!"

Don Juan's eyes were shining with contained laughter. He was putting me in my place, but he was laughing at it.

Don Juan left me alone in the room for perhaps an hour. I wanted to organize my thoughts and feelings. I had no way to do that. I knew without any doubt that my assemblage point was at a position where reasoning does not prevail, yet I was moved by reasonable concerns. Don Juan had said that technically, as soon as the assemblage point shifts, we are asleep. I wondered, for instance, if I was sound asleep from the stand of an onlooker, just as Genaro had been asleep to me.

I asked don Juan about it as soon as he returned.

"You are absolutely asleep without having to be stretched out," he replied. "If people in a normal state of awareness saw you now, you would appear to them to be a bit dizzy, even drunk."

He explained that during normal sleep, the shift of the assemblage point runs along either edge of man's band. Such shifts are always coupled with slumber. Shifts that are induced by practice occur along the midsection of man's band and are not coupled with slumber, yet a *dreamer* is asleep.

"Right at this juncture is where the new and the old seers made their separate bids for power," he went on. "The old seers wanted a replica of the body, but with more physical strength, so they made their assemblage points slide along the right edge of man's band. The deeper they moved along the right edge the more bizarre their *dreaming body* became. You, yourself, witnessed last night the monstrous result of a deep shift along the right edge."

He said that the new seers were completely different, that they maintain their assemblage points along the midsection of man's band. If the shift is a shallow one, like the shift into heightened awareness, the *dreamer* is almost like anyone else in the street, except for a slight vulnerability to emotions, such as fear and doubt. But at a certain degree of depth, the *dreamer* who is shifting along the midsection becomes a blob of light. A blob of light is the *dreaming body* of the new seers.

He also said that such an impersonal *dreaming body* is more conducive to understanding and examination, which are the basis of all the new seers do. The intensely humanized *dreaming body* of the old seers drove them to look for answers that were equally personal, humanized.

Don Juan suddenly seemed to be groping for words.

"There is another death defier," he said curtly, "so unlike the four you've *seen* that he's indistinguishable from the average man in the street. He's accomplished this unique feat by being able to open and close his gap whenever he wants."

He played with his fingers almost nervously.

"The ancient seer that the nagual Sebastian found in 1723 is that death defier," he went on. "We count

251

that day as the beginning of our line, the second beginning. That death defier, who's been on the earth for hundreds of years, has changed the lives of every nagual he met, some more profoundly than others. And he has met every single nagual of our line since that day in 1723."

Don Juan looked fixedly at me. I got strangely embarrassed. I thought my embarrassment was the result of a dilemma. I had very serious doubts about the content of the story, and at the same time I had the most disconcerting trust that everything he had said was true. I expressed my quandary to him.

"The problem of rational disbelief is not yours alone," don Juan said. "My benefactor was at first plagued by the same question. Of course, later on he remembered everything. But it took him a long time to do so. When I met him he had already recollected everything, so I never witnessed his doubts. I only heard about them.

"The weird part is that people who have never set eyes on the man have less difficulty accepting that he's one of the original seers. My benefactor said that his quandaries stemmed from the fact that the shock of meeting such a creature had lumped together a number of emanations. It takes time for those emanations to separate themselves."

Don Juan went on to explain that as my assemblage point kept on shifting, a moment would come when it would hit the proper combination of emanations; at that moment the proof of the existence of that man would become overwhelmingly evident to me.

I felt compelled to talk again about my ambivalence.

"We're deviating from our subject," he said. "It may seem that I'm trying to convince you of the existence of that man; and what I meant to talk about is the fact that the old seer knows how to handle the rolling force. Whether or not you believe that he exists is not important. Someday you'll know for a fact that he certainly succeeded in closing his gap. The energy that he borrows from the nagual every generation he uses exclusively to close his gap."

"How did he succeed in closing it?" I asked.

"There is no way of knowing that," he replied. "I've talked to two other naguals who saw that man face to face, the nagual Julian and the nagual Elias. Neither of them knew how. The man never revealed how he closes that opening, which I suppose begins to expand after a time. The nagual Sebastian said that when he first saw the old seer, the man was very weak, actually dying. But my benefactor found him prancing vigorously, like a young man."

Don Juan said that the nagual Sebastian nicknamed that nameless man "the tenant," for they struck an arrangement by which the man was given energy, lodging so to speak, and he paid rent in the form of favors and knowledge.

"Did anybody ever get hurt in the exchange?" I asked.

"None of the naguals who exchanged energy with him was injured," he replied. "The man's commitment was that he'd only take a bit of superfluous energy from the nagual in exchange for gifts, for extraordinary abilities. For instance, the nagual Julian got the gait of power. With it, he could activate or make dormant the emanations inside his cocoon in order to look young or old at will."

Don Juan explained that the death defiers in general went as far as rendering dormant all the emanations inside their cocoons, except those that matched the emanations of the allies. In this fashion they were able to imitate the allies in some form.

Each of the death defiers we had encountered at the rock, don Juan said, had been able to move his assemblage point to a precise spot on his cocoon in order to emphasize the emanations shared with the allies and to interact with them. But they were all unable to move it back to its usual position and interact with people. The tenant, on the other hand, is capable of shifting his assemblage point to assemble the everyday world as if nothing had ever happened.

Don Juan also said that his benefactor was convinced—and he fully agreed with him—that what takes place during the borrowing of energy is that the old sorcerer moves the nagual's assemblage point to emphasize the ally's emanations inside the nagual's cocoon. He then uses the great jolt of energy produced by those emanations that suddenly become aligned after being so deeply dormant.

He said that the energy locked within us, in the dormant emanations, has a tremendous force and an incalculable scope. We can only vaguely assess the scope of that tremendous force, if we consider that the energy involved in perceiving and acting in the world of everyday life is a product of the alignment of hardly one-tenth of the emanations encased in man's cocoon.

"What happens at the moment of death is that all that energy is released at once," he continued. "Living beings at that moment become flooded by the most inconceivable force. It is not the rolling force that has cracked their gaps, because that force never enters inside the cocoon; it only makes it collapse. What floods them is the force of all the emanations that are suddenly aligned after being dormant for a lifetime. There is no outlet for such a giant force except to escape through the gap."

He added that the old sorcerer has found a way to tap that energy. By aligning a limited and very specific spectrum of the dormant emanations inside the nagual's cocoon, the old seer taps a limited but gigantic jolt.

"How do you think he takes that energy into his own body?" I asked.

"By cracking the nagual's gap," he replied. "He moves the nagual's assemblage point until the gap opens a little. When the energy of newly aligned emanations is released through that opening, he takes it into his own gap."

"Why is that old seer doing what he's doing?" I asked.

"My opinion is that he's caught in a circle he can't break," he replied. "We got into an agreement with him. He's doing his best to keep it, and so are we. We can't judge him, yet we have to know that his path doesn't lead to freedom. He knows that, and he also knows he can't change it; he's trapped in a situation of his own making. The only thing he can do is to prolong his ally-like existence as long as he possibly can."

16
The Mold of Man

Right after lunch, don Juan and I sat down to talk. He
started without any preamble. He announced that we
had come to the end of his explanation. He said that
he had discussed with me, in painstaking detail, all the
truths about awareness that the old seers had discovered. He stressed that I now knew the order in which
the new seers had arranged them. In the last sessions
of his explanation, he said, he had given me a detailed
account of the two forces that aid our assemblage
points to move: the earth's boost and the rolling force.
He had also explained the three techniques worked
out by the new seers—*stalking, intent,* and *dreaming*
—and their effects on the movement of the assemblage point.

"Now, the only thing left for you to do before the
explanation of the mastery of awareness is completed," he went on, "is to break the barrier of perception by yourself. You must move your assemblage
point, unaided by anyone, and align another great
band of emanations.

"Not to do this will turn everything you've learned
and done with me into merely talk, just words. And
words are fairly cheap."

He explained that when the assemblage point is moving away from its customary position and reaches a certain depth, it breaks a barrier that momentarily disrupts its capacity to align emanations. We experience it as a moment of perceptual blankness. The old seers called that moment the wall of fog, because a bank of fog appears whenever the alignment of emanations falters.

He said that there were three ways of dealing with it. It could be taken abstractly as a barrier of perception; it could be felt as the act of piercing a tight paper screen with the entire body; or it could be *seen* as a wall of fog.

In the course of my apprenticeship with don Juan, he had guided me countless times to *see* the barrier of perception. At first I had liked the idea of a wall of fog. Don Juan had warned me that the old seers had also preferred to *see* it that way. He had said that there is great comfort and ease in *seeing* it as a wall of fog, but that there is also the grave danger of turning something incomprehensible into something somber and foreboding; hence, his recommendation was to keep incomprehensible things incomprehensible rather than making them part of the inventory of the first attention.

After a short-lived feeling of comfort in *seeing* the wall of fog I had to agree with don Juan that it was better to keep the transition period as an incomprehensible abstraction, but by then it was impossible for me to break the fixation of my awareness. Every time I was placed in a position to break the barrier of perception I *saw* the wall of fog.

On one occasion, in the past, I had complained to don Juan and Genaro that although I wanted to *see* it as something else, I couldn't change it. Don Juan had commented that that was understandable, because I was morbid and somber, that he and I were very different in this respect. He was lighthearted and practical and he did not worship the human inventory. I, on the other hand, was unwilling to throw my inventory out the window and consequently I was heavy, sinister, and impractical. I had been shocked and saddened by his harsh criticism and became very gloomy. Don Juan and Genaro had laughed until tears rolled down their cheeks.

Genaro had added that on top of all that I was vindictive and had a tendency to get fat. They had laughed so hard I finally felt obliged to join them.

Don Juan had told me then that exercises of assembling other worlds allowed the assemblage point to gain experience in shifting. I had always wondered, however, how to get the initial boost to dislodge my assemblage point from its usual position. When I'd questioned him about it in the past he'd pointed out that since alignment is the force that is involved in everything, *intent* is what makes the assemblage point move.

I asked him again about it.

"You're in a position now to answer that question yourself," he replied. "The mastery of awareness is what gives the assemblage point its boost. After all, there is really very little to us human beings; we are, in essence, an assemblage point fixed at a certain position. Our enemy and at the same time our friend is our internal dialogue, our inventory. Be a warrior; shut off your internal dialogue; make your inventory and then throw it away. The new seers make accurate inventories and then laugh at them. Without the inventory the assemblage point becomes free."

Don Juan reminded me that he had talked a great deal about one of the most sturdy aspects of our inventory: our idea of God. That aspect, he said, was like a powerful glue that bound the assemblage point to its original position. If I were going to assemble another true world with another great band of emanations, I had to take an obligatory step in order to release all ties from my assemblage point.

"That step is to *see* the mold of man," he said. "You must do that today unaided."

"What's the mold of man?" I asked.

"I've helped you *see* it many times," he replied. "You know what I'm talking about."

I refrained from saying that I did not know what he was talking about. If he said that I had *seen* the mold of man, I must have done that, although I did not have the foggiest idea what it was like.

He knew what was going through my mind. He gave me a knowing smile and slowly shook his head from side to side.

"The mold of man is a huge cluster of emanations in the great band of organic life," he said. "It is called the mold of man because the cluster appears only inside the cocoon of man.

"The mold of man is the portion of the Eagle's emanations that seers can *see* directly without any danger to themselves."

There was a long pause before he spoke again.

"To break the barrier of perception is the last task of the mastery of awareness," he said. "In order to move your assemblage point to that position you must gather enough energy. Make a journey of recovery. Remember what you've done!"

I tried unsuccessfully to recall what was the mold of man. I felt an excruciating frustration that soon turned into real anger. I was furious with myself, with don Juan, with everybody.

Don Juan was untouched by my fury. He said matter-of-factly that anger was a natural reaction to the hesitation of the assemblage point to move on command.

"It will be a long time before you can apply the principle that your command is the Eagle's command," he said. "That's the essence of the mastery of *intent*. In the meantime, make a command now not to fret, not even at the worst moments of doubt. It will be a slow process until that command is heard and obeyed as if it were the Eagle's command."

He also said that there was an unmeasurable area of awareness in between the customary position of the assemblage point and the position where there are no more doubts, which is almost the place where the barrier of perception makes its appearance. In that unmeasurable area, warriors fall prey to every conceivable misdeed. He warned me to be on the lookout and not lose confidence, for I would unavoidably be struck at one time or another by gripping feelings of defeat.

"The new seers recommend a very simple act when impatience, or despair, or anger, or sadness comes their way," he continued. "They recommend that warriors roll their eyes. Any direction will do; I prefer to roll mine clockwise.

"The movement of the eyes makes the assemblage point shift momentarily. In that movement, you will find relief. This is in lieu of true mastery of *intent*."

I complained that there was not enough time for him to tell me more about *intent*.

"It will all come back to you someday," he assured me. "One thing will trigger another. One key word and all of it will tumble out of you as if the door of an overstuffed closet had given way."

He went back then to discussing the mold of man. He said that to *see* it on my own, unaided by anyone, was an important step, because all of us have certain ideas that must be broken before we are free; the seer who travels into the unknown to *see* the unknowable must be in an impeccable state of being.

He winked at me and said that to be in an impeccable state of being is to be free of rational assumptions and rational fears. He added that both my rational assumptions and my rational fears were preventing me at that moment from realigning the emanations that would make me remember *seeing* the mold of man. He urged me to relax and move my eyes in order to make my assemblage point shift. He repeated over and over that it was really important to remember having *seen* the mold before I *see* it again. And since he was pressed for time there was no room for my usual slowness.

I moved my eyes as he suggested. Almost immediately I forgot my discomfort and then a sudden flash of memory came to me and I remembered that I had *seen* the mold of man. It had happened years earlier on an occasion that had been quite memorable to me, because from the point of view of my Catholic upbringing, don Juan had made the most sacrilegious statements I had ever heard.

It had all started as a casual conversation while we hiked in the foothills of the Sonoran desert. He was explaining to me the implications of what he was doing to me with his teachings. We had stopped to rest and had sat down on some large boulders. He had continued explaining his teaching procedure, and this had encouraged me to try for the hundredth time to give him an account of how I felt about it. It was evident that he did not want to hear about it anymore. He made me change levels of awareness and told me that if I would *see* the mold of man, I might understand everything he was doing and thus save us both years of toil.

He gave me a detailed explanation of what the mold of man was. He did not talk about it in terms of the Eagle's emanations, but in terms of a pattern of energy that serves to stamp the qualities of humanness on an amorphous blob of biological matter. At least, I understood it that way, especially after he further described the mold of man using a mechanical analogy. He said that it was like a gigantic die that stamps out human beings endlessly as if they were coming to it on a mass-production conveyor belt. He vividly mimed the process by bringing the palms of his hands together with great force, as if the die molded a human being each time its two halves were clapped.

He also said that every species has a mold of its own, and every individual of every species molded by the process shows characteristics particular to its own kind.

He began then an extremely disturbing elucidation about the mold of man. He said that the old seers as well as the mystics of our world have one thing in common—they have been able to *see* the mold of man but not understand what it is. Mystics, throughout the centuries, have given us moving accounts of their experiences. But these accounts, however beautiful, are flawed by the gross and despairing mistake of believing the mold of man to be an omnipotent, omniscient creator; and so is the interpretation of the old seers, who called the mold of man a friendly spirit, a protector of man.

He said that the new seers are the only ones who have the sobriety to *see* the mold of man and understand what it is. What they have come to realize is that the mold of man is not a creator, but the pattern of every human attribute we can think of and some we cannot even conceive. The mold is our God because we are what it stamps us with and not because it has created us from nothing and made us in its image and likeness. Don Juan said that in his opinion to fall on our knees in the presence of the mold of man reeks of arrogance and human self-centeredness.

As I heard don Juan's explanation I got terribly worried. Even though I had never considered myself to be a practicing Catholic, I was shocked by his blasphemous implications. I had been politely listening to him, yet I had been yearning for a pause in his barrage of sacrilegious judgments in order to change the subject. But he went on drumming his point in a merciless way. I finally interrupted him and told him that I believed that God exists.

He retorted that my belief was based on faith and, as such, was a secondhand conviction that did not amount to anything; my belief in the existence of God was, like everyone else's, based on hearsay and not on the act of *seeing*, he said.

He assured me that even if I was able to *see*, I was bound to make the same misjudgment that mystics have made. Anyone who *sees* the mold of man automatically assumes that it is God.

He called the mystical experience a chance *seeing*, a one-shot affair that has no significance whatsoever because it is the result of a random movement of the assemblage point. He asserted that the new seers are indeed the only ones who can pass a fair judgment on this matter, because they have ruled out chance *seeings* and are capable of *seeing* the mold of man as often as they please.

They have *seen*, therefore, that what we call God is a static prototype of humanness without any power. For the mold of man cannot under any circumstances help us by intervening in our behalf, or punish our wrongdoings, or reward us in any way. We are simply the product of its stamp; we are its impression. The mold of man is exactly what its name tells us it is, a pattern, a form, a cast that groups together a particular bunch of fiberlike elements, which we call man.

What he had said put me in a state of great distress. But he seemed unconcerned with my genuine turmoil. He kept on needling me with what he called the unforgivable crime of the chance seers, which makes us focus our irreplaceable energy on something that has no power whatsoever to do anything. The more he talked, the greater my annoyance. When I became so annoyed that I was about to shout at him, he had me change into yet a deeper state of heightened awareness. He hit me on my right side, between my hipbone and my rib cage. That blow sent me soaring into a radiant light, into a diaphanous source of the most peaceful and exquisite beatitude. That light was a haven, an oasis in the blackness around me.

From my subjective point of view, I *saw* that light for an immeasurable length of time. The splendor of the sight was beyond anything I can say, and yet I could not figure out what it was that made it so beautiful. Then the idea came to me that its beauty grew out of a sense of harmony, a sense of peace and rest, of having arrived, of being safe at long last. I felt myself inhaling and exhaling in quietude and relief. What a gorgeous sense of plenitude! I knew beyond a shadow of doubt that I had come face to face with God, the source of everything. And I knew that God loved me. God was love and forgiveness. The light bathed me, and I felt clean, delivered. I wept uncontrollably, mainly for myself. The sight of that resplendent light made me feel unworthy, villainous.

Suddenly, I heard don Juan's voice in my ear. He said that I had to go beyond the mold, that the mold was merely a stage, a stopover that brought temporary peace and serenity to those who journey into the unknown, but that it was sterile, static. It was at the same time a flat reflected image in a mirror and the mirror itself. And the image was man's image.

I passionately resented what don Juan was saying; I rebelled against his blasphemous, sacrilegious words. I wanted to tell him off, but I could not break the binding power of my *seeing*. I was caught in it. Don Juan seemed to know exactly how I felt and what I wanted to tell him.

"You can't tell the nagual off," he said in my ear. "It is the nagual who's enabling you to *see*. It is the nagual's technique, the nagual's power. The nagual is the guide.''

It was at that point that I realized something about the voice in my ear. It was not don Juan's, although it sounded very much like his voice. Also, the voice was right. The instigator of that *seeing* was the nagual Juan Matus. It was his technique and his power that was making me *see* God. He said it was not God, but the mold of man; I knew that he was right. Yet I could not admit that, not out of annoyance or stubbornness, but simply out of a sense of ultimate loyalty to and love for the divinity that was in front of me.

As I gazed into the light with all the passion I was capable of, the light seemed to condense and I *saw* a man. A shiny man that exuded charisma, love, understanding, sincerity, truth. A man that was the sum total of all that is good.

The fervor I felt on *seeing* that man was well beyond anything I had ever felt in my life. I did fall on my knees. I wanted to worship God personified, but don Juan intervened and whacked me on my left upper chest, close to my clavicle, and I lost sight of God.

I was left with a tantalizing feeling, a mixture of remorse, elation, certainties, and doubts. Don Juan made fun of me. He called me pious and careless and said I would make a great priest; now I could even pass for a spiritual leader who had had a chance *seeing* of God. He urged me, in a jocular way, to start preaching and describe what I had *seen* to everyone.

In a very casual but seemingly interested manner he made a statement that was part question, part assertion.

''And the man?'' he asked. ''You can't forget that God is a male.''

The immensity of something indefinable began to dawn on me as I entered into a state of great clarity.

''Very cozy, eh?'' don Juan added, smiling. ''God is a male. What a relief!''

After recounting to don Juan what I had remembered, I asked him about something that had just struck me as being terribly odd. To *see* the mold of man, I had obviously gone through a shift of my assemblage point. The recollection of the feelings and realizations I had had then was so vivid that it gave me a sense of utter futility. Everything I had done and felt at that time I was feeling now. I asked him how it was possible that having had such a clear comprehension, I could have forgotten it so completely. It was as if nothing of what had happened to me had mattered, for I always had to start from point one regardless of how much I might have advanced in the past.

"That's only an emotional impression," he said. "A total misapprehension. Whatever you did years ago is solidly enclosed in some unused emanations. That day when I made you *see* the mold of man, for instance, I had a true misapprehension myself. I thought that if you *saw* it, you would be able to understand it. It was a true misunderstanding on my part."

Don Juan explained that he had always regarded himself as being very slow to understand. He had never had any chance of testing his belief, because he did not have a point of reference. When I came along and he became a teacher, which was something totally new to him, he realized that there is no way to speed up understanding and that to dislodge the assemblage point is not enough. He had thought that it would be sufficient. Soon he became aware that since the assemblage point normally shifts during dreams, sometimes to extraordinarily distant positions, whenever we undergo an induced shift we are all experts at immediately compensating for it. We rebalance ourselves constantly and activity goes on as if nothing has happened to us.

He remarked that the value of the new seers' conclusions does not become evident until one tries to move someone else's assemblage point. The new seers said that what counts in this respect is the effort to reinforce the stability of the assemblage point in its new position. They considered this to be the only teaching procedure worth discussing. And they knew that it is a long process that has to be carried out little by little at a snail's pace.

Don Juan said then that he had used power plants at the beginning of my apprenticeship in accordance with a recommendation of the new seers. They knew by experience and by *seeing* that power plants shake the assemblage point way out of its normal setting. The effect of power plants on the assemblage point is in principle very much like that of dreams: dreams make it move; but power plants manage the shift on a greater and more engulfing scale. A teacher then uses the disorienting effects of such a shift to reinforce the notion that the perception of the world is never final.

I remembered then that I had *seen* the mold of man five more times over the years. With each new time I had become less passionate about it. I could never get over the fact, however, that I always *saw* God as a male. At the end it stopped being God for me and became the mold of man, not because of what don Juan had said, but because the position of a male God became untenable. I could then understand don Juan's statements about it. They had not been blasphemous or sacrilegious in the least; he had not made them from within the context of the daily world. He was right in saying that the new seers have an edge in being capable of *seeing* the mold of man as often as they want. But what was more important to me was that they had sobriety in order to examine what they *saw*.

I asked him why it was that I always *saw* the mold of man as a male. He said that it was because my assemblage point did not have the stability then to remain completely glued to its new position and shifted laterally in man's band. It was the same case as *seeing* the barrier of perception as a wall of fog.

What made the assemblage point move laterally was a nearly unavoidable desire, or necessity, to render the incomprehensible in terms of what is most familiar to us: a barrier is a wall and the mold of man cannot be anything else but a man. He thought that if I were a woman I would see the mold as a woman.

Don Juan stood up then and said that it was time for us to take a stroll in town, that I should *see* the mold of man among people. We walked in silence to the square, but before we got there I had an uncontainable surge of energy and ran down the street to the outskirts of town. I came to a bridge, and right there, as if it had been waiting for me, I *saw* the mold of man as a resplendent, warm, amber light.

I fell on my knees, not so much out of piety, but as physical reaction to awe. The sight of the mold of man was more astonishing than ever. I felt, without any arrogance, that I had gone through an enormous change since the first time I had *seen* it. However, all the things I had *seen* and learned had only given me a greater, more profound appreciation for the miracle that I had in front of my eyes.

The mold of man was superimposed on the bridge at first, then I refocused my eyes and *saw* that the mold of man extended up and down into infinity; the bridge was but a meager shell, a tiny sketch superimposed on the eternal. And so were the minute figures of people who moved around me, looking at me with unabashed curiosity. But I was beyond their touch, although at that moment I was as vulnerable as I could be. The mold of man had no power to protect me or spare me, yet I loved it with a passion that knew no limits.

I thought that I understood then something that don Juan had told me repeatedly, that real affection cannot be an investment. I would have gladly remained the servant of the mold of man, not for what it could give me, for it has nothing to give, but for the sheer affection I felt for it.

I had the sensation of something pulling me away, and before I disappeared from its presence I shouted a promise to the mold of man, but a great force whisked me away before I could finish stating what I meant. I was suddenly kneeling at the bridge while a group of peasants looked at me and laughed.

Don Juan got to my side and helped me up and walked me back to the house.

"There are two ways of *seeing* the mold of man," don Juan began as soon as we sat down. "You can *see* it as a man or you can *see* it as a light. That depends on the shift of the assemblage point. If the shift is lateral, the mold is a human being; if the shift is in the midsection of man's band, the mold is a light. The only value of what you've done today is that your assemblage point shifted in the midsection."

He said that the position where one *sees* the mold of man is very close to that where the *dreaming body* and the barrier of perception appear. That was the reason the new seers recommend that the mold of man be *seen* and understood.

"Are you sure you understand what the mold of man really is?" he asked with a smile.

"I assure you, don Juan, that I'm perfectly aware of what the mold of man is," I said.

"I heard you shouting inanities to the mold of man when I got to the bridge," he said with a most malicious smile.

I told him that I had felt like a worthless servant worshiping a worthless master, and yet I was moved out of sheer affection to promise undying love.

He found it all hilarious and laughed until he was choking.

"The promise of a worthless servant to a worthless

269

master is worthless," he said and choked again with laughter.

I did not feel like defending my position. My affection for the mold of man was offered freely without thought of recompense. It did not matter to me that my promise was worthless.

17
The Journey
of the <u>Dreaming</u> <u>Body</u>

Don Juan told me that the two of us were going to drive to the city of Oaxaca for the last time. He made it very clear that we would never be there together again. Perhaps his feeling might return to the place, he said, but never again the totality of himself.

In Oaxaca, don Juan spent hours looking at mundane, trivial things, the faded color of walls, the shape of distant mountains, the pattern on cracked cement, the faces of people. Then we went to the square and sat on his favorite bench, which was unoccupied, as it always was when he wanted it.

During our long walk in the city, I had tried my best to work myself into a mood of sadness and moroseness, but I just could not do it. There was something festive about his departure. He explained it as the unrestrainable vigor of total freedom.

"Freedom is like a contagious disease," he said. "It is transmitted; its carrier is an impeccable nagual. People might not appreciate that, and that's because they don't want to be free. Freedom is frightening. Remember that. But not for us. I've groomed myself nearly all my life for this moment. And so will you."

He repeated over and over that at the stage where I

was, no rational assumptions should interfere with my actions. He said that the *dreaming body* and the barrier of perception are positions of the assemblage point, and that that knowledge is as vital to seers as knowing how to read and write is to modern man. Both are accomplishments attained after years of practice.

"It is very important that you remember, right now, the time when your assemblage point reached that position and it created your *dreaming body,*" he said with tremendous urgency.

Then he smiled and remarked that time was extremely short; he said that the recollection of the main journey of my *dreaming body* would put my assemblage point in a position to break the barrier of perception in order to assemble another world.

"The *dreaming body* is known by different names," he said after a long pause. "The name I like the best is, the other. That term belongs to the old seers, together with the mood. I don't particularly care for their mood, but I have to admit that I like their term. The other. It's mysterious and forbidden. Just like the old seers, it gives me the feeling of darkness, of shadows. The old seers said that the other always comes shrouded in wind."

Over the years don Juan and other members of his party had tried to make me aware that we can be in two places at once, that we can experience a sort of perceptual dualism.

As don Juan spoke, I began to remember something so deeply forgotten that at first it was as if I had only heard about it. Then, step by step, I realized that I had lived that experience myself.

I had been in two places at once. It happened one night in the mountains of northern Mexico. I had been collecting plants with don Juan all day. We had stopped for the night and I had nearly fallen asleep from fatigue when suddenly there was a gust of wind and don Genaro sprang up from the darkness right in front of me and nearly scared me to death.

My first thought was one of suspicion. I believed that don Genaro had been hiding in the bushes all day, waiting for darkness to set in before making his terrifying appearance. As I looked at him prancing around, I noticed that there was something truly odd about him that night. Something palpable, real, and yet something I could not pinpoint.

He joked with me and horsed around, performing acts that defied my reason. Don Juan laughed like an idiot at my dismay. When he judged that the time was right, he made me shift into heightened awareness and for a moment I was able to *see* don Juan and don Genaro as two blobs of light. Genaro was not the flesh-and-blood don Genaro that I knew in my state of normal awareness but his *dreaming body*. I could tell, because I *saw* him as a ball of fire that was above the ground. He was not rooted as don Juan was. It was as if Genaro, the blob of light, were on the verge of taking off, already up in the air, a couple of feet off the ground, ready to zoom away.

Another thing I had done that night, which suddenly became clear to me as I recollected the event, was that I knew automatically that I had to move my eyes in order to make my assemblage point shift. I could, with my *intent,* align the emanations that made me *see* Genaro as a blob of light, or I could align the emanations that made me *see* him as merely odd, unknown, strange.

When I *saw* Genaro as odd, his eyes had a malevolent glare, like the eyes of a beast in the darkness. But they were eyes, nonetheless. I did not *see* them as points of amber light.

That night don Juan said that Genaro was going to help my assemblage point shift very deeply, that I should imitate him and follow everything he did. Genaro stuck out his rear end and then thrust his pelvis forward with great force. I thought it was an obscene gesture. He repeated it over and over again, moving around as if he were dancing.

Don Juan nudged me on the arm, urging me to imitate Genaro, and I did. Both of us sort of romped around, performing that grotesque movement. After a while, I had the feeling that my body was executing the movement on its own, without what seemed to be the real me. The separation between my body and the real me became even more pronounced, and then at a given instant I was looking at some ludicrous scene where two men were making lewd gestures at each other.

I watched in fascination and realized that I was one of the two men. The moment I became aware of it I felt something pulling me and I found myself again thrusting my pelvis backward and forward in unison with Genaro. Almost immediately, I noticed that another man standing next to don Juan was watching us. The wind was blowing around him. I could see his hair being ruffled. He was naked and seemed embarrassed. The wind gathered around him as if protecting him, or perhaps the opposite, as if trying to blow him away.

I was slow to realize that I was the other man. When I did, I got the shock of my life. An imponderable physical force pulled me apart as if I were made out of fibers, and I was again looking at a man that was me, romping around with Genaro, gaping at me while I looked. And at the same time, I was looking at a naked man that was me, gaping at me while I made lewd gestures with Genaro. The shock was so great that I broke the rhythm of my movements and fell down.

The next thing I knew, don Juan was helping me to stand up. Genaro and the other me, the naked one, had disappeared.

I had also remembered that don Juan had refused to discuss the event. He did not explain it except to say that Genaro was an expert in creating his double, or the other, and that I had had long interactions with Genaro's double in states of normal awareness without ever detecting it.

"That night, as he has done hundreds of times before, Genaro made your assemblage point shift very deep into your left side," don Juan commented after I had recounted to him everything I had remembered. "His power was such that he dragged your assemblage point to the position where the *dreaming body* appears. You *saw* your *dreaming body* watching you. And his dancing did the trick."

I asked him to explain to me how Genaro's lewd movement could have produced such a drastic effect.

"You're a prude," he said. "Genaro used your immediate displeasure and embarrassment at having to perform a lewd gesture. Since he was in his *dreaming body*, he had the power to *see* the Eagle's emanations; from that advantage it was a cinch to make your assemblage point move."

He said that whatever Genaro had helped me to do that night was minor, that Genaro had moved my assemblage point and made it produce a *dreaming body* many, many times, but that those events were not what he wanted me to remember.

"I want you to realign the proper emanations and remember the time when you really woke up in a *dreaming position*," he said.

A strange surge of energy seemed to explode inside me and I knew what he wanted me to remember. I could not, however, focus my memory on the complete event. I could only recall a fragment of it.

I remembered that one morning, don Juan, don Genaro, and I had sat on that very same bench while I was in a state of normal awareness. Don Genaro had said, all of a sudden, that he was going to make his body leave the bench without getting up. The statement was completely out of the context of what we had been discussing. I was accustomed to don Juan's orderly, didactic words and actions. I turned to don Juan, expecting a clue, but he remained impassive, looking straight ahead as if don Genaro and I were not there at all.

Don Genaro nudged me to attract my attention, and then I witnessed a most disturbing sight. I actually *saw* Genaro on the other side of the square. He was beckoning me to come. But I also saw don Genaro sitting next to me, looking straight ahead, just as don Juan was.

I wanted to say something, to express my awe, but I found myself dumbstruck, imprisoned by some force around me that did not let me talk. I again looked at Genaro across the park. He was still there, motioning to me with a gesture of his head to join him.

My emotional distress mounted by the second. My stomach was getting upset, and finally I had tunnel vision, a tunnel that led directly to Genaro on the other side of the square. And then a great curiosity, or a great fear, which seemed to be the same thing at that moment, pulled me to where he was. I actually soared through the air and got to where he was. He made me turn around and pointed to the three people who were sitting on a bench in a static position, as if time had been suspended.

I felt a terrible discomfort, an internal itching, as if the soft organs in the cavity of my body were on fire, and then I was back on the bench, but Genaro was gone. He waved goodbye to me from across the square and disappeared among the people going to the market.

Don Juan became very animated. He kept on looking at me. He stood up and walked around me. He sat down again and could not keep a straight face as he talked to me.

I realized why he was acting that way. I had entered into a state of heightened awareness without being helped by don Juan. Genaro had succeeded in making my assemblage point move by itself.

I laughed involuntarily upon seeing my writing pad, which don Juan solemnly put inside his pocket. He said that he was going to use my state of heightened awareness to show me that there is no end to the mystery of man and to the mystery of the world.

I focused all my concentration on his words. However, don Juan said something I did not understand. I asked him to repeat what he had said. He began talking very softly. I thought he had lowered his voice so as not to be overheard by other people. I listened carefully, but I could not understand a word of what he was saying; he was either speaking in a language foreign to me or it was mumbo jumbo. The strange part of it was that something had caught my undivided attention, either the rhythm of his voice or the fact that I had forced myself to understand. I had the feeling that my mind was different from usual, although I could not figure out what the difference was. I had a hard time thinking, reasoning out what was taking place.

Don Juan talked to me very softly in my ear. He said that since I had entered into heightened awareness without any help from him my assemblage point was very loose, and that I could let it shift into the left side by relaxing, by falling half asleep on that bench. He assured me that he was watching over me, that I had nothing to fear. He urged me to relax, to let my assemblage point move.

I instantly felt the heaviness of being deeply asleep. At one moment, I became aware that I was having a dream. I saw a house that I had seen before. I was approaching it as if I were walking on the street. There were other houses, but I could not pay any attention to them. Something had fixed my awareness on the particular house I was seeing. It was a big modern stucco house with a front lawn.

When I got closer to that house, I had a feeling of familiarity with it, as if I had dreamed of it before. I walked on a gravel path to the front door; it was open and I walked inside. There was a dark hall and a large living room to the right, furnished with a dark-red couch and matching armchairs set in a corner. I was definitely having tunnel vision; I could see only what was in front of my eyes.

A young woman was standing by the couch as if she had just stood up as I came in. She was lean and tall, exquisitely dressed in a tailored green suit. She was perhaps in her late twenties. She had dark-brown hair, burning brown eyes that seemed to smile, and a pointed, finely chiseled nose. Her complexion was fair but had been tanned to a gorgeous brown. I found her ravishingly beautiful. She seemed to be an American. She nodded at me, smiling, and extended her hands with the palms down as if she were helping me up.

I clasped her hands in a most awkward movement. I scared myself and tried to back away, but she held me firmly and yet so gently. Her hands were long and beautiful. She spoke to me in Spanish with a faint trace of an accent. She begged me to relax, to feel her hands, to concentrate my attention on her face and to follow the movement of her mouth. I wanted to ask her who she was, but I could not utter a word.

Then I heard don Juan's voice in my ear. He said, "Oh, there you are," as if he had just found me. I was sitting on the park bench with him. But I could also hear the young woman's voice. She said, "Come and sit with me." I did just that and began a most incredible shifting of points of view. I was alternately with don Juan and with that young woman. I could see both of them as clearly as anything.

Don Juan asked me if I liked her, if I found her appealing and soothing. I could not speak, but somehow I conveyed to him the feeling that I did like that lady immensely. I thought, without any overt reason, that she was a paragon of kindness, that she was indispensable to what don Juan was doing with me.

Don Juan spoke in my ear again and said that if I liked her that much I should wake up in her house, that my feeling of warmth and affection for her would guide me. I felt giggly and reckless. A sensation of overwhelming excitation rippled through my body. I felt as if the excitation were actually disintegrating me. I did not care what happened to me. I gladly plunged into a blackness, black beyond words, and then I found myself in the young woman's house. I was sitting with her on the couch.

After an instant of sheer animal panic, I realized that somehow I was not complete. Something was missing in me. I did not, however, find the situation threatening. The thought crossed my mind that I was *dreaming* and that I was presently going to wake up on the park bench in Oaxaca with don Juan, where I really was, where I really belonged.

The young woman helped me to get up and took me to a bathroom where a large tub was filled with water. I realized then that I was stark naked. She gently made me get into the tub and held my head up while I half floated in it.

After a while she helped me out of the tub. I felt weak and flimsy. I lay down on the living-room couch and she came close to me. I could hear the beating of her heart and the pressure of blood rushing through her body. Her eyes were like two radiant sources of something that was not light, or heat, but curiously in between the two. I knew that I was *seeing* the force of life projecting out of her body through her eyes. Her whole body was like a live furnace; it glowed.

I felt a weird tremor that agitated my whole being. It was as if my nerves were exposed and someone was plucking them. The sensation was agonizing. Then I either fainted or fell asleep.

When I woke up, someone was putting face towels soaked in cold water on my face and the back of my neck. I saw the young woman sitting by my head on the bed where I was lying. She had a pail of water on a night table. Don Juan was standing at the foot of the bed with my clothes draped over his arm.

I was fully awake then. I sat up. They had covered me with a blanket.

"How's the traveler?" don Juan asked, smiling. "Are you in one piece now?"

That was all I could remember. I narrated this episode to don Juan, and as I talked, I recalled another fragment. I remembered that don Juan had taunted and teased me about finding me naked in the lady's bed. I had gotten terribly irritated at his remarks. I had put on my clothes and stomped out of the house in a fury.

Don Juan had caught up with me on the front lawn. In a very serious tone he had remarked that I was my ugly stupid self again, that I had put myself together by being embarrassed, which had proved to him that there was still no end to my self-importance. But he had added in a conciliatory tone that that was not important at the moment; what was significant was the fact that I had moved my assemblage point very deeply into the left side and consequently I had traveled an enormous distance.

He had spoken of wonders and mysteries, but I had not been able to listen to him, for I had been caught in the crossfire between fear and self-importance. I was actually fuming. I was certain that don Juan had hypnotized me in the park and had then taken me to that lady's house, and that the two of them had done terrible things to me.

My fury was interrupted. Something out there in the street was so horrifying, so shocking to me, that my anger stopped instantaneously. But before my thoughts became fully rearranged, don Juan hit me on my back and nothing of what had just taken place remained. I found myself back in my blissful everyday-life stupidity, happily listening to don Juan, worrying about whether or not he liked me.

As I was telling don Juan about the new fragment that I had just remembered I realized that one of his methods for handling my emotional turmoil was to make me shift into normal awareness.

"The only thing that soothes those who journey into the unknown is oblivion," he said. "What a relief to be in the ordinary world!

"That day, you accomplished a marvelous feat. The sober thing for me to do was not to let you focus on it at all. Just as you began to really panic I made you shift into normal awareness; I moved your assemblage point beyond the position where there are no more doubts. There are two such positions for warriors. In one you have no more doubts because you know everything. In the other, which is normal awareness, you have no doubts because you don't know anything.

"It was too soon then for you to know what had really happened. But I think the right time to know is now. Looking at that street, you were about to find out where your *dreaming position* had been. You traveled an enormous distance that day."

Don Juan scrutinized me with a mixture of glee and sadness. I was trying my best to keep under control the strange agitation I was feeling. I sensed that something terribly important to me was lost inside my memory, or, as don Juan would have put it, inside some unused emanations that at one time had been aligned.

My struggle to keep calm proved to be the wrong thing to do. All at once, my knees wobbled and nervous spasms ran through my midsection. I mumbled, unable to voice a question. I had to swallow hard and breathe deeply before I regained my calmness.

"When we first sat down here to talk, I said that no rational assumptions should interfere with the actions of a seer," he continued in a stern tone. "I knew that in order to reclaim what you've done, you'd have to dispense with rationality, but you'd have to do it in the level of awareness you are in now."

He explained that I had to understand that rationality is a condition of alignment, merely the result of the position of the assemblage point. He emphasized that I had to understand this when I was in a state of great vulnerability, as I was at that moment. To understand it when my assemblage point had reached the position where there are no doubts was useless, because realizations of that nature are commonplace in that position. It was equally useless to understand it in a state of normal awareness; in that state, such realizations are emotional outbursts that are valid only for as long as the emotion lasts.

"I've said that you traveled a great distance that day," he said calmly. "And I said that because I know it. I was there, remember?"

I was sweating profusely out of nervousness and anxiety.

"You traveled because you woke up at a distant *dreaming position*," he continued. "When Genaro pulled you across the plaza, right here from this bench, he paved the way for your assemblage point to move from normal awareness all the way to the position where the *dreaming body* appears. Your *dreaming body* actually flew over an incredible distance in the blink of an eyelid. Yet that's not the important part. The mystery is in the *dreaming position*. If it is strong enough to pull you, you can go to the ends of this world or beyond it, just as the old seers did. They disappeared from this world because they woke up at a *dreaming position* beyond the limits of the known. Your *dreaming position* that day was in this world, but quite a distance from the city of Oaxaca."

"How does a journey like that take place?" I asked.

"There is no way of knowing how it is done," he said. "Strong emotion, or unbending intent, or great interest serves as a guide; then the assemblage point gets powerfully fixed at the *dreaming position,* long enough to drag there all the emanations that are inside the cocoon."

Don Juan said then that he had made me *see* countless times over the years of our association, either in states of normal awareness or in states of heightened awareness; I had *seen* countless things that I was now beginning to understand in a more coherent fashion. This coherence was not logical or rational, but it clarified, nonetheless, in whatever strange way, everything I had done, everything that was done to me, and everything I had *seen* in all those years with him. He said that now I needed to have one last clarification: the coherent but irrational realization that everything in the world we have learned to perceive is inextricably tied to the position where the assemblage point is located. If the assemblage point is displaced from that position, the world will cease to be what it is to us.

Don Juan stated that a displacement of the assemblage point beyond the midline of the cocoon of man makes the entire world we know vanish from our view in one instant, as if it had been erased—for the stability, the substantiality, that seems to belong to our perceivable world is just the force of alignment. Certain emanations are routinely aligned because of the fixation of the assemblage point on one specific spot; that is all there is to our world.

"The soundness of the world is not the mirage," he

continued, "the mirage is the fixation of the assemblage point on any spot. When seers shift their assemblage points, they are not confronted with an illusion, they are confronted with another world; that new world is as real as the one we are watching now, but the new fixation of their assemblage points, which produces that new world, is as much of a mirage as the old fixation.

"Take yourself, for example; you are now in a state of heightened awareness. Whatever you are capable of doing in such a state is not an illusion; it is as real as the world you will face tomorrow in your daily life, and yet tomorrow the world you are witnessing now won't exist. It exists only when your assemblage point moves to the particular spot where you are now."

He added that the task warriors are faced with, after they finish their training, is one of integration. In the course of training, warriors, especially nagual men, are made to shift to as many individual spots as possible. He said that in my case I had moved to countless positions that I would have to integrate someday into a coherent whole.

"For instance, if you would shift your assemblage point to a specific position, you'd remember who that lady is," he continued with a strange smile. "Your assemblage point has been at that spot hundreds of times. It should be the easiest thing for you to integrate it."

As though my recollection depended on his suggestion, I began to have vague memories, feelings of sorts. There was a feeling of boundless affection that seemed to attract me; a most pleasant sweetness filled the air, exactly as if someone had just come up from behind me and poured that scent over me. I even turned around. And then I remembered. She was Carol, the nagual woman! I had been with her only the day before. How could I have forgotten her?

I had an indescribable moment in which I think all

the feelings of my psychological repertory ran through my mind. Was it possible, I asked myself, that I had woken up in her house in Tucson, Arizona, two thousand miles away? And are each of the instances of heightened awareness so isolated that one cannot remember them?

Don Juan came to my side and put his arm on my shoulder. He said that he knew exactly how I felt. His benefactor had made him go through a similar experience. And just as he himself was now trying to do with me, his benefactor had tried to do with him: soothe with words. He had appreciated his benefactor's attempt, but he doubted then as he doubted now that there is a way to soothe anyone who realizes the journey of the *dreaming body*.

There was no doubt in my mind now. Something in me had traveled the distance between the cities of Oaxaca, Mexico, and Tucson, Arizona. I felt a strange relief, as if I had been purged of guilt at long last.

During the years I had spent with don Juan, I had had lapses of continuity in my memory. My being in Tucson with him on that day was one of those lapses. I remembered not being able to recall how I had gotten to Tucson. I did not pay any attention to it, however. I thought the lapse was the result of my activities with don Juan. He was always very careful not to arouse my rational suspicions in states of normal awareness, but if suspicions were unavoidable he always curtly explained them away by suggesting that the nature of our activities fostered serious disparities of memory.

I told don Juan that since both of us had ended up that day in the same place, I wondered whether it was possible for two or more people to wake up at the same *dreaming position*.

"Of course," he said. "That's the way the old Toltec sorcerers took off into the unknown in packs. They followed one another. There is no way of knowing how one follows someone else. It's just done. The *dreaming body* just does it. The presence of another *dreamer* spurs it to do it. That day you pulled me with you. And I followed because I wanted to be with you."

I had so many questions to ask him, but every one of them seemed superfluous.

"How is it possible that I didn't remember the nagual woman?" I muttered, and a horrible anguish and longing gripped me. I was trying not to feel sad anymore, but suddenly sadness ripped through me like pain.

"You still don't remember her," he said. "Only when your assemblage point shifts can you recollect her. She is like a phantom to you, and so are you to her. You've seen her once while you were in normal awareness, but she's never seen you in her normal awareness. To her you are as much a personage as she is to you. With the difference that you may wake up someday and integrate it all. You may have enough time to do that, but she won't. Her time here is short."

I felt like protesting a terrible injustice. I mentally prepared a barrage of objections, but I never voiced them. Don Juan's smile was beaming. His eyes shone with sheer glee and mischief. I had the sensation that he was waiting for my statements, because he knew what I was going to say. And that sensation stopped me, or rather I did not say anything because my assemblage point had again moved by itself. And I knew then that the nagual woman could not be pitied for not having time, nor could I rejoice for having it.

Don Juan was reading me like a book. He urged me to finish my realization and voice the reason for not feeling sorry or for not rejoicing. I felt for an instant that I knew why. But then I lost the thread.

"The excitation of having time is equal to the excitation of not having it," he said. "It's all the same."

286

"To feel sad is not the same as feeling sorry," I said. "And I feel terribly sad."

"Who cares about sadness?" he said. "Think only of the mysteries; mystery is all that matters. We are living beings; we have to die and relinquish our awareness. But if we could change just a tinge of that, what mysteries must await us! What mysteries!"

18
Breaking the
Barrier of Perception

In the late afternoon, still in Oaxaca, don Juan and I strolled around the square leisurely. As we approached his favorite bench the people who were sitting there got up and left. We hurried over to it and sat down.

"We've come to the end of my explanation of awareness," he said. "And today, you are going to assemble another world by yourself and leave all doubts aside forever.

"There must be no mistake about what you are going to do. Today, from the vantage point of heightened awareness, you are going to make your assemblage point move and in one instant you are going to align the emanations of another world.

"In a few days, when Genaro and I meet you on a mountaintop, you are going to do the same from the disadvantage of normal awareness. You will have to align the emanations of another world on a moment's notice; if you don't you will die the death of an average man who falls from a precipice."

He was alluding to an act that he would have me perform as the last of his teachings for the right side: the act of jumping from a mountaintop into an abyss.

Don Juan stated that warriors ended their training when they were capable of breaking the barrier of perception, unaided, starting from a normal state of awareness. The nagual led warriors to that threshold, but success was up to the individual. The nagual merely tested them by continually pushing them to fend for themselves.

"The only force that can temporarily cancel out alignment is alignment," he continued. "You will have to cancel the alignment that keeps you perceiving the world of daily affairs. By *intending* a new position for your assemblage point and by *intending* to keep it fixed there long enough, you will assemble another world and escape this one.

"The old seers are still defying death, to this day, by doing just that, *intending* their assemblage points to remain fixed on positions that place them in any of the seven worlds."

"What will happen if I succeed in aligning another world?" I asked.

"You will go to it," he replied. "As Genaro did, one night in this very place when he was showing you the mystery of alignment."

"Where will I be, don Juan?"

"In another world, of course. Where else?"

"What about the people around me, and the buildings, and the mountains, and everything else?"

"You'll be separated from all that by the very barrier that you have broken: the barrier of perception. And just like the seers who have buried themselves to defy death, you won't be in this world."

There was a battle raging inside me as I heard his statements. Some part of me clamored that don Juan's position was untenable, while another part knew beyond any question that he was right.

I asked him what would happen if I moved my assemblage point while I was in the street, in the middle of traffic in Los Angeles.

"Los Angeles will vanish, like a puff of air," he replied with a serious expression. "But you will remain.

"That is the mystery I've been trying to explain to you. You've experienced it, but you haven't understood it yet, and today you will."

He said that I could not as yet use the boost of the earth to shift into another great band of emanations, but that since I had an imperative need to shift, that need was going to serve me as a launcher.

Don Juan looked up at the sky. He stretched his arms above his head as if he had been sitting for too long and was pushing physical weariness out of his body. He commanded me to turn off my internal dialogue and enter into inner silence. Then he stood up and began to walk away from the square; he signaled me to follow him. He took a deserted side street. I recognized it as being the same street where Genaro had given me his demonstration of alignment. The moment I recollected that, I found myself walking with don Juan in a place that by then was very familiar to me: a deserted plain with yellow dunes of what seemed to be sulfur.

I recalled then that don Juan had made me perceive that world hundreds of times. I also recalled that beyond the desolate landscape of the dunes there was another world shining with an exquisite, uniform, pure white light.

When don Juan and I entered into it this time, I sensed that the light, which came from every direction, was not an invigorating light, but was so soothing that it gave me the feeling that it was sacred.

As that sacred light bathed me a rational thought exploded in my inner silence. I thought it was quite possible that mystics and saints had made this journey of the assemblage point. They had seen God in the mold of man. They had seen hell in the sulfur dunes.

And then they had seen the glory of heaven in the diaphanous light.

My rational thought burned out almost immediately under the onslaughts of what I was perceiving. My awareness was taken by a multitude of shapes, figures of men, women, and children of all ages, and other incomprehensible apparitions gleaming with a blinding white light.

I saw don Juan, walking by my side, staring at me and not at the apparitions, but the next instant I *saw* him as a ball of luminosity, bobbing up and down a few feet away from me. The ball made an abrupt and frightening movement and came closer to me and I *saw* inside it.

Don Juan was working his glow of awareness for my benefit. The glow suddenly shone on four or five threadlike filaments on his left side. It remained fixed there. All my concentration was on it; something pulled me slowly as if through a tube and I *saw* the allies—three dark, long, rigid figures agitated by a tremor, like leaves in a breeze. They were against an almost fluorescent pink background. The moment I focused my eyes on them, they came to where I was, not walking or gliding or flying, but by pulling themselves along some fibers of whiteness that came out of me. The whiteness was not a light or a glow but lines that seemed to be drawn with heavy powder chalk. They disintegrated quickly, yet not quickly enough. The allies were on me before the lines faded away.

They crowded me. I became annoyed, and the allies immediately moved away as if I had chastised them. I felt sorry for them, and my feeling pulled them back instantly. And they again came and rubbed themselves against me. I *saw* then something I had *seen* in the mirror at the stream. The allies had no inner glow. They had no inner mobility. There was no life in them. And yet they were obviously alive. They were strange grotesque shapes that resembled zippered-up sleeping bags. The thin line in the middle of their elongated shapes made them look as if they had been sewed up.

They were not pleasing figures. The sensation that they were totally alien to me made me feel uncomfortable, impatient. I *saw* that the three allies were moving as if they were jumping up and down; there was a faint glow inside them. The glow grew in intensity until, in at least one of the allies, it was quite brilliant.

The instant I *saw* that, I was facing a black world. I do not mean that it was dark as night is dark. It was rather that everything around me was pitch-black. I looked up at the sky and I could not find light anywhere. The sky was also black and literally covered with lines and irregular circles of various degrees of blackness. The sky looked like a black piece of wood where the grain showed in relief.

I looked down at the ground. It was fluffy. It seemed to be made of flakes of agar-agar; they were not dull flakes, but they were not shiny either. It was something in between, which I had never seen in my life: black agar-agar.

I heard then the voice of *seeing*. It said that my assemblage point had assembled a total world with other great bands of emanations: a black world.

I wanted to absorb every word I was hearing; in order to do that I had to split my concentration. The voice stopped; my eyes became focused again. I was standing with don Juan just a few blocks away from the square.

I instantly felt that I had no time to rest, that it would be useless to indulge in being shocked. I rallied all my strength and asked don Juan if I had done what he had expected.

"You did exactly what you were expected to do," he said reassuringly. "Let's go back to the square and stroll around it one more time, for the last time in this world."

I refused to think about don Juan's leaving, so I

asked him about the black world. I had vague recollections of having *seen* it before.

"It's the easiest world to assemble," he said. "And of all you've experienced, only the black world is worth considering. It is the only true alignment of another great band you have ever made. Everything else has been a lateral shift along man's band, but still within the same great band. The wall of fog, the plain with yellow dunes, the world of the apparitions—all are lateral alignments that our assemblage points make as they approach a crucial position."

He explained as we walked back to the square that one of the strange qualities of the black world is that it does not have the same emanations that account for time in our world. They are different emanations that produce a different result. Seers that journey into the black world feel that they have been in it for an eternity, but in our world that turns out to be an instant.

"The black world is a dreadful world because it ages the body," he said emphatically.

I asked him to clarify his statements. He slowed down his pace and looked at me. He reminded me that Genaro, in his direct way, had tried to point that out to me once, when he told me that we had plodded in hell for an eternity while not even a minute had passed in the world we know.

Don Juan remarked that in his youth he had become obsessed with the black world. He had wondered, in front of his benefactor, about what would happen to him if he went into it and stayed there for a while. But as his benefactor was not given to explanations, he had simply plunged don Juan into the black world to let him find out for himself.

"The nagual Julian's power was so extraordinary," don Juan continued, "that it took me days to come back from that black world."

"You mean it took you days to return your assemblage point to its normal position, don't you?'' I asked.

"Yes. I mean that," he said.

He explained that in the few days that he was lost in the black world he aged at least ten years, if not more. The emanations inside his cocoon felt the strain of years of solitary struggle.

Silvio Manuel was a totally different case. The nagual Julian also plunged him into the unknown, but Silvio Manuel assembled another world with another set of bands, a world also without the emanations of time but one which has the opposite effect on seers. He disappeared for seven years and yet he felt he had been gone only a moment.

"To assemble other worlds is not only a matter of practice, but a matter of *intent*,'' he continued. "And it isn't merely an exercise of bouncing out of those worlds, like being pulled by a rubber band. You see, a seer has to be daring. Once you break the barrier of perception, you don't have to come back to the same place in the world. See what I mean?''

It slowly dawned on me what he was saying. I had an almost invincible desire to laugh at such a preposterous idea, but before the idea coalesced into a certainty, don Juan spoke to me and disrupted what I was about to remember.

He said that for warriors the danger of assembling other worlds is that those worlds are as possessive as our world. The force of alignment is such that once the assemblage point breaks away from its normal position, it becomes fixed at other positions, by other alignments. And warriors run the risk of getting stranded in inconceivable aloneness.

The inquisitive, rational part of me commented that I had *seen* him in the black world as a ball of luminosity. It was possible, therefore, to be in that world with people.

"Only if people follow you around by moving their

294

own assemblage points when you move yours," he replied. "I shifted mine in order to be with you; otherwise you would have been there alone with the allies."

We stopped walking, and don Juan said that it was time for me to go.

"I want you to bypass all lateral shifts," he said, "and go directly to the next total world: the black world. In a couple of days you'll have to do the same thing by yourself. You won't have time to piddle around. You'll have to do it in order to escape death."

He said that breaking the barrier of perception is the culmination of everything seers do. From the moment that barrier is broken, man and his fate take on a different meaning for warriors. Because of the transcendental importance of breaking that barrier, the new seers use the act of breaking it as a final test. The test consists of jumping from a mountaintop into an abyss while in a state of normal awareness. If the warrior jumping into the abyss does not erase the daily world and assemble another one before he reaches bottom, he dies.

"What you are going to do is to make this world vanish," he went on, "but you are going to remain somewhat yourself. This is the ultimate bastion of awareness, the one the new seers count on. They know that after they burn with consciousness, they somewhat retain the sense of being themselves."

He smiled and pointed to a street that we could see from where we were standing—the street where Genaro had shown me the mysteries of alignment.

"That street, like any other, leads to eternity," he said. "All you have to do is follow it in total silence. It's time. Go now! Go!"

He turned around and walked away from me. Genaro was waiting for him at the corner. Genaro waved at me and then made a gesture of urging me to come on. Don Juan kept on walking without turning to look.

Genaro joined him. I started to follow them, but I knew that it was wrong. Instead, I went in the opposite direction. The street was dark, lonely, and bleak. I did not indulge in feelings of failure or inadequacy. I walked in inner silence. My assemblage point was moving at great speed. I *saw* the three allies. The line of their middle made them look as if they were smiling sideways. I felt that I was being frivolous. And then a windlike force blew the world away.

Epilogue

A couple of days later, all the nagual's party and all the apprentices got together on the flat mountaintop don Juan had told me about.

Don Juan said that each of the apprentices had already said goodbye to everybody, and that all of us were in a state of awareness that admitted no sentimentalism. For us, he said, there was only action. We were warriors in a state of total war.

Everyone, with the exception of don Juan, Genaro, Pablito, Nestor, and me, moved a short distance away from the flat mountaintop, in order to allow Pablito, Nestor, and me privacy to enter into a state of normal awareness.

But before we did, don Juan took us by the arms and walked us around the flat top.

"In a moment, you're going to *intend* the movement of your assemblage points," he said. "And no one will help you. You are now alone. You must remember then that *intent* begins with a command.

"The old seers used to say that if warriors are going to have an internal dialogue, they should have the proper dialogue. For the old seers that meant a dialogue about sorcery and the enhancement of their self-reflection. For the new seers, it doesn't mean dialogue, but the detached manipulation of *intent* through sober commands."

He said over and over again that the manipulation of *intent* begins with a command given to oneself; the command is then repeated until it becomes the Eagle's command, and then the assemblage point shifts, accordingly, the moment warriors reach inner silence.

The fact that such a maneuver is possible, he said, is something of the most singular importance to seers, old and new alike, but for reasons diametrically opposed. Knowing about it allowed the old seers to move their assemblage point to inconceivable *dreaming positions* in the incommensurable unknown; for the new seers it means refusing to be food, it means escaping the Eagle by moving their assemblage points to a particular *dreaming position* called total freedom.

He explained that the old seers discovered that it is possible to move the assemblage point to the limit of the known and keep it fixed there in a state of prime heightened awareness. From that position, they *saw* the feasibility of slowly shifting their assemblage points permanently to other positions beyond that limit—a stupendous feat fraught with daring but lacking sobriety, for they could never retract the movement of their assemblage points, or perhaps they never wanted to.

Don Juan said that adventurous men, faced with the choice of dying in the world of ordinary affairs or dying in unknown worlds, will unavoidably choose the latter, and that the new seers, realizing that their predecessors had chosen merely to change the locale of their death, came to understand the futility of it all; the futility of struggling to control their fellow men, the futility of assembling other worlds, and, above all, the futility of self-importance.

One of the most fortunate decisions that the new seers made, he said, was never to allow their assemblage points to move permanently to any position other than heightened awareness. From that position, they actually resolved their dilemma of futility and found out that the solution is not simply to choose an alternate world in which to die, but to choose total consciousness, total freedom.

Don Juan commented that by choosing total freedom, the new seers unwittingly continued in the tradition of their predecessors and became the quintessence of the death defiers.

He explained that the new seers discovered that if the assemblage point is made to shift constantly to the confines of the unknown, but is made to return to a position at the limit of the known, then when it is suddenly released it moves like lightning across the entire cocoon of man, aligning all the emanations inside the cocoon at once.

"The new seers burn with the force of alignment," don Juan went on, "with the force of *will,* which they have turned into the force of *intent* through a life of impeccability. *Intent* is the alignment of all the amber emanations of awareness, so it is correct to say that total freedom means total awareness."

"Is that what all of you are going to do, don Juan?" I asked.

"We most certainly will, if we have sufficient energy," he replied. "Freedom is the Eagle's gift to man. Unfortunately, very few men understand that all we need, in order to accept such a magnificent gift, is to have sufficient energy.

"If that's all we need, then, by all means, we must become misers of energy."

After that, don Juan made us enter into a state of normal awareness. At dusk, Pablito, Nestor, and I jumped into the abyss. And don Juan and the nagual's party burned with the fire from within. They entered into total awareness, for they had sufficient energy to accept the mind-boggling gift of freedom.

Pablito, Nestor, and I didn't die at the bottom of that gorge—and neither did the other apprentices who had jumped at an earlier time—because we never reached it; all of us, under the impact of such a tremendous and incomprehensible act as jumping to our deaths, moved our assemblage points and assembled other worlds.

We know now that we were left to remember heightened awareness and to regain the totality of ourselves. And we also know that the more we remember, the more intense our elation, our wondering, but also the greater our doubts, our turmoil.

So far, it is as if we were left only to be tantalized by the most far-reaching questions about the nature and the fate of man, until the time when we may have sufficient energy not only to verify everything don Juan taught us, but also to accept the Eagle's gift ourselves.